Cornell Studies in Civil Liberty

FEDERAL SERVICE AND THE CONSTITUTION

THE DEVELOPMENT OF THE
PUBLIC EMPLOYMENT RELATIONSHIP

Federal Service and the Constitution

THE DEVELOPMENT OF THE
PUBLIC EMPLOYMENT RELATIONSHIP

David H. Rosenbloom

Cornell University Press

ITHACA AND LONDON

International Standard Book Number 0-8014-0614-5
Library of Congress Catalog Card Number 74-140462

PRINTED IN THE UNITED STATES OF AMERICA
BY VAIL-BALLOU PRESS, INC.

Acknowledgments

I am indebted to several of my former professors and associates at the University of Chicago for their contributions to this project. I am particularly grateful to Professor Herbert J. Storing for his encouragement and assistance in formulating the study, to Professors C. Herman Pritchett, Lloyd I. Rudolph, and George E. Von der Muhll for their help throughout its development and for their undying aversion to intellectual imperialism, and to Professor Theodore J. Lowi for useful suggestions concerning publication. I am also indebted to Professor Herman D. Lujan of the University of Kansas for his thoughtful critique of the manuscript. My greatest debt is to my wife for her support and encouragement. Nevertheless, I have rejected far more advice than I have accepted, and the responsibility for whatever shortcomings remain is clearly my own.

Finally, I am thankful to the *Public Personnel Review* (July 1970) for permission to use material from my article "Citizenship Rights and Civil Service"; to the *University of Kansas Law Review* (Summer 1970) for permission to use material from another article, "The Constitution and the Civil Service: Some Recent Developments, Judicial and Political"; and to the University of Minnesota Press for permission to use the material appearing in Table 2.

D. H. R.

Washington, D.C.
January 1971

Contents

Tables

Figure

FEDERAL SERVICE AND THE CONSTITUTION

THE DEVELOPMENT OF THE
PUBLIC EMPLOYMENT RELATIONSHIP

Introduction

The constitutional relationship between the citizen and the state in public employment is an important feature of the United States political system, but one which has not been adequately conceptualized and analyzed.[1] It has been a partial determinant of the gross characteristics of public bureaucracy in America and of the fundamental rights of a sizable segment of the population. In recent years the significance of the public employment relationship has been increased by important changes in its content, by the growing importance of the federal and state bureaucracies, and by the corresponding expansion of public employment which is presented in Tables 1 and 2.

The relationship is most usefully thought of as the degree of differentiation between the constitutional rights [2] of citi-

[1] Earlier studies involving the public employment relationship have tended to focus on specific issues, such as political neutrality and loyalty-security, and few, if any, have sought to analyze its historical development. For the more general approaches see Sterling D. Spero, *Government as Employer* (New York: Remsen Press, 1948), and "Employer and Employee in the Public Service," in Carl J. Friedrich *et al., Problems of the American Public Service* (New York: McGraw-Hill, 1935), pp. 171–239; and Morton R. Godine, *The Labor Problem in Public Service* (Cambridge: Harvard University Press, 1953), especially chap. iii. See also Arch Dotson, "A General Theory of Public Employment," *Public Administration Review,* XVI (Summer 1956), 197–211.

[2] Because the relationship is between the citizen and the state, rather than the employee and the state, only constitutional rights are considered. Differentiation of legal rights based upon the societal special-

1

Table 1. Civilian employment in the federal civil service,
1821–1967 (selected years)

Year	Number of employees	Year	Number of employees
1821	6,914	1911	395,905
1831	11,491	1921	561,143
1841	18,038	1931	609,746
1851	26,274	1941	1,437,682
1861	36,672	1951	2,482,666
1871	51,020	1961	2,435,808
1881	100,020	1964	2,500,492
1891	157,442	1966	2,759,019
1901	239,476	1967	3,002,461

Sources: Through 1951, U.S., Bureau of the Census and Social Science Research Council, *Statistical History of the United States from Colonial Times to the Present* (Stamford: Fairfield Publishers, 1965), p. 710. The figures for 1961–1967 are from U.S., Civil Service Commission, *Annual Report*, Vol. LXXVIII (1961), Vol. LXXXI (1964), Vol. LXXXIII (1966), Vol. LXXXIV (1967), Appendix A. All figures are as of June 30, except those for 1921, which are as of July 31.

zens when in or in application for, and when out of or not in application for, public employment.[3] The concept of such a relationship is intended to comprehend the distinction be-

---

ization of function (division of labor) is a more common phenomenon than the differentiation of constitutional rights upon this basis, and is less fundamental. In studying the relationship in political systems having ill-defined constitutional citizenship guarantees it would be necessary to determine the degree of differentiation of those rights granted to citizens which could be said to characterize the regime.

[3] In *Scott* v. *Macy*, 349 F. 2d 182, 184 (1965), it was reasoned that "the Constitution does not distinguish between applicants and employees." Throughout United States history generally there has been no significant difference between the constitutional rights of citizens in public employment and those in application for such employment. Henceforth, the term "in public employment" will include "in application" as well.

Table 2. Civilian public employment as a percentage of the labor force, 1929–1966 (selected years)

Year	Federal government	State and local governments	Total [a]
1929	1.1	5.1	6.2
1930	1.1	5.2	6.3
1933	1.1	5.0	6.1
1935	1.4	5.1	6.6
1939	1.6	5.6	7.2
1944	4.4	4.7	9.2
1949	3.0	6.2	9.2
1954	3.2	6.7	10.0
1959	3.1	8.3	11.4
1961	3.1	8.8	11.9
1962	3.1	9.2	12.3
1966	——	——	17.0

Sources: U.S., Bureau of Labor Statistics, *Employment and Earnings Statistics.* Also S. Krislov, *The Negro in Federal Employment* (Minneapolis: University of Minnesota Press, 1967), p. 90. For 1966 see Robert Moberly, "The Strike and Its Alternatives in Public Employment," *University of Wisconsin Law Review*, CMLXVI (Spring 1966), 549.

[a] Because of rounding, the figures for federal government and state and local employment sometimes exceeds the totals.

tween citizens in public employment and others with respect to the ways in which the state may legitimately act upon the constitutional rights of one or the other, but not both. Therefore, the relationship can take two general forms. It is nondiscriminatory when the roles of citizen and public employee are thought to be entirely compatible and there is no differentiation between the constitutional rights of citizens which is dependent upon public employment. The relationship is discriminatory when the roles of public employee and citizen are not believed to be wholly compatible and differentiation of constitutional rights is dependent upon the fact of public employment. The relationship is negatively discriminatory when the constitutional rights of public employees are subject to greater restriction, and it is positively discriminatory when they are afforded additional constitutional rights. It is logically possible for the relationship to have positive and negative elements at the same time and for these elements to balance each other to cause a neutrally discriminatory relationship.[4]

A few examples may serve to clarify these definitions. In the United States, regulations concerning political neutrality represent an important example of negative discrimination because the constitutional political rights of citizens are differentiated upon the basis of public employment, and the civil servant's rights are subject to greater restriction. Another example would be a legitimate regulation providing for personnel actions to be taken on the basis of race or religion. A third example, under the United States Constitution, would be the refusal of employment or dismissal from employment of persons who have refused to answer questions before a governmental hearing body or a court on the ground that answering might tend to incriminate them. There have been numerous other examples of negative discrimination which will be discussed throughout this study.

Examples of positive discrimination are less common. One example would be the constitutional right of a civil servant to treat his public office as private property. In such instances the civil servant's constitutional rights are increased because, unlike other citizens, he literally owns a unit of the government, and whatever powers pertain to the office are constitutionally vested in the "owner." For example, in England until the sixteenth century,

[4] For an alternative analytical framework see Reinhard Bendix, *Nation Building and Citizenship* (New York: John Wiley and Sons, 1964), pp. 116–17.

offices could be disposed of as if they were cattle or real estate. They could be bought, inherited, and divided between different persons. The proprietary rights extended to the fees attached to the offices and not even the king could deprive the official of these benefits without proper indemnification.[5]

The concept of property in public office continued well after the actual sale of office was uncommon. Until the nineteenth century "no Government post could be taken from its occupant or suppressed, nor even could its character be changed without violating the right of private property." [6] Another example of positive discrimination would be an arrangement providing civil servants with special and greater parliamentary representation.[7] There have also been some examples in the United States. For instance, from 1842 until 1939 federal employees were constitutionally immune from state taxation,[8] and at the present time civil servants have the right of absolutely privileged speech under certain circumstances.[9]

The public employment relationship is best conceptualized as existing along a continuum from entirely nondiscriminatory

[5] K. W. Swart, *Sale of Offices in the Seventeenth Century* (The Hague: Martinus Nijhoff, 1949), p. 47.

[6] Elie Halévy, *A History of the English People* (New York: Harcourt, Brace and Co., 1924), p. 14.

[7] A representational system along these lines was instituted by the State of Victoria, Australia, in 1903. Civil servants and state railway workers were deprived of their general franchise and instead allowed to elect one of the 35 members of the Legislative Council, the upper chamber, and 3 of 68 members of the Legislative Assembly, the lower chamber. The system was designed as a means to take public employees out of the ordinary political process and was abandoned because the special representatives failed to attain parliamentary influence. See Spero, *Government as Employer*, p. 57.

[8] This situation was the result of judicial decisions. See C. Herman Pritchett, *The American Constitution* (New York: McGraw-Hill, 1959), pp. 215, 218n.

[9] See chap. 8, *infra*.

to entirely discriminatory. The range of discrimination—that is, the amount of overall differentiation of constitutional rights dependent upon public employment—can be scaled in correlation with two other dimensions. One is the degree of discrimination, that is, the perceived relative importance of the differentiated rights. This can be indexed according to the relative importance as perceived by members of the political system generally, by institutions such as the courts, by a panel of experts, or by some group, organization, or individual thought to be especially well qualified to do so. For example, if the justices of the Supreme Court were used as the relevant indicator of perceived relative importance and they agreed that free speech was more important than the right to bear firearms, the degree of discrimination would be greater when an employee's freedom of speech was restricted than when his right to bear firearms was. However, in order to construct a more useful index, it would be necessary to assign a relative numerical value to each differentiated right. Thus, free speech might be given a relative value of ten while the right to bear firearms might be given a value of two. The hypothetical upper limit of the degree of discrimination in the negative direction would be the civil servant's forfeiture of all constitutional rights. In the positive direction, it would be the granting of rights only to civil servants.

The other dimension is the domain of discrimination, that is, the number of employees or persons having their rights restricted or increased in connection with public employment at various degree levels. In historical comparisons, it would be necessary to express the domain of discrimination as a proportion. This dimension is helpful because it is common for discrimination to vary in accordance with the civil servant's rank, functions, or authority, and for restrictions on equality of access to civil service positions to apply only to limited groups such as women or Negroes. For example, regulations concerning political neutrality might apply only to higher ranking civil servants, and a loyalty-security provision might apply only to employees in sensitive positions. If this dimension were ignored it would be necessary to conclude that when the degree of discrimination approached its upper limit for a minority of civil servants, the range of discrimination did likewise. The range of discrimination may therefore be said to vary directly with the degree and domain of discrimination. More specifically, when there is more than one type of discrimination of the public employment relationship, the range can be said to vary with the sum of the products of the other two dimensions.[10] Figure 1 illustrates some of the principles involved, although the examples are largely hypothetical, the degree of discrimination arbitrarily assigned, and the domain held constant.

There are, however, several obstacles to the mathematical application of the principles involved. The greatest difficulty lies in assignment of relative values to differentiated rights. It is also sometimes impossible, especially in historical cases, to estimate the domain of discrimination. Nevertheless, the

[10] This relationship can be expressed mathematically as follows. If r represents the range of discrimination, d the domain of discrimination, and D the degree of discrimination, $r = d_1(D_1) + d_2(D_2) + \ldots d_n(D_n)$. Therefore, in the previous example involving free speech and firearms, if r_1, d_1, and D_1 are for free speech, and r_2, d_2, and D_2 are for firearms, r_1 is greater than r_2 when $d_2 = D_1/D_2d_1 + 1$, or 6 d_1. The formula can be used to indicate the direction of discrimination by making D negative when employees' rights are abridged. Therefore, using the previous example, if civil servants' right of free speech were restricted while they were granted extraordinary rights to bear firearms, dd, the direction of discrimination, would equal $d_1(-D_1) + d_2(D_2)$ and would be negative when d_2 was less than D_1/D_2d_1 or $5d_1$; positive when $d_2 = D_1/D_2d_1 + 1$ or $6d_1$; and neutral when $d_2 = D_1/D_2d_1$ or $5d_1$.

framework is useful for analyzing the United States experience because almost all important discriminations have been negative, and it is usually possible to make a rough determination of the importance of those discriminated rights which have been most fundamental to the overall development of the public employment relationship.

+	Extraordinary right to bear firearms	Right to special parliamentary representation		+
Nondiscriminatory – – – – – – – (range) – – – – – – – – Discriminatory				
–	Loss of right to bear firearms	Loss of right not to testify against self	Political neutrality regulations	–

Figure 1. The public employment relationship as a continuum

There are some discriminations that are inevitable due to the nature of employment generally.[11] The employee must report to work at a specific time. It could be said that this restricts his freedom of movement. He must also perform his assigned tasks, rather than spend his time in religious contemplation. This could be viewed as a restriction of his religious freedom. Civil servants may have access to files and information which is not granted to ordinary citizens, and this could be viewed as a positive discrimination. In this study, however, any limitation or grant of constitutional rights which is a direct attribute of the job and which applies only when in the place of work or during the hours of work will be considered to be of trivial importance and will not be ana-

[11] See *Graves* v. *Walton County Board of Education*, 410 F. 2d 1153 (1969).

lyzed. This distinction, for example, would make restrictions on speech only at work unimportant, but restrictions applying off the job important. Any restriction of a constitutional right which does not involve overt activity on the part of the employee will be considered important. The right not to be excluded from public employment on the basis of race or religious affiliation is an example of such a right.

Another category of differentiation of rights which, in this study, is not considered to be an important part of the public employment relationship is that of conflict of interest regulations. These regulations usually affect property rights or the right to engage in extragovernmental employment. While the rights involved are important to the citizen, they have been less fundamental and central to the overall development of the public employment relationship than the differentiation of political and other civil rights has been. They are often much closer to being direct attributes of the job and are generally intended to prevent corruption rather than to achieve direct political affects.

In this study the public employment relationship is further limited to civilian employment in the executive branch of the federal government. This is desirable in order to make the subject matter more manageable. The positions under consideration represent the largest number of civil service posts under relatively common regulations, and excepting judges, they represent the most important public employment positions. Noncivilian public employees' constitutional rights are also differentiated on the basis of the societal specialization of function, but this differentiation is based primarily upon their military status rather than their status as public employees. However, in analyzing the development of the relationship involving federal employment it is often helpful to consider Supreme Court and other judicial opinions involving state employment. This is useful because there has been no significant distinction between the two types of employment concerning the public employment relationship,[12] and some of the more important judicial opinions on the relationship have involved state employees.

Although the range of discrimination has varied widely over time, this variance cannot be correlated with a few explanatory variables. It has been due to a host of political, social, and economic factors. It has been related to regime ideology, the sociological representativeness of the bureaucracy, the separation of powers, changes in technology, international tension, and several other factors. Despite the diversity of variables affecting the range of discrimination, it is possible to make some generalizations concerning the systemic origin of the negatively discriminatory relationship.

The development of a discriminatory public employment relationship is related to the specialization of function and the problem of controlling bureaucracy. As Max Weber pointed out,

under normal conditions, the power of a fully developed bureaucracy is always overtowering. The "political master" finds himself in the position of the "dilettante" who stands opposite the "expert" facing the trained official who stands within the management of administration.[13]

In democratic political systems the problem of controlling bureaucracy is often more acute. As Weber indicated, "Democracy inevitably comes into conflict with the bureaucratic

[12] Therefore, although this study concentrates on federal employment, the constitutional relationship under consideration is equally applicable to state and local employees as well.

[13] Max Weber, *From Max Weber: Essays in Sociology,* trans. and ed. by H. H. Gerth and C. Wright Mills (New York: Oxford University Press, 1958), p. 232.

tendencies which by its fight against notable rule, democracy has produced." [14] By comparing some of the general requirements of bureaucracy with those of democracy it becomes evident that there is a tension between the two. Bureaucracy requires unity, hierarchy, command, long duration in office, and recognition of differentiated competence, while democracy requires plurality, equality, liberty (freedom), rotation in office, and the recognition of all men as being competent. The tension makes it necessary for democracy either to abandon bureaucracy or to control it. The first alternative, it is generally agreed, is not feasible because "an essential part of the present structure of governance consists of its far-flung system of professionalized administration and its hierarchy of appointed officials upon whom society is thoroughly dependent." [15] Therefore, democratic political systems must, in order to maintain their essential variables within the democratic range, develop techniques for controlling their bureaucratic components.

In the United States the problem of control has been complicated by the system of separated and shared powers, and instances in which the "political master" has been unable to compel bureaucratic performance are common. For example, President Franklin D. Roosevelt, in a reported conversation with one of his top administrators, remarked that

when I woke up this morning, the first thing I saw was a headline in the *New York Times* to the effect that our Navy was going to spend two billion dollars on a shipbuilding program. Here I am, the Commander-In-Chief of the Navy having to read about that for the first time in the press. . . .

The Treasury . . . is so large and far-flung and ingrained in

---

[14] *Ibid.*, p. 226.

[15] Hans Rosenberg, *Bureaucracy, Aristocracy, and Autocracy: The Prussian Experience, 1660–1815* (Boston: Beacon Press, 1966), p. 1.

its practices that I find is almost impossible to get the action and results I want. . . .

But the Treasury is not to be compared with the State Department. You should go through the experience of trying to get any changes in the thinking, policy, and action of the career diplomats and then you'd know what a real problem was.[16]

Another well-known statement of the problem was made by President Truman in the summer of 1952 while contemplating the possibility of General Eisenhower as the next president. Truman said, "He'll sit here, and he'll say 'Do this! Do that!' *And nothing will happen.* Poor Ike—it won't be a bit like the Army. He'll find it very frustrating." [17]

Today it is generally agreed that bureaucracy cannot be controlled in any simple sense because:

No general statement can be so exhaustive as to permit the civil servant to act on the basis of a series of purely technical calculations, even if he were willing to do so. He is inevitably left with some discretion; he has to participate in the making of policy. This is, of course, especially true at the higher levels, but the same principle applies, often in very significant ways at lower levels as well.

. . . . .

Not only do civil servants exercise discretion in interpreting and applying the commands of their political superiors, they participate intimately in the formulation of those commands. They make proposals of their own and fight for them; they comment on the proposals of their political superiors—and may fight against them. They make a vital contribution to the process of deciding what is to be done. Government would come to a standstill if our

---

[16] Quoted in Sidney Hyman (ed.), *Beckoning Frontiers* (New York: Alfred A. Knopf, 1951), p. 336.

[17] Quoted in Richard E. Neustadt, *Presidential Power: The Politics of Leadership* (New York: John Wiley and Sons, 1960), p. 9.

"closest statesmen" in the civil service suddenly started doing only what they were told.[18]

Not only it is difficult for the "political master" to control the behavior of civil servants, but their policy-making abilities and political influence, in many ways, lack democratic legitimacy. This lack of legitimacy largely stems from the fact that civil servants are not popularly elected. If they are political appointees they are often suspected by some of being incompetent "party hacks" whose real function is to make life difficult for the political opposition. On the other hand, when they are selected by other means, such as the merit system, their loyalties to the party in power and democracy itself may be suspect. Furthermore, they may not be considered to be a legitimate interest group within the pluralist framework. Although their influence is often great, who they are and what they do is largely unknown to most citizens. In the United States the suspicion which attaches to the bureaucracy is indicated by election campaigns, which, as some have pointed out, "always ring with denunciations of the 'dictatorial bureaucracy,' its 'demand for more power,' its 'incompetence,' and its 'corruption.' " [19]

In the United States, and some other Western democracies as well, a negatively discriminatory public employment rela-

[18] Herbert Storing, "Political Parties and the Bureaucracy," in Robert A. Goldwin (ed.), *Political Parties, U.S.A.* (Chicago: Rand McNally, 1964), pp. 145, 152.

[19] Herman Miles Somers, "The President, The Congress, and the Federal Government Service," in Wallace Sayre (ed.), *The Federal Government Service* (Englewood Cliffs: Prentice-Hall, 1965), p. 95. For example, the *New York Times,* October 17, 1968, p. 1, reported: "Richard M. Nixon said yesterday that the chief revolt in America was against 'an increasingly impersonal' Federal bureaucracy that saps individual initiative."

tionship has been an important method of controlling some
of the general characteristics of bureaucracy through regulation of the behavior of public employees. For example, provisions concerning loyalty-security have been intended to insure that the bureaucracy as a whole will be loyal to the
United States and to its Constitution, and that civil servants
as individuals will not use their official positions to subvert
the government. Regulations or practices which exclude members of a social class or racial group have also been intended
to place or maintain the bureaucracy in "safe hands." Political neutrality has been intended, in part, to prevent the
bureaucracy from being openly partisan and to reduce the
extent to which a civil servant can use whatever political
influence and official authority he has in the political arena.
In other words, in democratic political systems it is sometimes believed to be desirable, in order to control bureaucracy, to abridge the constitutional rights of civil servants because an injudicious use of these rights might seriously interfere with the ability of the system to maintain its essential
variables within the democratic range.

In democratic political systems a discriminatory public
employment relationship presents theoretical problems. When
the system is formally dedicated to the preservation of individual liberty, a negatively discriminatory relationship must
be ideologically and judicially justified. In the United States
the ideological justification has been based on a concept of
sovereignty. It has been pointed out that "the state-employer
insists that its role as sovereign entitles it to special privileges
as an employer to which other employers may lay no claim." [20]
It is generally alleged that the state's sovereignty resides in
the people as a whole, and therefore "a public employee has
as his employer all of the people [and] the people cannot

[20] Spero, "Employer and Employee," p. 171.

tolerate an attack upon themselves" by striking or subversive civil servants.[21] Nor can the people allow a civil servant to use any special ability derived from his position "to influence the political judgment of the people." [22] In short, it is argued that public servants have a public trust and therefore some of their constitutional rights must be sacrificed for the good of the political system and its members.[23]

The judicial justification of negative discrimination has also been of importance. In recent years the courts have played a major role in determining the acceptable range of discrimination. Under the Constitution arguments concerning the public employment relationship can be divided into those dealing with substantive rights and those dealing with procedural rights. Substantively, the central issue has been whether removal from, or refusal of, public employment for reasons of speech, association, religious and political beliefs, or the exercise of other individual rights should be considered to be unconstitutional violations of those rights. Procedurally, the major questions have been whether government employment should be considered to be property, whether removals or refusals of employment should be considered to be denials of liberty, and if so what forms of procedural due process under the Fifth Amendment should pre-

[21] Thomas E. Dewey, quoted in Frederick L. Mosher, "Features and Problems of the Federal Service," in Sayre (ed.), *Federal Government Service*, p. 166.

[22] *Ibid.* Mosher is summarizing an argument commonly made rather than advocating this position.

[23] The concept of public trust is deeply ingrained in American political life. In *People* v. *Murrary*, 307 Ill. 349 (1923) the Illinois Supreme Court stated: "That a public office is a public trust is a principle of law as well as a political maxim." More recently it was held to be "a living tenet of our society and not mere rhetoric that a public office is a public trust." *Neusse* v. *Camp*, 385 F. 2d 694, 706 (1967).

vail; and whether refusal of, or removal from, public employment for reasons which stigmatize the individual's reputation, such as disloyalty, immorality, or dishonesty, should be considered to be punishment and require a jury trial and other Sixth Amendment procedures.

The traditional doctrine has been the "doctrine of privilege." This doctrine is based on the premise that because there is no constitutional right to public employment, there are few or no constitutional rights which cannot be restricted while the citizen is in public employment. The most concise statement of the principle has been Justice Holmes's well-known dictum that "the petitioner may have a constitutional right to talk politics, but he has no constitutional right to be a policeman." [24] Under this doctrine, when the citizen accepts public employment he accepts all the conditions which go along with it. If these conditions specify political neutrality or some other negative discrimination the employee's constitutional rights are not violated, because his acceptance of these restrictions is voluntary rather than compelled. The doctrine has been summarized as follows:

Its central tenet is that office is held at the pleasure of the government. Its general effect is that the government may impose any requirement it sees fit as conditional to employment. From the point of view of the state, public employment is maintained as an indulgence; from the position of the citizen, his job is a grant concerning which he has no independent rights.[25]

[24] *McAuliffe* v. *New Bedford,* 155 Mass. 216, 220 (1892). Holmes was then a judge on the Massachusetts Supreme Court.

[25] Arch Dotson, "The Emerging Doctrine of Privilege in Public Employment," *Public Administration Review,* XV (Spring 1955), 77. Dotson called the doctrine "emerging" because it was not until 1947 that the Supreme Court appeared to accept it, although the doctrine had been the basis of several lower federal court decisions and state court decisions by that time.

This doctrine began to undergo important modification in the 1940's and was completely rejected in the 1960's.

The doctrine which presently determines the constitutional acceptability of negative discriminations is the "doctrine of substantial interest." This doctrine starts "with the premise that a state [or the federal government] cannot condition an individual's privilege of public employment on his non-participation in conduct which under the Constitution is protected from direct interference by the state." [26] The doctrine is not simply one of unconstitutional substantive conditions, however; it also requires that "whenever there is a substantial interest, other than employment by the state, involved in the discharge of a public employee, he can be removed neither on arbitrary grounds nor without a procedure calculated to determine whether legitimate grounds do exist." [27] The newer doctrine accepts the old premise that there is no constitutional right to public employment, but rejects the conclusion that therefore there are no constitutional rights which cannot be abridged while in office. In developing this doctrine, the courts have recently redefined the public employment relationship.

In the remainder of this study the development of the public employment relationship is analyzed. This analysis does not examine every discrimination of the relationship but rather seeks to explain its historical development. Special emphasis has been given to the judicial doctrines concerning the relationship, and especially to the change from the doctrine of privilege to that of substantial interest. It has been possible to proceed in this fashion because the areas of discrimination which have been of greatest importance to the development of judicial doctrines concerning the relationship—that is, po-

[26] *Gilmore* v. *James,* 274 F. Supp. 75, 91 (1967).
[27] *Birnbaum* v. *Trussell,* 371 F. 2d 672, 678 (1966).

litical neutrality, equality of access to civil service positions, and loyalty-security—have also included the most important discriminations of the public employment relationship itself. The analysis has not, however, been confined to judicial decisions, but has sought to explain the origin of discriminations of the public employment relationship as well.

1 | Development of the Public Employment Relationship, 1776-1829

I

During the period 1776–1829 a discriminatory public employment relationship developed in the United States. The direction of discrimination was negative, as it has been ever since, although there were important factors tending toward positive discrimination as well. The immediate development of negative discrimination was largely due to a prevailing suspicion against public officials which had evolved during the colonial period. The predisposition of Americans to regulate the behavior and authority of public officers strictly was indicated by their complaint in the Declaration of Independence that King George III had "erected a multitude of new offices, and sent hither swarms of officers to harass our people, and eat out their substance." The major factor encouraging positive discrimination was a tendency to regard office as a form of property. This tendency was also a legacy of Colonial administration, in which office was sometimes bought and sold,[1]

[1] This practice was not uncommon. In 1739 the buying and selling of county clerkships in Maryland was criticized in the Lower House in which it was declared that practice tended to ruin the colony. See Charles A. Barker, *Background of the Revolution in Maryland* (New Haven: Yale University Press, 1940), pp. 226, 230; Md., *Lower House Journal* XL, 392–95 (1739); Donnell M. Owings, *His Lordship's Patronage* (Baltimore: Maryland Historical Society, 1953), p.

tenure was often for life, kinship was important and office was often "inherited" on an informal basis, and office was generally reserved for members of the upper social classes.

The public employment relationship became negatively discriminatory under the authority of the Continental Congress, which attempted to circumvent the widespread use of patronage, which had been common during the colonial era, by adopting the following resolution:

Whereas it may be highly injurious to the interest of these United States, to permit candidates for public offices to vote in or other ways influence their own elections: *"Resolved,* That Congress will not appoint any member thereof during the term of his sitting, or within six months after he shall have been in Congress, to any office under the said states for which he or any others for his benefit may receive any salary, fees or other emolument." [2]

The resolution established a negatively discriminatory relationship because it prohibited the employment of persons, although for a limited period, on the basis of their legitimate previous political activity, that is, membership in Congress. [3]

----

32. In 1737 South Carolina outlawed the practice; see S.C., *Statutes at Large of South Carolina,* III, 468, No. 623 (1737). As late as 1775–1776 an officeholder wrote Governor Martin of North Carolina that "the office which I have for some years past executed . . . was an honest purchase." William L. Sanders (ed.), *Colonial Records of North Carolina* (Raleigh: Josephus Daniels, 1890), X, 333. The sale of office was also practiced in Virginia. See K. W. Swart, *The Sale of Offices in the Seventeenth Century* (The Hague: Martinus Nijhoff, 1949), p. 65; and also Leonard Woods Labaree, *Royal Government in America* (New Haven: Yale University Press, 1930), pp. 40–41, 50.

[2] U.S., *Journals of The Continental Congress,* XV, 1269 (November 15, 1779).

[3] The prohibition on dual officeholding can be considered either a separation-of-powers provision, or a conflict-of-interest regulation and therefore outside the relationship.

The range of discrimination was, of course, very limited because the degree and domain of discrimination were both minor.

Earlier, in 1777, the Congress had indicated its suspicion of public officers by instituting a limited "loyalty program." It adopted the following resolution:

It being represented in Congress, that persons disaffected with the American cause, have, through inadvertence, been employed as deputy post masters and post riders; which, if true, must be attended with the most mischievous effects:

Resolved, that the post master general be and hereby is directed to transmit to Congress, a list of names of the persons so employed, and by whose recommendations they were introduced, that Congress may consider, and, if necessary, take orders thereon.[4]

Two years later, after a committee of Congress sought means to "prevent persons disaffected to the interests of the United States from being employed in any of the important offices thereof," Congress required all federal civilian and military officers to take the following oath:

I_____ do acknowledge the United States of America to be free, independent and sovereign states, and declare the people thereof owe no allegiance or obedience to George the 3d, King of Great Britain; and I renounce, refuse and abjure any allegiance or obedience to him; and I do swear (or affirm) that I will, to the utmost of my power, support, maintain, and defend the United States against the said King . . . and his heirs and successors, and his and their abettors, assistants and adherents and I will serve the said United States in the office of _____ which I now hold, with fidelity, according to the best of my skill and understanding. So help me God.[5]

[4] U.S., *Journals of the Continental Congress,* VII, 29–30 (January 11, 1777).

[5] See Harold M. Hyman, *To Try Men's Souls* (Berkeley: University of California Press, 1959), pp. 82–83.

Although the resolution and the oath tended toward negative discrimination, they did not establish it because the right to be disloyal to the American cause, despite the disloyalty of a large proportion of the population, was not, at the time, an ordinary citizen right. It is also unclear whether any action was taken under the resolution. These measures provided, however, a precedent for excluding citizens from the civil service on the basis of their political beliefs.

The belief that the government or the public interest might be betrayed by disloyal civil servants was the basis of the first restriction of any importance on the behavior of public servants. Article VI of the Articles of Confederation provided that no "person holding any office of profit or trust under the United States, or any of them, [shall] accept any present, emolument, office or title of any kind whatever, from any king, prince or foreign state." Therefore behavior which could be legitimate for ordinary citizens was not legitimate for civil servants. The major importance of the provision was less in its extension of the range of discrimination than in its creation of a precedent for restricting the ordinary rights of citizens while they are in public employment.

The Constitution contains several provisions affecting the public employment relationship, and under the government it established the range of discrimination has become as extensive as that in any modern democratic political system.[6] Article I, section 3, allowed formal disqualification for public service under certain circumstances: "Impeachment shall not extend further than to removal from office and disqualification to hold and enjoy any office of honor, trust or profit under

[6] The framers, of course, could not have anticipated this development or the importance of several constitutional provisions upon it. It should be remembered that the word "administration" does not even appear in the Constitution.

the United States." Article I, section 6, prohibited the appointment of former members of Congress to "any civil office under the authority of the United States, which shall have been created, or the emoluments whereof shall have been increased during such time." [7] Article I, section 9, repeated Article VI of the Articles of Confederation, but allowed public officers to receive presents, emoluments, and the like if Congress gave its consent, and Article II, section 1, prohibited persons "holding an office of trust or profit under the United States" from being electors in the electoral college. Article VI established a significant increase in the range of discrimination: "All executive and judicial officers, both of the United States and of the several States, shall be bound by oath or affirmation, to support this Constitution." This provision can be used to exclude citizens on the basis of their political beliefs and thereby restrict their ordinary First Amendment rights. At the time of the adoption of the Constitution the provision was important because it could be used to exclude anti-federalists who were an important segment of the population, and who until 1791 were able to prevent ratification of the Constitution in North Carolina and Rhode Island. Article VI also made formal negative discrimination on the basis of religious beliefs unconstitutional by providing that "no religious test shall ever be required as a qualification to any office or public trust under the United States."

Several other constitutional provisions have had an indirect effect on the development of the public employment relationship. The most important provision in this respect, aside from

[7] Article V of the Articles of Confederation had removed the six-month restriction on the appointment of congressmen. The constitutional provision was the center of lengthy debate at the Constitutional Convention. See Max Farrand (ed.), *Records of the Federal Convention* (New Haven: Yale University Press, 1911), I, 386ff., II, 282ff., 489ff.

the Bill of Rights, was Article II, section 2, which anticipated the formation of executive departments but did not establish them. It provides that the president

shall nominate, and by and with the advice and consent of the Senate, shall appoint ambassadors, other public ministers and consuls, judges of the Supreme Court, and all other officers of the United States whose appointments are not otherwise herein provided for, and which shall be established by law: but the Congress may by law vest the appointment of such inferior officers, as they think proper, in the President alone, in the Courts of law, or in the heads of departments.

This provision is extensive in its scope. It limits the appointment power, provides that offices must be created by law rather than by executive fiat, and allows Congress to regulate the appointment of lesser civil servants.[8]

The Constitution was silent on two administrative features which are of great importance to the public employment relationship. It did not overtly, except in the instance of impeachment,[9] determine the tenure or method of removal of appointed executive officers and employees. These features are important because constitutionally guaranteed tenure or removal only after elaborate procedures, such as impeachment, can encourage the development of positive discrimination and tend to make the public employment relationship less nega-

---

[8] This provision was changed very late in the Constitutional Convention. Originally, it was to allow the president to appoint "to all offices which may hereafter be created by law." The change has been of great importance to administration because it gives Congress an important share of authority in regulating the civil service. See *ibid.,* II, 23, 405, 406, 627–28.

[9] Article II, section 4: "The President, Vice President and all civil officers of the United States, shall be removed from office on impeachment for, and conviction of, treason, bribery, or other high crimes and misdemeanors."

tively discriminatory by making it more difficult to enforce restrictions through the threat of removal. For example, if tenure were during good behavior and the only constitutional method of removal were through impeachment, a common negative discrimination, that of dismissal on the basis of political beliefs, could not occur. On the other hand, when tenure and removal are unregulated, it is easier to establish formal legal and informal negative discriminations. Madison and Hamilton attempted to clarify the constitutional intention with respect to removal in the *Federalist Papers,* but only succeeded in obscuring the issue. In number thirty-nine, Madison wrote that a republic "is administered by persons holding their offices during pleasure for a limited period or during good behavior." [10] He went on to say that "the tenure of ministerial offices generally will be a subject of legal regulation." [11] In number seventy-seven, however, Hamilton indicated that the Constitution defined the removal power in the case of presidential officers.[12] He wrote:

It has been mentioned as one of the advantages to be expected from the cooperation of the Senate in the business of appointment, that it would contribute to the stability of the administration. The consent of that body would be necessary to displace as well as to appoint. A change of the Chief Magistrate, therefore, would not occasion so violent or so general revolution in the officers of the government as might be expected if he were the sole disposer of offices. Where a man in any station had given satisfactory evidence of his fitness for it, a new President would be restrained from attempting a change in favor of a person more agreeable to him by the apprehension that a discontenance of the

[10] *The Federalist Papers,* ed. Clinton Rossiter (New York: The New American Library, 1961), p. 241.

[11] *Ibid.,* p. 242.

[12] Presidential officers are those appointed by the president with the advice and consent of the Senate.

Senate might frustrate the attempt, and bring some degree of discredit upon himself.[13]

The questions of tenure and removal for presidential officers was settled in practice by congressional action in 1789.

II

The "Decision of 1789" has had an important effect on the public employment relationship. It was made in the House during the course of establishing a Department of Foreign Affairs and it concerned the president's power to remove the department head. By implication the decision might have been applicable to other presidential officers as well. The following major positions were put forward.

1. The power to remove was part of the executive power granted to the president by the Constitution and therefore he could exercise it without the advice and consent of the Senate.

2. The power to remove was connected to the power to appoint and therefore the Constitution required the Senate's concurrence.

3. The only constitutional means of removal was impeachment.

4. The Constitution gave Congress the authority to decide where the removal power should be vested.

    A. Congress should vest it in the president alone.

    B. Congress should vest it in the president and the Senate.

The final decision gave the removal power to the president alone through an alliance between those holding positions 1 and 4A above.[14]

[13] *Federalist Papers*, p. 459.

[14] The act hedged the constitutional question by allowing removal "whenever the said principal officer shall be removed by the presi-

If position 3 had been chosen the public employment relationship would almost certainly have been less negatively discriminatory, and possibly partially positively discriminatory. This position would have given presidential officers tenure during good behavior, rather than at pleasure, and important procedural rights in removals. These rights might have been extended to lesser officers as well.[15] If position 2 or 4B had been chosen the development of the relationship would also have been quite different. This position probably would have led to a less negatively discriminatory relationship because the president would have had to supply reasons for the proposed removal and the Senate would have had to deliberate upon them. Under this decision removals might have become similar to trials or impeachment proceedings. If this position had been adopted, it might have been extended to lesser officers as a matter of policy.

Although the primary importance of the congressional debate involved the extent of the executive power, several arguments concerning the public employment relationship

---

dent." The vote in the House was 31 to 19 with 9 not voting. It was passed in the Senate upon the tie-breaking vote of Vice President Adams. See U.S., *Annals of the Congress of the United States,* 1st Cong., 1st Session, I, 578, 580, 585 (June 16–22, 1789). The decision was nullified by the Tenure of Office Act of 1867, U.S., *Statutes at Large,* XIV, 430 (March 2, 1867), but was held to be the *only* constitutional means of removal, aside from impeachment, in *Myers* v. *United States,* 272 U.S. 552 (1926). See also *Humphrey's Executor* v. *United States,* 295 U.S. 602 (1935) and *Weiner* v. *United States,* 357 U.S. 349 (1958).

[15] Madison understood this to be the case. He argued that if impeachment were the only constitutional means of removal for presidential officers, it would constitutionally be the only means for removing all officers. Representative Smith of South Carolina, the major proponent of impeachment, disagreed, citing Congress' authority to establish inferior officers on whatever terms it thought proper. See *Annals of Congress,* I, 547–48.

were made. These arguments tended to center on two distinct positions which have been relevant to the development of the public employment relationship throughout United States history. On the one hand, it was argued that removal had an adverse effect on the dismissed which warranted a procedural check on the removal power in order to insure fair treatment of the individual. On the other hand, it was argued that removal free of cumbersome procedures was necessary to prevent officers from using their authority against their superiors or the public interest.

Representative Smith of South Carolina put forward the most extreme arguments in favor of protection for the individual. Although his arguments had little practical chance of success at the time, they represented an alternative under consideration, had some logical force, and were in some ways similar to arguments currently forming the basis of the doctrine of substantial interest. Smith's question was, "For what cause should a man be removed from office?"

If you desire an officer to be a man of capacity and integrity, you may be disappointed. A gentleman possessed of these qualities, knowing he may be removed at the pleasure of the President, will be loath to risk his reputation on such insecure ground. As the matter stands in the Constitution, he knows if he is suspected of doing anything wrong, he shall have a fair trial [i.e., impeachment] . . . But if he is subjected to the whim of any man, it may deter him from entering into the service of his country; because if he is not subservient to that person's pleasure, he may be turned out, and the public may be led to suppose, for improper behavior. . . . The public suppose him guilty of malpractices. Hence his reputation is blasted, his property sacrificed. I say his property is sacrificed, because I consider his office as property. He is stripped of this, and left exposed to the malevolence of the world, contrary to the principles of all free governments, which are, that no man shall be despoiled of his property but by a fair and impartial trial.[16]

For Smith such dismissal was "to inflict the punishment without trial, when the Constitution requires it to be done on impeachment and conviction." [17]

Smith, although advocating a decidedly minority position, was not alone. Representative Livermore of New Hampshire agreed that

when an important and confidential trust is placed in a man, it is worse than death to him to be displaced without cause; his reputation depends on the single will of the President, who may ruin him on bare suspicion. Nay, a new President may turn him out on mere caprice, or in order to make room for a favorite. This contradicts all my notions of property; everything of this sort should be with due deliberation; every person ought to have a hearing before he is punished.[18]

Although during this period removals generally indicated fault, Smith's and Livermore's arguments were apparently enhanced by the not uncommon practice of overtly stigmatizing individuals in the process of dismissal. For example, in 1780 it was recommended that two members of the Treasury Board under the Continental Congress be dismissed for "disgusting conduct," [19] and several years later, John Quincy

[16] *Ibid.*, pp. 457–58.

[17] *Ibid.*, p. 471. Smith changed his position in later years. See Leonard D. White, *The Federalists* (New York: The Free Press, 1965), p. 21.

[18] *Annals of Congress*, I, 479.

[19] See Jay Caesar Guggenheimer, "The Development of the Executive Departments," in J. Franklin Jameson (ed.), *Essays in Constitutional History of the United States in the Formative Period, 1775–1789* (Boston: Houghton, Mifflin and Co., 1889), pp. 135–36.

Adams dismissed a clerk for "neglect of duty and groveling vices." [20]

Representative Gerry of Massachusetts based his argument in favor of protection of the individual on the requirements of of republican government:

Suppose an officer discharges his duty as the law directs, yet the President will remove him; he will be guided by some other criterion; perhaps the officer is not good-natured enough; he makes an ungraceful bow, or does it left leg foremost; this is unbecoming in a great officer at the President's levee. Now because he is so unfortunate as not to be so good a dancer and he is a worthy officer, he must be removed. The Senate, and this House, may think it necessary to inquire why a good officer is dismissed. The President will say it is my pleasure; I am authorized by law to exercise this prerogative; I have my reasons for it, but you have no right to require them of me. This language may be proper in a monarchy; but in a republic every action out is to be accounted for.[21]

This argument is similar to present-day arguments against the dismissal of civil servants for arbitrary reasons, especially when those reasons extend the range of discrimination.

Arguing against these views were those who believed the good of the community should come before the good of the individual officer whose position made it possible for him to injure the public interest. Representative Hartley of Pennsylvania rejected the concept of property in office:

The gentleman [Smith] further contends, that every man has a property in his office, and ought not to be removed but for criminal conduct. . . . I hope this doctrine will never be admitted in this country. A man when in office ought to have abilities to dis-

[20] See Leonard D. White, *The Jeffersonians* (New York: The Free Press, 1965), p. 190.

[21] *Annals of Congress,* I, 574.

charge the duties of it; if he is discovered to be unfit, he ought to be immediately removed. . . . If he has an estate in his office, his right must be purchased, and a practice like what obtains in England will be adopted here; we shall be unable to dismiss an officer without allowing him a pension for the interest he is deprived of.[22]

Several members of Congress shared Hartley's sentiments and made arguments similar to those favoring and justifying negative discrimination. Ames of Massachusetts thought that an officer "ought to be removed at any time, when, instead of doing the greatest possible good, he is likely to do an injury to the public interest."[23] He feared that "It will be as frequently necessary to prevent crimes as to punish them, and it may often happen that the only prevention is by removal."[24] This argument is similar to some of those presently made in defense of loyalty-security provisions which seek to prevent injury, rather than to punish civil servants after the injury has been done.

Madison was the leading proponent of vesting the removal power in the President alone. He believed that "the danger to liberty, the danger to maladministration, has not yet been found to lie so much in the facility of introducing improper persons into office, as in the difficulty of displacing those who are unworthy of public trust."[25] Similarly, Vining of Delaware asked, "If he cannot be removed, I should suppose he cannot be suspended; and what security have the people against the machinations of a bad man in office?"[26]

In answer to those who foresaw an injury to the dismissed officer, some congressmen adopted arguments similar to those used under the doctrine of privilege. Representative Boudinot of New Jersey stated:

[22] *Ibid.*, p. 480.   [23] *Ibid.*, p. 474.   [24] *Ibid.*, p. 475.
[25] *Ibid.*, p. 496.   [26] *Ibid.*, p. 373.

If it is said that this is an injury to the individual, I confess that it is possible that it may be so. But ought we not in the first place to consult the public good? But on mature consideration, I do not apprehend any very great injury will result to the individual from this practice, because . . . he knows the tenure by which he is to hold it, and ought to be prepared against every contingency.[27]

Hartley believed that "it does not always imply criminality to be removed from office, because it may be proper to remove for other causes." [28]

Representative Stone of Maryland accepted the right of removal, but was apprehensive that it might not be exercised for proper reasons: "In public and private life, it may be proper to discharge an agent without divulging the reason; yet clearly a good reason ought to precede the dismission, because otherwise you do an act of injustice by a breach of [implied] contract." [29] Representatives Benson and Baldwin argued that the president would be restrained from unjustly removing officers because his power of appointment was limited and he would therefore have nothing to gain from such removals.[30] Others argued that even if the president did make unjust removals, the check on the appointment power would prevent injury to the nation. Representative Clymer of Pennsylvania asked, "What great danger would arise from the removal of a worthy man, when the Senate must be consulted in the appointment of his successor?" [31] and Boudinot argued:

If he removes a good officer, he cannot appoint his successor without the consent of the Senate; and it is fairly to be presumed, that if at any time he should be guilty of such an oversight, as to remove a useful and valuable officer, the evil will be small, because another as valuable will be placed in his stead.[32]

[27] *Ibid.*, p. 529.　　[28] *Ibid.*, p. 481.　　[29] *Ibid.*, p. 567.
[30] *Ibid.*, pp. 382, 559.　　[31] *Ibid.*, p. 489.　　[32] *Ibid.*, p. 529.

The two schools of thought expressed during the debate have persistently influenced the development of the public employment relationship throughout United States history. The position favoring easy removal and its judicial counterpart, the doctrine of privilege, have, for the most part, been dominant. In recent years, however, arguments placing greater importance on the injury to the individual's reputation or constitutional rights which may be caused by removal or exclusion have become the basis of the doctrine of substantial interest. Similarly, although the belief that a check on appointment is an adequate check on removal has been dominant for most of United States history, civil servants have, in recent years, been afforded important procedural rights in removals.[33]

III

The public employment relationship underwent significant and substantially uniform development during the administrations of the first six presidents. President Washington was concerned with establishing the new government on a firm and lasting basis. He considered "the successful administration of the general government as an object of almost infinite consequence to the present and future happiness of the citizens of the United States." [34] He sought to establish proper precedents because

many things which appear of little importance in themselves at the beginning may have great and durable consequences from their having been established at the commencement of a new general government. It will be much easier to commence the administration, upon a well adjusted system, built on tenable grounds,

[33] See chaps, 3, 5, 7, 8, *infra*.
[34] George Washington, *The Writings of George Washington*, ed. John Fitzpatrick (Washington: U.S. Government Printing Office, 1931), XXX, 510.

than to correct errors or other inconveniences after they shall have been confirmed by habit.[35]

The precedential nature of the negative discrimination created during this period has had lasting effects upon the public employment relationship.

Washington probably had greater political and legal freedom in appointment and removal [36] than any other president. From a political standpoint, his election generated no campaign debts, being the first president he had no removal problem, and political competition was not as important as it would later become. The only significant legal restriction on his appointment authority was a law implementing the constitutional provision requiring civil servants to swear their allegiance to the Constitution.[37] Tenure was generally at the

[35] *Ibid.*, p. 321.

[36] Throughout this discussion, presidential appointment and removal policies concern only presidential officers unless otherwise indicated. This restriction is necessary because data concerning lesser officers are not available. The discussion is based on the following: Paul P. Van Riper, *History of the United States Civil Service* (Evanston: Row, Peterson and Co., 1958), especially pp. 16–23; Leonard D. White, *The Federalists*, pp. 258–85; White, *Jeffersonians*, pp. 347–69; Carl R. Fish, *The Civil Service and the Patronage* (New York: Longmans, Green and Co., 1905), especially pp. 1–79; Sidney Aronson, *Status and Kinship: Standards of Selection in the Administrations of John Adams, Thomas Jefferson, and Andrew Jackson* (Cambridge: Harvard University Press, 1964); Herbert Kaufman, "The Growth of the Federal Personnel System," in Wallace Sayre (ed.), *The Federal Government Service* (Englewood Cliffs: Prentice-Hall, 1965), pp. 12–20.

[37] U.S., *Statutes at Large*, I, 23 (June 1, 1789). There were some others of lesser importance. For example, a law enacted on September 2, 1789, prohibited persons in the Treasury Department from being connected with the carrying trade, to own part or all of a "seavessel," or to be connected with the purchase or disposal of public securities and the purchase of public property. An offense was punishable by a $3,000 fine and, of importance to the public employment

pleasure of the appointing officer [38] and removal was unrestricted by procedural requirements.

In making appointments, Washington's "primary object" was "fitness of character." [39] For Washington fitness of character meant standing in the community and personal integrity. His appointments to significant civil service positions therefore tended to be restricted to members of the upper social classes. At the time, this practice appeared to be in the natural order of things, and no real alternative had been suggested by English or Colonial administration. Although it was a nonspecialized age and upper social class status often coincided with education and competence, this was not always the case. In a colonial Virginia, for example, county justices were generally members of the upper social classes, but often had no knowledge of law when they were appointed.[40] During Washington's administration, "nowhere in the Department [of State] was there a single person other than the Secretary who had experience or training in foreign affairs." [41] Washington's appointment policy was an important negative discrimination and extension of the range of discrimination because it restricted access to civil service positions to members of the upper social classes and thereby abridged the

relationship, disqualification forever from holding any appointive office under the United States. See *ibid.*, p. 68, section 8.

[38] There were some exceptions. The Judiciary Act of 1789 provided for marshalls with a four-year term but removable at pleasure as well. *Ibid.*, p. 88 (September 24, 1789). In 1801, Congress established a five-year term for justices of the peace in the District of Columbia. *Ibid.*, II, 107 (February 27, 1801).

[39] Washington, *Writings*, XXX, 469.

[40] Charles S. Sydnor, *Gentlemen Freeholders: Political Practices in Washington's Virginia* (Chapel Hill: University of North Carolina Press, 1952), pp. 6–7.

[41] White, *Federalists*, p. 128.

basic equality of citizens implied if not overtly provided for in the Constitution.

Several other elements in Washington's appointment policy also interfered with citizen equality. Place of residence, military service, previous service under the Confederation or state governments, and financial needs were also considered. For the public employment relationship a requirement of loyalty to the new government [42] and of political orthodoxy were of greatest importance. In 1795, Washington wrote,

I shall not, whilst I have the honor to administer the government, bring a man into any office, of consequence knowingly whose political tenets are adverse to the measures which the general government are pursuing; for this, in my opinion, would be a sort of political suicide.[43]

This was an important negative discrimination and extension of the range of discrimination because it interfered with the citizen's First Amendment rights and was destined to become one of the most common discriminations of the public employment relationship.[44]

President Adams' personnel practices were similar to Washington's but were more politically oriented. He once stated, "Political principles, and discretion, will always be considered with other qualifications, and well weighed, in all appointments." [45] He also said that "Washington appointed a multitude of democrats and jacobins of the deepest die. I have

---

[42] *Ibid.,* p. 271.   [43] Washington, *Writings,* XXXIV, 315.

[44] Washington made only 17 removals, none of which were important to the public employment relationship. See Fish, *Civil Service,* p. 13. Table 3 presents the removal of presidential officers between 1789 and 1869.

[45] Quoted in Howard Lee McBain, *De Witt Clinton and the Origin of the Spoils System in New York* (New York: Columbia University Press, 1907), p. 58.

been more cautious in this respect." [46] Adams did not wholly proscribe Republicans, but he certainly favored Federalists. When Jefferson became president, he found that "out of about six-hundred officers named by the President there were six Republicans only . . . and these were chiefly halfbreeds." [47] Adams, it will be recalled, was also responsible for the midnight appointees of *Marbury* v. *Madison* fame. Adams' appointment policy with respect to social class standing was similar to that of Washington in its results. Adams sought talent rather than upper social class status in making appointments, but he defined talent mainly in terms of a college education and realized that it was largely confined to members of the upper class.[48] At the time of his presidency, Adams apparently also believed that appointments from the upper social classes were better for all members of the political system because: "The proposition that they [the people] are the best keepers of their liberties, is not true. They are the worst conceivable; they are no keepers at all. They can neither act, judge, think, or will." [49] Adams' appointment policy, therefore continued the negative discriminations with regard to access to the civil service which had been established by Washington, and increased the importance of partisan political commitment.

Adams' Removal policy was also more politically motivated and he established important precedents for making removals on the basis of political beliefs and activities. As Table 3 indicates, he made twenty-one removals; and while

[46] Quoted in White, *Federalists*, p. 273.

[47] Thomas Jefferson, *The Works of Thomas Jefferson*, ed. P. L. Ford (New York: G. P. Putnam's Sons, 1904), X, 393–94.

[48] Aronson, *Status and Kinship*, p. 3.

[49] John Adams, *The Works of John Adams*, ed. Charles F. Adams (Boston: Little, Brown and Co., 1850), VI, 7. The statement is quoted by Aronson, *Status and Kinship*, p. 5, who believes it is representative of Adams' thought during his presidency.

most of these were for cause, some were clearly for political reasons. Adams' dismissal in 1797 of Trench Coxe, Commissioner of Revenue, was "the first" removal for party reasons in the history of the federal government.[50] Two of Adams' best-known removals were based on a combination of political activity and loyalty factors. Two federal officers in New Hampshire were dismissed after failing to support Federalist policy with respect to France. Adams dismissed them because "their political conduct has been disrespectful to the government and offensive to good men in the extreme." [51]

The range of discrimination of the public employment relationship became more extended under Jefferson and his political followers. By the election of 1800, political competition organized around identifiable partisan groups had become important, and Jefferson became the first president to succeed an incumbent of the opposition party. His personnel policies were consequently more politically oriented than those of Washington or Adams. Jefferson complained of Adams' appointment policy and especially of his midnight appointees.[52] He sought to redress the balance by appointing

[50] Fish, *Civil Service*, p. 19.

[51] Quoted in H. Eliot Kaplan, "Political Neutrality of the Civil Service," *Public Personnel Review*, I (April 1940), 11. Prior to their removal the *Columbia Centinel* said, "They want only for a safe occasion to betray our country to France." See Fish, *Civil Service*, p. 20.

[52] Jefferson was somewhat bitter about these appointees. He once stated that "one act of Mr. Adams life, and one only, ever gave me a moment's displeasure. I did consider his last appointments to office as personally unkind. They were from among my most ardent political enemies, from whom no faithful cooperation could ever be expected, and laid me under the embarrassment of acting through men whose views were to defeat mine, or to encounter the odium of putting others in their places." Quoted in William C. Deming, *The Application of the Merit System in the United States Civil Service* (Washington: U.S. Government Printing Office, 1928), p. 43.

only Republicans until the proportion of Federalists and Republicans in the civil service roughly approximated the proportion of each in the nation. He originally intended, at least overtly, to ignore political opinions and affiliation once the balance was reached and to appoint only on the basis of honesty, capability, and faithfulness to the Constitution. In practice, however, he continued to appoint only Republicans after a balance was reached.[53]

Jefferson was also politically motivated in his removal policy. He believed that in order to redress the balance some removals were necessary. Although his right to remove higher officers was accepted by both Federalists and Republicans, many believed lesser civil servants should be left undisturbed.[54] He was therefore cautious in making removals:

I proceed in the operation with deliberation and inquiry, that it may injure the best men least, and effect the purposes of justice and political utility with the least private distress; that it may be thrown, as much as possible, on delinquency, on oppression, on intolerance, on incompetence, on ante-revolutionary adherence to our enemies.[55]

One of the most significant aspects of Jefferson's removal policy was his development of a concept of political neutrality for civil servants. In 1801, he issued the following circular:

the President of the United States has seen with dissatisfaction officers of the general government taking on various occasions active parts in the elections of public functionaries, whether of the general or state governments. . . . The right of any officer to give his vote at elections as a qualified citizen is not meant to be

[53] Fish, *Civil Service,* p. 44. See also Nobel E. Cunningham, *The Jeffersonian Republicans in Power* (Chapel Hill: University of North Carolina Press, 1963), chaps. i–iii.

[54] White, *Jeffersonians,* p. 347.

[55] Jefferson, *Works,* IX, 273–74.

restrained, nor, however given, shall it have any effect to his prejudice; but it is expected that he will not attempt to influence the votes of others, nor take any part in the business of electioneering, that being deemed inconsistent with the spirit of the Constitution and his duties to it.[56]

The circular was ineffective, and Jefferson removed primarily those officers engaging in political activity against his administration. In 1802 he wrote Elbridge Gerry:

After twelve months' trial I have at length been induced to remove three or four more of those most marked for their bitterness and active zeal in slandering and in electioneering . . . such officers as shall afterwards continue to bid us defiance shall as certainly be removed, if the case shall become known.[57]

With respect to the Massachusetts election of that year he said, "I think it not amiss that it would be known that we are determined to remove officers who are active or open mouthed against the government, by which I mean the legislative as well as the executive." [58] In all, Jefferson removed 109 out of 433 officers in the presidential class, and there were changes in several hundred lesser posts as well.[59]

Although Jefferson's appointments were politically different from those of the Federalist presidents, their social class status was approximately the same. Jefferson sought to appoint members of the "natural aristocracy," that is, an educated elite, rather than members of the "artificial aristocracy," which he believed was "a mischievous ingredient in government." [60]

[56] James D. Richardson (ed.), *A Compilation of the Messages and Papers of the Presidents, 1789–1897* (Washington: U.S. Government Printing Office, 1899), X, 98–99.

[57] Jefferson, *Works,* IX, 392–93.

[58] *Ibid.,* pp. 401–402.

[59] Fish, *Civil Service,* p. 42; Kaufman, "Federal Personnel," p. 16. See also Table 3.

[60] Quoted in Aronson, *Status and Kinship,* p. 8.

However, he also sought "respectability in the public estimation," [61] and as in Adams' case, his emphasis on education led him to restrict appointment primarily to members of the upper social classes.[62]

The appointment and removal policies of Presidents Madison, Monroe, and John Quincy Adams did little to alter the range of discrimination established under Jefferson. For the most part, they took over civil services to their liking and made few, if any political removals. They continued to make appointments on the basis of partisanship and upper social

[61] Jefferson, *Works*, IX, 255.

[62] Aronson, *Status and Kinship*, pp. 11–14, *passim*. It is probable, although by no means certain, that Jefferson made the civil service somewhat more representative. See Fish, *Civil Service*, pp. 49–50; Van Riper, *History*, pp. 23–24; White, *Jeffersonians*, pp. 4–5. Aronson concluded that Jefferson's "elite" civil service appointments were more representative, but deficiencies in his analysis make this conclusion questionable. One problem in his analysis is that it is confined to elite positions, which were defined as "full time, civil positions filled by presidential appointment which involved responsibilities affecting the nation as a whole and which were not guaranteed tenure by the Constitution" (p. 31). This definition is misleading though, because judges, whose tenure was guaranteed by the Constitution, were included. Aronson's elite positions include the following: the six cabinet members; eleven members of the Treasury Department excluding the Secretary; territorial governors, secretaries, and judges; ministers plenipotentiary and/or extraordinary; five officers in the land office; five other executive officers; Supreme Court Justices and circuit and district court judges. The total number of position titles was 36. Out of these position titles 5 were judges and 1 was attorney general. These officers were likely to be lawyers, and Aronson considered occupation to be a major indicator of social status, and law to be an upper social class profession (pp. 33, 38). His analysis is therefore somewhat tautological. The defect is especially severe when one considers the fact that Adams appointed 44 judges and 2 attorneys general out of a total of 96 appointments; Jefferson 46 and 4 out of 100; and Jackson 44 and 3 out of 127 (p. 170 and Appendix C). Another serious problem is the large proportion of unknowns, sometimes reaching 50 per cent and not uncommonly between 10 and 20 per cent.

class standing. During their administrations, however, there were some laws enacted which had an important effect on the development of the public employment relationship. In 1810 the range of discrimination was increased when the employment of Negroes in the postal service was prohibited.[63] From a systemic point of view, the enactment of the Tenure of Office Act of 1820 [64] was more significant. The act established a tenure of four years for most officers handling public monies, but in no way restricted removals within the term of appointment. It was important to the development of the public employment relationship because it confirmed the absence of a legal right to office and encouraged the adoption of the spoils system.[65] John Q. Adams, the first president to have a large number of appointments expire, generally reappointed any officer not guilty of misconduct and the act was unimportant until Andrew Jackson became president.[66]

Despite the Tenure of Office Act, the Decision of 1789, and Jefferson's early removals, tenure in most of the civil service was *de facto* during good behavior. At the time, dismissals connoted fault or delinquency and were by common agreement only for adequate cause.[67] Thomas L. Kinney, Superintendent of Indian Trade in 1816, expressed this widespread view:

To dismiss from office, in those days, without cause, would have been deemed an outrage, not less against the public interest, than

[63] U.S., *Statutes at Large*, II, 594 (April 30, 1810); re-enacted *ibid.*, IV, 104 (March 13, 1825). See chap. 5 for greater detail.

[64] *Ibid.*, III, 582 (May 15, 1820).

[65] The act was the work of William Crawford who either sought to increase patronage or viewed it as a means of compelling better administrative performance. See Carl R. Fish, "The Crime of Crawford," *American Historical Review*, XXV (April 1916), 545–46. President Monroe regretted having signed it. White, *Jeffersonians*, p. 388.

[66] White, *Jeffersonians*, p. 390.   [67] *Ibid.*, p. 378.

the party proscribed. Hence competency, zeal and honesty, being the characteristics of the clerks I found in the Office of Indian Trade, when I succeeded to its management, it no more occurred to me to turn them out, than it did to cut their throats.[68]

Moreover, "it was uniformly the practice to give notice to the person accused of the charges, if they implicated his character." [69]

Throughout the period under consideration kinship was of informal, but real importance in the appointment of civil servants. It was related to selection from among the upper social classes and to conscious efforts on the part of some officers to find positions for their relatives.[70] In John Adams' administration 37 per cent of his "elite" appointments were related to persons within the same elite, 31 per cent to previous elites, and 40 per cent to persons in the same or previous elites: for Jefferson's elite the figures were 22, 22, and 34 per cent, respectively.[71] The importance of kinship was often indicated by succession in office from father to son. Strictly speaking, it was not inheritance, but it tended in that direction. For example, Henry Dearborn, William Ellery, Abraham Bishop, and John Page were all followed into office by their sons.[72] The tendency was great enough to prompt John Calhoun to write President Monroe in 1819 that

it is certainly painful to do an act, which may leave the family of the late collector in want, yet the tendency to hereditary principle

[68] Quoted *ibid.*, p. 511.

[69] U.S., Congress, Senate, Document 73, 21st Cong., 2d Sess., p. 89 (March 3, 1831).

[70] One of the most successful at this was Timothy Pickering, Secretary of State under Washington and Adams, who found positions for two sons, two nephews, and one cousin. See White, *Federalists,* pp. 280–84 for this and other cases.

[71] Aronson, *Status and Kinship,* pp. 141–42.

[72] White, *Jeffersonians,* p. 357.

from this very cause in the inferior offices of our country merits great consideration. What is humanity now, may in the course of one or two generations ripen into a claim on the government.[73]

The long tenure, the upper social class basis of the civil service, the importance of kinship, and the "inheritance" of office were important factors tending toward positive discrimination of the public employment relationship. These factors enhanced the pre-existing concept of property in office, despite the Decision of 1789, Jefferson's removals, the Tenure of Office Act, and the development of important negative discriminations. If these factors had continued to be important they might eventually have given privileged individuals, in Calhoun's words, "a claim on the government." However, Andrew Jackson and the spoils system destroyed the concept of property in office and stunted the development of positive discrimination along these lines.

IV

Between 1776 and 1829 the public employment relationship underwent important development. The major factors influencing this development were a prevailing suspicion against public officials which had evolved as a consequence of colonial administration, a general restriction of civil service positions to members of the upper social classes, and the evolution of political competition organized around clearly identifiable factions. Under the influence of these factors almost every component of the relationship which assumed greater importance in later years was present during this early period. The issues of political neutrality, equality of access to civil service positions, loyalty-security, and stigmatizing dismissals were raised; and the nature of the relationship itself was debated in making the Decision of 1789.

[73] Quoted *ibid.*

Although there were important factors encouraging positive discrimination, the direction of actual discrimination was negative, as it has been ever since. The most important discrimination of this type was inequality of access and removal for political opinions or activities. Neither of these discriminations was wholly accepted. In Washington's words, it "would be repugnant to the vital principles of our government, virtually to exclude from public trusts, talents and virtue unless accompanied by wealth." [74] Political removal was attacked by John Haywood, Treasurer of North Carolina, in a letter to John Steele, Comptroller of the United States Treasury, in 1800:

I should feel not only pain but mortification, as a citizen of the United States, were I to suppose for one moment, that we are ever to have a president capable of acting on a scale so narrow and illiberal as to be led to discharge and oust from office a meritorious and informed officer merely because he may chance to have been opposed to his election; or may hold political opinions differing from his own.[75]

The contradiction between the Constitution and political removal and appointment was also acknowledged by Andrew Jackson in 1824. He wrote: "The Constitution secures to every man equal rights and privileges; and the very moment I proscribe an individual from office, on account of his political opinion; I become myself a despot." [76] Perhaps the subtleties of the public employment relationship were most clearly perceived by Duff Green, a mail contractor threatened with the

[74] Washington, *Writings*, XXXV, 317–18. Washington was requesting Congress to appropriate higher salaries for civil servants and was trying to convince Republicans that such salaries would be beneficial. Nevertheless the statement is significant.

[75] Quoted in White, *Federalists*, p. 48.

[76] Andrew Jackson, *The Correspondence of Andrew Jackson*, ed. J. S. Bassett (Washington: Carnegie Institution, 1926), III, 247.

loss of his contract for what he believed to be political reasons. In 1826 he wrote the postmaster general:

I regret to see an admission . . . from you, which goes so far to strengthen the prevailing opinion that every man who refuses to give his adhesion to the present dynasty shall be proscribed. . . . Although it is my fixed purpose to use all lawful and honorable means to prevent the re-election of Mr. Adams, it is not therefore proper that I should be denied the rights of a citizen.[77]

During this period the domain of discrimination was generally fixed by practice rather than by law and is difficult to estimate. For example, whether Jefferson was willing to remove almost all officers who openly opposed him, or only a moderate proportion, is unknown.[78] However, the inequalities of access to civil service positions and political removals of the time must be considered to represent a high degree of discrimination, and the range of discrimination which had developed by 1829 was significant in itself and in its precedential effects.

[77] Quoted in White, *Jeffersonians*, pp. 332–33.
[78] Jefferson failed to remove at least one officer who was obviously attempting to sabotage the embargo. See *ibid.*, pp. 414, 454–55.

2 | The Spoils System
and the Public
Employment Relationship

The application of the spoils system to the federal civil service was of great and continuing importance to the development of the public employment relationship. The system consisted of two major elements: rotation in office and a highly politicized personnel system and bureaucracy. Although the system reached the pinnacle of its importance between 1829 and 1865, some of its elements are still significant features of the United States political system. The spoils system created new negative discriminations and abandoned pre-existent ones, it influenced the channels later taken by reform, and it provided the background against which political neutrality developed. The system was introduced into the federal government in 1829 by President Andrew Jackson.

By the time Jackson became president, the spoils system had been operating in New York and Pennsylvania for a number of years,[1] and the principle of rotation in office had been implied, for federal employees, by the Tenure of Office Act.[2] Jackson was the first president to provide an ideological justification of the spoils system and attempt to establish it

[1] Carl R. Fish, *The Civil Service and the Patronage* (New York: Longmans, Green and Co., 1905), pp. 86–94.

[2] U.S., *Statutes at Large,* III, 582 (May 15, 1820). For the background of rotation generally, see Fish, *Civil Service,* pp. 79–104.

in the federal government. He believed the system could serve at least three purposes. First, it could destroy the concept of property in office and reduce the importance of the upper social classes in American politics. Second, it could provide a rationalization for the many civil service removals Jackson, who was the first president since Jefferson to be elected in opposition to an incumbent administration, would find it politically desirable to make. Finally, it could solve the problems of disability and superannuation in the civil service, which were caused by the reluctance of presidents and appointing officers prior to 1829 to make removals.

In his Inaugural Address, Jackson explained:

The recent demonstration of public sentiment inscribes on the list of executive duties, in characters too legible to be overlooked, the task of *reform,* which will require particularly the correction of those abuses that have brought the patronage of the Federal Government into conflict with the freedom of elections and the counteraction of those causes which have disturbed the rightful course of appointment and have placed or continued power in unfaithful or incompetent hands.[3]

In his First Annual Message, Jackson elaborated upon his concept of reform and introduced the principles upon which the spoils system was later established.

There are, perhaps, few men who can for any great length of time enjoy office and power without being more or less under the influence of feelings unfavorable to the faithful discharge of their public duties. . . . [T]hey are apt to acquire a habit of looking with indifference upon the public interests and of tolerating conduct from which an unpracticed man would revolt. Office is considered a species of property, and government rather as a means

[3] James D. Richardson (ed.), *A Compilation of the Messages and Papers of the Presidents of the United States, 1789–1897* (Washington: U.S. Government Printing Office, 1896), II, 438.

of promoting individual interests than as an instrument created solely for the service of the people. Corruption in some and in others a perversion of the correct feelings and principles divert government from its legitimate end and make it an engine for the support of the few at the expense of the many. The duties of all public officers are, or at least admit of being made, so plain and simple that men of intelligence may readily qualify themselves for their performance; and I cannot but believe that more is lost by the long continuance of men in office than is generally to be gained by their experience.[4]

Jackson went on to endorse the principle of equality of access to civil service positions and an extension of the Tenure of Office Act.[5]

In a country where offices are created solely for the benefit of the people no one man has any more intrinsic right to official station than another. Offices were not established to give support to particular men at the public expense. No individual wrong is, therefore, done by removal, since neither appointment to nor continuance in office is a matter of right. . . . The proposed limitation [four years] would destroy the idea of property now so generally connected with official station, and although individual distress may be sometimes produced, it would, by promoting that rotation which constitutes a leading principle in the republican creed, give healthful action to the system.[6]

[4] *Ibid.*, pp. 448–49. As Sidney Aronson, *Status and Kinship: Standards of Selection in the Administrations of John Adams, Thomas Jefferson, and Andrew Jackson* (Cambridge: Harvard University Press, 1964), p. 243, points out, there is a striking similarity between the last sentence of Jackson's statement as quoted above, and the following one by Lenin: "The majority of functions of the old 'state power' have become so simplified and can be reduced to such simple operations of registration filing, and checking that they will be quite within the reach of every literate person."

[5] Such an extension came in 1836 when postmasters were given a four-year term. See U.S., *Statutes at Large*, V, 80 (July 2, 1836).

[6] Richardson, *Messages and Papers*, II, 449.

Jackson had, therefore, developed an elaborate ideological justification for what he proposed to do—that is, make the civil service more sociologically representative, and institute the principle of rotation.[7] However, before Jackson could put his program into operation and before the spoils system could become important on the national level, certain conditions had to be present. Two of these conditions which have also been an integral part of the public employment relationship are the authority of the president to remove presidential officers without senatorial concurrence, and the right of superior officers to remove subordinate employees for any cause.

The authority of the president to remove presidential officers without senatorial concurrence was basically established by the Decision of 1789, but it was subjected to several challenges during Jackson's presidency.[8] The Whigs opposed the development of the spoils system under Jackson, as the following statement by Daniel Webster indicates:

The army is the army of the country; the navy is the navy of the country; neither of them is either the mere instrument of the administration for the time being, or of him who is at the head of it. The Post Office, the Land Office, the Customs-house, are, in

---

[7] The two were connected, at least to some extent, as historian James Parton observed: "Men of intelligence, ability, and virtue universally desire to fix their affairs on a basis of permanence. It is the nature of such men to make each year do something for all the years to come." *The Life of Andrew Jackson* (Boston: Houghton, Mifflin and Co., 1887), III, 220.

[8] For example, see U.S., Congress, Senate, Document 41, 22d Cong., 1st Sess. (January 26, 1832); and Document 108, 23d Cong., 2d Sess. (February 9, 1835). After Jackson's administration it was challenged at various times until 1867 when the Tenure of Office Act was passed. See U.S., Congress, House, Select Committee on Civil Service and Retrenchment, *Reorganization of Executive Departments*, Report 741, 27th Cong., 2d Sess. (May 23, 1842), and Senate, Document 399, 28th Cong., 1st Sess. (June 15, 1844).

like manner, institutions of the country, established for the good of the people; and it may well alarm the lovers of free institutions, when all the offices in these several departments are spoken of, in high places, as being but "spoils of victory." [9]

As part of their opposition to the spoils system and their overall dislike of executive power, the Whigs challenged the president's removal power in 1834. Jackson, in connection with the destruction of the Second Bank of the United States, had removed Secretary of the Treasury Duane for exercising authority vested in that officer by law.[10] Senator Henry Clay introduced the following resolutions:

1. *Resolved,* that the Constitution of the United States does vest in the President power to remove at pleasure, officers under the government . . . whose offices have been established by law.

2. *Resolved,* that, in all cases of offices created by law, the tenure of holding which is not prescribed by the Constitution, Congress is authorized by the Constitution to prescribe the tenure, terms, and conditions, on which they are to be holden.

3. *Resolved,* that the Committee on the Judiciary be instructed to inquire into the expediency of providing by law that, in all instances of appointment to office by the President, by and with the advice and consent of the Senate, other than diplomatic appointments, the power of removal shall be exercised only in concurrence with the Senate.[11]

Although bills to implement these resolutions gained support in the Senate,[12] they were never reported out of committee

[9] U.S., *Register of Debates in Congress,* 23d Cong., 2d Sess. XI, Part 1, p. 461 (February 16, 1835).

[10] See Leonard D. White, *The Jacksonians* (New York: The Free Press, 1965), pp. 33–44; and Wilfred F. Binkley, *President and Congress* (New York: Vintage Books, 1947), pp. 93–104.

[11] U.S., Congress, Senate, Document 155, 23d Cong., 1st Sess. (March 7, 1834).

[12] *Register of Debates in Congress,* XI, Part 1, 418–575 (February 13–21, 1835).

in the House and the presidential removal power remained unrestricted until after the Civil War.

A challenge to the removal power of greater importance to the overall development of the public employment relationship was presented in the case of *Ex parte Hennen* in 1839.[13] The central issue was whether a public employee, not guaranteed tenure by the Constitution, could be removed for reasons having nothing to do with his capacity and on-the-job performance. The case involved the removal of a clerk of the District Court of the Eastern District of Louisiana. The judge who removed him sent him a letter in which it was observed:

Unreservedly, that the business of the office for the last two years had been conducted promptly, skilfully and uprightly, and that in appointing Mr. Winthrop to succeed him, he had been actuated purely by a sense of duty and feelings of kindness towards one whom he had long known, and between whom and himself the closest friendship had ever subsisted.[14]

The fact that the officer was in the judicial branch, which has traditionally been somewhat divorced from partisan politics, that he admittedly performed his duties well, and that his removal was for a rather arbitrary reason might have been the basis of a decision making the right of removal less than absolute. The Supreme Court found, however, that "it cannot, for a moment, be admitted that it was the intention of the Constitution that those offices which are denominated inferior offices should be held during life," [15] and therefore that Hennen had no right to office and could be removed for any reason by the person or body possessing the authority to dismiss him.

The *Hennen* case was the first important one of its kind to reach the Supreme Court, and the Court relied mainly on state precedents. One alternative before the Court was *Hoke*

[13] 13 Peters 230.   [14] *Ibid.*, p. 256.   [15] *Ibid.*, p. 259.

v. *Henderson*,[16] in which the Supreme Court of North Carolina held that public office was a property right. In *Hennen,* the Court held the precedent to be inapplicable because Hoke held office during good behavior under North Carolina law.[17] Nevertheless the difference in language and decision in the two cases is striking and clearly suggests a compromise under which office would not be considered property, and removals for wholly arbitrary reasons would not be legitimate. *Hennen,* however, was in accord with the spoils system and the prevailing political climate, and the case may be considered the first important decision in the doctrine of privilege.[18]

The development of the spoils system was also dependent, as Jackson indicated in his First Annual Message, upon the nature of civil service tasks. This variable is also of general importance to the public employment relationship because the domain of discrimination is often dependent upon it, as it was in the instance of discrimination applied under the spoils system. During the period in which the spoils system reached the peak of its importance, government was predominantly laissez-faire, public policy was distributional, and as Jackson indicated, for the most part the tasks of the civil service were relatively plain and simple. By 1860 technological advances had done little to alter the office skills of 1800.[19] However,

[16] 15 N.C. 1 (1833).

[17] The Hoke case was overruled in *Mial* v. *Ellington,* 134 N.C. 131 (1903).

[18] During the period under consideration, *Hennen* was reinforced by *Butler* v. *Pennsylvania,* 51 U.S. 402 (1850), in which it was held that public employment was not a contract within the meaning of Article I, section 10, of the Constitution, which forbade any state from passing a "law impairing the obligation of contracts." This decision eliminated the possibility that state civil servants would be subject to a different body of constitutional law than federal employees.

[19] White, *Jacksonians,* p. 548.

in those parts of the civil service in which technical knowledge and skills were required the spoils system was less significant.[20] For example, in 1882 Superintendent of the Life-Saving Service, Sumner I. Kimball, who was not opposed to the spoils principle, explained that "the Life-Saving Service is an expert service; a technical one, in which it is absolutely indispensable to have the very best obtainable men. In organizing it . . . I found it necessary to adopt such means as would exclude politics."[21] For the same reasons the Patent Office remained relatively free of spoils throughout its history.[22]

In order for the spoils system to be established, it was also necessary for the major political parties to accept it in principle, or at least in practice; and for them to have the opportunity to apply it. The spoils system was of greatest importance during the period of United States history in which the partisanship of the presidency changed most frequently. It has been estimated that overall removals under Jackson were somewhere between 10 and 20 per cent of the total number of federal employees.[23] As Table 3 indicates, he removed 252 out of 610 presidential officers. If the Democrats had remained in office for a period of more than twenty years, as did the Jeffersonian Republicans, the spoils system

[20] *Ibid.,* pp. 14, 15, 315, 354, 357; Fish, *Civil Service,* p. 182.

[21] U.S., Congress, Senate, Committee on Civil Service and Retrenchment, Report 576, 47th Cong., 1st Sess., p. 21 (March 18, 1882).

[22] White, *Jacksonians,* p. 211. One Senatorial opponent of reform in 1872 explained that the military service, which had training schools and long tenure, was different from civilian service "because their duties require scientific knowledge and long experience for their proper performance." U.S., *Congressional Globe,* 42d Cong., 2d Sess., Part 1, p. 457 (January 18, 1872).

[23] Erik M. Eriksson, "The Federal Civil Service Under President Jackson," *Mississippi Valley Historical Review,* XIII (March 1927), 529.

probably would not have developed to the extent that it did. Van Buren was in favor of the spoils system, but being in political agreement with Jackson he found it unnecessary to make many removals. The Democrats, however, were defeated by the Whigs in 1840. Shortly after taking office, President William Henry Harrison died and was succeeded by Vice-President John Tyler, who was really more of a Democrat than a Whig. The Democrats won the election of 1844, but were defeated by the Whigs in 1848. From 1853 to 1861 differing Democratic factions were in office, and in 1861 the Republicans began a long period of one party dominance during which the importance of spoils declined and civil service reform took place.

In retrospect, the Harrison-Tyler administration was of greatest importance for the development of the spoils system. Prior to Harrison's election the Whigs had opposed the spoils system, but during the Harrison-Tyler administration the largest number of removals up to that time were made, as Table 3 indicates. Moreover, most of these were made by Harrison, a true Whig.[24] The Whigs undoubtedly found it politically desirable to practice spoils because there was no just reason for leaving the partisan appointments of Jackson and Van Buren in office, especially while a mob of Whigs were seeking office.[25] Moreover, the spoils system paid party workers with civil service jobs, and there was a strong economic motivation for one party to engage in spoils after another did.

II

The spoils system had a dual effect on the range of discrimination of the public employment relationship. Along with

[24] Fish, *Civil Service,* pp. 150–51.
[25] White, *Jacksonians,* pp. 303–304.

Jackson's efforts, it increased the degree of equality of access to civil service positions by seeking characteristics in appointees which were not confined largely to members of the upper social class. At the same time, however, it continued and increased inequality of access based on partisan affiliation and standing. The spoils system also encouraged and often coerced political activity and financial contribution from civil servants, which were important negative discriminations.

Jackson was hostile to a civil service composed mainly of members of the upper social class. He once stated that

the road to office and preferment being accessible alike to the rich and poor, the farmer and printer, honesty, probity and capability constituting the sole and exclusive test, will I am persuaded, have the happiest tendency to preserve unimpaired, freedom of political action; change it and let it be known that any class or portion of citizens are and ought to be proscribed and discontent and dissatisfaction will be engendered.[26]

The rough draft of his first inaugural address stated that he would "fill the various offices at the disposal of the Executive with individuals uniting as far as possible the qualities of the head and heart, always recollecting that in a free government the demand for moral qualities should be made superior to that of talents." [27] On the other hand, he believed that the highest appointments "required the best talents that the country could furnish." [28]

Several historians and political scientists have concluded that Jackson succeeded in altering the social class basis of the

[26] Andrew Jackson, *The Correspondence of Andrew Jackson*, ed. J. S. Bassett (Washington: Carnegie Institution, 1926), IV, 32. For Jackson's appointment ideology see Aronson, *Status and Kinship,* especially pp. 14–21.

[27] Jackson, *Correspondence,* IV, 11–12.

[28] *Ibid.,* pp. 100–101; rough draft of his first annual message.

civil service and made it more sociologically representative of the nation as a whole.[29] Leonard White, for example, says that "certain it is that the year 1820 marked the end of an era, politically and administratively. The gentlemen who since 1789 had taken the responsibility of government were driven from the scene to be replaced by a new type of public servant and by other ideals of official action." [30] Although the change was important at all levels, it was probably less radical in the higher positions.[31] After Jackson's administration the trend toward a civil service not dominated by the upper social classes continued under the influence of the spoils system. One historian of the period concluded,

the government formerly served by the elite of the nation, is now served to a very considerable extent by its refuse. . . . In the year of our Lord 1859, the fact of a man's holding office under

[29] See Fish, *Civil Service,* pp. 49–50, 109; Arthur Schlesinger, Jr., *The Age of Jackson* (Boston: Little, Brown and Co., 1945), pp. 46–47; Paul P. Van Riper, *History of the United States Civil Service* (Evanston: Row, Peterson and Co., 1958), pp. 23–24, 32; Richard Hofstadter, *Anti-Intellectualism in American Life* (New York: Vintage Books, 1963), pp. 168–70.

[30] Leonard D. White, *The Jeffersonians* (New York: The Free Press, 1965), p. viii.

[31] Aronson, *Status and Kinship,* p. 60, concludes that "although Jackson's was the most representative of all the elites, there were important differences between those of Adams and Jefferson. In fact, there was a closer correspondence between Jeffersonians and Jacksonians than between Jeffersonians and Federalists." Aronson's methodological defects, as noted in Chapter 1, make his conclusions unreliable. Although he studied only elites, he suggested that "it may have been that the major democratization of the civil service in Jackson's administration took place in the lower ranks of the federal civil service" (p. 179). Within the elite, kinship retained its importance and 23 per cent of Jackson's elite appointments were related to other members of the elite, 29 per cent to members of a previous elite, and 34 per cent to the same or previous elites (pp. 141–42). See also White, *Jacksonians,* pp. 98–100.

the government is presumptive evidence that he is one of three characters, namely, an adventurer, an incompetent person, or a scoundrel. From this remark must be excepted those who hold offices that have never been subjected to the spoils system, or offices which have been "taken out of politics." [32]

Under the spoils system, recruitment for civil service positions was based not only upon partisan affiliation but upon the expectation of future partisan service as well. John Calhoun, a perceptive political thinker, was quick to recognize the implications of this method of selection:

So long as offices were considered as public trusts, to be conferred on the honest, the faithful, and capable, for the common good, and not for the benefit or gain of the incumbent or his party, and so long as it was the practice of the government to continue in office those who faithfully performed their duties, its patronage, in point of fact was limited to the mere power of nominating to accidental vacancies or newly created offices, and could, of course, exercise but a moderate influence, either over the body of the community, or of the office-holders themselves: but when this practice was reversed—when offices, instead of being considered as public trusts, to be conferred on the deserving, were regarded as the spoils of victory, to be bestowed as rewards for partisan services, without respect to merit; when it became understood that all who hold office, hold it by the tenure of partisan zeal and party service, it is easy to see that the certain, direct, and inevitable tendency of such a state of things is to convert the entire body of those in office into corrupt and supple instruments of power, and to raise up a host of hungry, greedy, and subservient partisans ready for every service, however base and corrupt.[33]

Under the spoils system political parties allocated civil service employment as remuneration for their workers. The

[32] Parton, *Jackson*, III, 220.
[33] U.S., Congress, Senate, Document 108, 23d Cong., 2d Sess., p. 3 (February 9, 1835).

parties also coerced partisan work through the threat of removal, and they taxed civil servants' salaries through political
assessment. The system resembled the sale of office, but the
sale was contingent on partisan work and a small percentage
of one's salary, rather than being an outright purchase.[34] An
employee might be dismissed or refused employment for
membership in the "wrong" party, for "wrong" political activity, for support of the "wrong" candidate, for "wrong"
voting, or for refusal to perform political services. These
practices significantly extended the range of discrimination.
Previously, dismissals were sometimes based on political
affiliation, but probably were never based on the refusal to
perform partisan tasks or vote for the party ticket. The new
elements abridged the implicit First Amendment right not to
engage in political activity against one's will, and the right
to vote free of official coercion.[35]

The political duties of civil servants under the spoils system
included such partisan activities as electioneering and con-
tributing money to the party in office. These activities could
be voluntary or coerced and were an official part of the system.
Sometimes the head of an office, appointed for political
reasons, would keep an efficient deputy to perform the actual
administrative tasks involved while he would occupy himself
with party work.[36] Several civil servants would be given leave
of absence to electioneer. This was especially true at the
larger customhouses such as those in New York and Phila-

[34] In a sense, the concept of property in office was turned on its
head. Under the spoils system office "belonged" to participation structures (political parties) which used it to gain and maintain control
of authority structures.

[35] There were some attempts during the spoils period to establish
political neutrality. These were, however, uniformly unsuccessful.
See chap. 4, *supra*.

[36] Fish, *Civil Service*, p. 182.

delphia. In 1842 a House Committee investigating the situation at New York was given the following testimony from an employee: "I have myself been absent attending the polls all day, and for two or three days in succession, for objects connected with elections." [37] Another civil servant stated: "I have known from twenty to thirty customhouse officers for two weeks or more at a time engaged in obtaining naturalization papers for foreigners, and making other arrangements preparatory to the elections." [38] Another House Committee found similar practices in existence at Philadelphia in 1856:

Being then the appraiser in the customhouse at Philadelphia, he was "absent on leave, in the state committee room" for some four months; during which time he rendered no service to the government, yet received his regular salary. The practice has also prevailed in the New York and other customhouses, of appointing men temporarily for the week preceding the election, and granting them leave of absence, that they might devote themselves to electioneering duties.[39]

If these activities were voluntarily performed and there was no coercion involved, they did not constitute a negative discrimination of the public employment relationship; and because some employees were paid by the government, in effect, to exercise their political rights, it might be viewed, in practice, as positive discrimination. That much of this political activity was voluntary is probable; however, there is evidence that much was coerced. Dorman B. Eaton, a leading civil service

[37] U.S., Congress, House, Document 212, 27th Cong., 2d Sess., p. 487 (May 9, 1842).

[38] *Ibid.*, p. 486.

[39] U.S., Congress, House, *Covode Investigation*, Report 648, 36th Cong., 1st Sess., p. 25 (June 16, 1860). Examples of such pre-election employment can be found on pp. 496–97, 519 (in the New York Post Office), 527, 533. In some cases the appointee thought the employment was permanent.

reformer, investigated the customhouse at New York and concluded that "control of occupation and salary is generally the control of men. No officer of the army or the navy has an authority half as despotic as that of a collector over the conduct, the income, and the political freedom of those whom he commands." [40]

It has also been concluded that under the spoils system "employees dared not express any opinion, however privately, which might offend those in power, lest stories be carried, and dismissals follow." [41] Actual examples of removal for "wrong" political activity are not difficult to find. One employee in the New York customhouse made the following statement:

I was informed . . . that I was to be removed. I was given to understand that [it was] on account of my politics. . . . It was understood, generally, by persons employed in the collection of customs . . . that no person could consider himself safe, in regard to retaining his place, unless he was orthodox in his politics, according to the locofoco creed.[42]

Another employee was told that "there were some little political matters that caused . . . [his] removal." [43] There were no secret ballots at the time and an employee might be dismissed for failing to vote as he was told. A United States District

[40] Dorman B. Eaton, *The Spoils System and Civil Service Reform in the Custom-House and Post-Office at New York* (New York: G. P. Putnam's Sons, 1882), p. 53.

[41] U.S., Civil Service Commission, *History of the Federal Civil Service* (Washington: U.S. Government Printing Office, 1941), p. 21. Parton, *Jackson*, III, 212, described the situation when Jackson began his presidency as follows: "Terror, meanwhile, reigned in Washington . . . the great body of officials awaited their fate in silent horror, glad when the office hours expired at having escaped another day. . . . No man deemed it safe and prudent to trust his neighbor, and the interior of the department presented a fearful scene of guarded silence, secret intrigue, espionage, and tale-bearing."

[42] House Document 212, p. 482.   [43] House Report 648, p. 363.

Attorney was asked, "Do you know of any effort on the part of collector Barker [in Philadelphia] to use his official position to force federal employees to vote at his dictation?" He answered, "It is generally understood with the mass of the party with whom I have acted that he has done so from the time he came into office. . . . I could have brought the names of many . . . who say they have been removed for that cause." [44] An employee in the Philadelphia customhouse said, "I have known several cases where men were removed because they did not vote for the same ticket that the collector was in favor of." [45]

An important political right is the right to contribute money for political causes. Without this right those of free speech and association would be considerably less significant. If a public employee is forced to contribute to a political party by the government it constitutes negative discrimination. Political assessments, or forced contributions, were common under the spoils system.[46] President Hayes once referred to assessments as "indirect robbery of the public treasury," [47] and others have viewed it as reducing "public office to the degraded character of merchandise, to be bought and sold to subordinates by a regulated annual stipend." [48] The system of assessment contained both elements.

The political parties could raise large sums of money

[44] *Ibid.,* p. 333.   [45] *Ibid.,* p. 369.

[46] President William Henry Harrison tried, but failed, to prevent assessment by declaring that payment of a contribution or assessment by officeholders would be cause for removal. This also would have been an important negative discrimination if it had been effective. See U.S., Congress, Senate, Document 26, 27th Cong., 1st Sess. (March 20, 1841).

[47] Quoted in Dorman B. Eaton, *Term and Tenure of Office* (New York: G. P. Putnam's Sons, 1882), p. 19.

[48] U.S., Congress, House, *Defalcations,* Report 313, 25th Cong., 3d Sess., p. 249 (February 27, 1839).

through assessment. For example, in 1853, workers in the New York customhouse were assessed the following amounts: 19 weighers, 15 measurers, and 7 gaugers, $25 each; 195 inspectors, $15 each; 184 clerks, $10 each; and 137 night watchmen $7.50 each; for a total of $6,817.50.[49] From the point of view of those concerned assessments were logical. One employee in the New York customhouse in the 1830's stated that "the weighers were called on to pay fifteen dollars each for support of the election; and when I declined . . . the deputy surveyor, observed, that I ought to consider whether my $1,500 per annum was not worth paying fifteen dollars for." [50] Generally the amount assessed was relatively small, somewhere between 1 and 6 per cent of the civil servant's salary.[51] In 1856 the assessment in the Philadelphia customhouse was $30 to $33 on a salary of $1,095, and assessment on clerks in the General Land Office was as low as $3.20 on a salary of $1,600.[52]

Some civil servants undoubtedly contributed voluntarily, but others felt coerced. One employee in Philadelphia remarked that "we knew the consequences of refusing to pay and did not wish to lose our situations." [53] A similarly situated employee had "never seen any refusal to pay the assessment," [54] and an employee in the New York customhouse in the 1830's said that "if the individual did not pay the amount he was taxed with the collector would remark, 'you will be reported to the general committee'—and everybody well understood that proscription would follow." [55] In the Land Office, clerks often did not receive their stated salaries because an

[49] White, *Jacksonians,* p. 335.   [50] House Report 313, p. 250.
[51] *Ibid.,* pp. 250–51. Also House Report 648, p. 567.
[52] House Report 648, pp. 22–23, 553, 561.
[53] *Ibid.,* p. 368.   [54] *Ibid.,* p. 367.
[55] House Report 313, p. 251.

assessment "was deducted from the pay of the clerks by the pay-clerk." [56]

Forced political activity and political assessment considerably extended the range of discrimination. It is, however, difficult to estimate the domain of discrimination because negative discrimination along these lines was applied informally by custom and practice rather than on a formal legal basis. Although such negative discrimination was common in customhouses and other highly partisan units of administration or havens for party hacks, it was certainly not confined to them. On the other hand, these forms of negative discrimination were almost wholly absent from technical agencies and positions. Any negative discrimination at the degree level of coerced political activity was, of course, an increase in the domain over that prior to 1829 when there is no record of such discrimination.

Under the spoils system the domain of negative discrimination at the degree level of removal for political opinion and affiliation also increased. The overwhelming majority of removals was based on the politics of the dismissed civil servants.

Table 3 presents the number of presidential officers removed from 1789 to 1869. The table demonstrates that the number of removals was roughly correlated with changes in the partisan affiliation of the president. This lends confirmation to the proposition that most removals were for political reasons, and that frequent changes in the partisan control of the presidency were a necessary condition for the establishment and operation of the spoils system. The number of removals does not adequately indicate the total turnover. There were many resignations in anticipation of removal. For example, in Polk's administration about 10,000 postmasters

[56] House Report 648, p. 568.

resigned while only 1,600 were removed,[57] and under Pierce, 2,802 presidential officers resigned.[58] The number of non-presidential employees removed is difficult to estimate because meaningful data are not generally available. However, in

Table 3. Removals of presidential officers, 1789–1869

President	Number removed	Estimated officers
Washington	17	
Adams	21	
Jefferson [a]	109	433 (1802)
Madison	27	
Monroe	27	824 (1816)
Adams [b]	12	
Jackson [a]	252	610 (1829)
Van Buren	80	924 (1839)
Harrison, Tyler [a]	458	
Polk [a]	342	
Taylor [a]	540	929 (1849)
Fillmore	88	
Pierce [a]	823	
Buchanan [c]	458	1,520 (1859)
Lincoln [a]	1,457	
Johnson	903	2,669 (1869)

Source: Carl R. Fish, "Removal of Officials by the Presidents of the United States," *American Historical Association Annual Report,* I (1899), 67–86, especially p. 84.

[a] Change in political party.

[b] John Q. Adams can be classified as either a Jeffersonian Republican or a Federalist.

[c] Change in faction.

some instances estimates are possible. The customhouse at New York was exceptional for its political involvement and therefore not representative of the bureaucracy as a whole, but

[57] White, *Jacksonians,* p. 312.   [58] Fish, *Civil Service,* p. 166.

it is one of the few bureaus for which removal figures are available. Dorman B. Eaton summarized removals there as follows:

Thus, in the period of five years, or 1,565 secular days next preceding the appointment of collector Arthur in 1871 there had been 1,678 removals . . . *more than at the rate of one for every day. The aggregate was very nearly equal to a removal of every official twice in that time.*[59]

The political activity, appointment, and removal of civil servants under the spoils system created several political and administrative effects which encouraged civil service reform.[60] The method of selection took a great deal of presidential time, as the following statement by President Polk indicates: "I am ready to exclaim, will the pressure for office never cease! It is one year today since I entered on the duties of my office, and still the pressure for office has not abated. I most sincerely wish I had no offices to bestow." [61] The system also encouraged corruption by appointing men unfit to perform their assigned functions and because, as Henry Clay correctly predicted in 1829,

incumbents, feeling the instability of their situation, and knowing their liability to periodic removals, at short terms, without any

[59] Eaton, *The Spoils System,* p. 23. Italics in original.

[60] The spoils system, of course, also had effects which did not directly influence reform. Probably the most important of these from a systematic point of view was to foster the development of strong political parties. For a general statement see Fred W. Riggs, "Bureaucracy and Political Development: A Paradoxical View," in Joseph LaPalombara (ed.), *Bureaucracy and Political Development* (Princeton: Princeton University Press, 1963), pp. 120–67, especially pp. 127–30.

[61] James K. Polk, *The Diary of James K. Polk During His Presidency, 1845 to 1849,* ed. Milo M. Quaife (Chicago: A. C. McClurg and Co., 1910), I, 261. See also White, *Jacksonians,* pp. 303–305; and Van Riper, *History,* pp. 50–51.

regard to the manner in which they have executed their trust, will be disposed to make the most of their uncertain offices while they have them, and hence we may expect immediate cases of fraud, predation and corruption.[62]

In 1868 an Indian Peace Commission cited the relationship between political activity, appointment, and removal, and corruption:

The records are abundant to show that agents have pocketed the funds appropriated by the government and driven the Indians to starvation. . . . For a long time these officers have been selected from partisan ranks, not so much on account of honesty and qualification as for devotion to party interests and their willingness to apply the money of the Indian to promote the selfish schemes of local politicians.[63]

The belief that the spoils system unavoidably caused corruption was reinforced in 1877 when a commission examining the customhouse at New York concluded that political appointment was

unsound in principle, dangerous in practice, demoralizing in its influence on all connected with the customs service, and calculated to encourage and perpetuate the official ignorance, inefficiency and corruption which, perverting the powers of Government to personal and party ends, have burdened the country with debt and taxes, and assisted to prostrate the trade and industry of the nation.[64]

[62] Quoted in Fish, *Civil Service,* p. 140.

[63] U.S., Congress, House, Executive Document 97, 40th Cong., 2d Sess., p. 21 (January 7, 1868).

[64] U.S., Congress, House, Executive Document 8, 45th Cong., 1st Sess., p. 15 (October 25, 1877). The New York Customhouse had a long history of corruption. In 1838 it was discovered that collector Swartwout had embezzled $1,225,705.69. See House Report 313, p. 8; White, *Jacksonians,* p. 426.

The spoils system also tended to encourage the creation of civil service positions for party workers, and at one time United States naval policy was partially based on the distribution of patronage in the navy yards.[65] The widespread political activity, appointment, and removal under the spoils system therefore not only extended the range of discrimination, but became associated with administrative effects which in turn encouraged reforms regulating these features of the system and further development of the public employment relationship.

III

The spoils system thoroughly altered the civil service and had important effects on the public employment relationship and its future development. It destroyed the concept of property in office, made long tenure unusual except in technical positions and agencies, and altered the social class composition of the bureaucracy. The spoils system immediately affected the public employment relationship in diverse ways. It established a greater degree of equality of access to civil service positions insofar as social class status was concerned, but it continued and increased the importance of political opinion and affiliation in recruitment. All things considered, therefore, it is reasonable to conclude that the spoils system decreased the range of discrimination with regard to equality of access. At the same time it extended the range by increasing political removals, and by coercing political contribution and activity. The degree of these discriminations, especially the latter, which often extended to voting, must be regarded as extensive, and although the domain is uncertain, it was substantial.

The spoils system marked an important turning point in

[65] House Executive Document 8, p. 51; and Leonard D. White, *The Republican Era* (New York: The Free Press, 1965), pp. 172–73.

the development of the public employment relationship. It was the last time partisan political activity on the part of the civil service would be encouraged and would be an important part of the political system. It was also the last time that most of the more important negative discriminations of the public employment relationship would be determined and applied on the basis of custom and practice rather than by law. Moreover, much of the future legislation affecting the relationship would be enacted as a reaction to perceived administrative and political effects created by the spoils system.

3 | Civil Service Reform
and the Public
Employment Relationship

I

The civil service reform movement and its legislative outcomes have had a lasting effect of great importance upon
the development of the public employment relationship. The
immediate influence of reform was, in conjunction with more
extensive goals, to encourage a decrease in the range of discrimination by increasing the degree of equality of access to
civil service positions, by making illegal the coercion of political activity and financial contribution, and by prohibiting
removals for reasons other than cause affecting the efficiency
of the civil service. The attempt to prevent coercion was
unsuccessful, however, and the concepts of reform eventually
encouraged restrictions on political activity which considerably
extended the range of discrimination. The reform movement
began toward the close of the Civil War as a reaction to the
spoils system, and although the movement itself became unimportant after the turn of the century, many of the concepts
of reform became political norms which are still accepted
and are of importance to the public employment relationship
at the present time.[1]

[1] The last time reform was challenged *in toto* by a political platform
and a presidential candidate was in 1896 when the Democratic platform contained an anti-reform plank, and William Jennings Bryan
echoed Jackson in declaring, "A permanent officeholding class is not
in harmony with our institutions. A fixed term in appointive offices

Civil service reform of some kind was almost inevitable as government became more positive, as public policy became more regulatory, as technology and business methods advanced, and as the size of the civil service grew in conjunction with these factors.[2] The reformers were aware of the fact that the spoils system was rapidly becoming anachronistic. One of their leaders, Carl Schurz, argued that

there are certain propositions so self evident and so easily understood that it would appear like discourtesy to argue them before persons of intelligence. Such a one it is, that as the functions of government grow in extent, importance and complexity, the necessity grows of their being administered not only with honesty, but also with trained ability and knowledge.[3]

Civil service reform, however, as the reformers understood it, was never intended simply to reform the civil service. As Schurz expressed it, "the question whether the Departments at Washington are managed well or badly is, in proportion to the whole problem, an insignificant question." [4] The overall goals of the reformers were related less to the condition of the civil service than to that of the nation and to the role of men like themselves in the political system.

The reformers were intellectual and social leaders, some of whom had been active abolitionists and later became anti-

---

. . . would open the public service to a larger number of citizens without impairing its efficiency." Quoted in William Dudley Foulke, *Fighting the Spoilsmen* (New York: G. P. Putnam's Sons, 1919), p. 111.

[2] Between 1871 and 1881 the civil service almost doubled in size. See Table 1.

[3] Carl Schurz, *Congress and the Spoils System* (New York: George G. Peck, 1895), p. 4.

[4] Carl Schurz, *Speeches, Correspondence, and Political Papers of Carl Schurz,* ed. Frederick Bancroft (New York: G. P. Putnam's Sons, 1913), II, 123.

imperialists. They were lawyers, editors, clergymen, professors, and mercantile and financial, rather than industrial, businessmen. They tended to be Protestant and to come from urban areas. They were especially prominent in the northeastern part of the country, and many were from prominent or old-established New England families. They were often descendants of merchants, clergymen, and public servants.[5] The reformers were sociologically similar to the social group which was important in political life before being displaced by the spoils system and the "common man." In advocating civil service reform they sought to change several characteristics of the political system. In Schurz's words, they wanted "to restore ability, high character, and true public spirit once more to their legitimate spheres in our public life, and to make active politics once more attractive to men of self-respect and high patriotic aspirations." [6]

The reformers hoped that civil service reform, as they proposed it, would decrease the ability of professional politicians to control the civil service for partisan purposes and therefore relegate them to a role of minor importance in the political system. They clearly understood the change in American political life which was brought about by the spoils system. George William Curtis, the leading advocate of reform, attacked the spoils system on the ground that it

creates a mercenary political class, an oligarchy of stipendiaries, a bureaucracy of the worst kind, which controls parties with relentless despotism, imposing upon them at the elections issues which are prescribed not by the actual feeling and interest of

[5] See Ari Hoogenboom, *Outlawing the Spoils* (Urbana: University of Illinois Press, 1961), pp. vii, ix–x, 21.

[6] Carl Schurz, editorial in *Harper's Weekly*, XXXVII (July 1, 1893), 614.

the country but solely by the necessities and profit of the oligarchy.[7]

He also condemned the system for "excluding able and upright men from public life." [8] Dorman B. Eaton, another leading reformer, declared that under the spoils system

we have seen a class of politicians become powerful in high places, who have not taken (and who by nature are not qualified to take) any large part in the social and educational life of the people. Politics have tended more and more to become a trade, or separate occupation. High character and capacity have become disassociated from public life in the popular mind.[9]

Schurz was in agreement with his colleagues, and he believed that an important task of reform was to

rescue our political parties, and in great measure the management of our public affairs, from the control of men whose whole statesmanship consists in the low arts of office mongering, and many of whom would never have risen to power had not the spoils system furnished them the means and opportunity for organizing gangs of political followers as mercenary as themselves.[10]

Aside from depriving men such as themselves from what they believed to be their proper role in the political system, a major defect of the spoils system and government by professional politicians, according to the reformers, was that "the moral tone of the country is debased. The national character

[7] George William Curtis, "Introduction" in Dorman B. Eaton, *The Civil Service in Great Britain* (New York: Harper and Bros., 1880), p. v.

[8] George William Curtis, *The Year's Work in Civil Service Reform* (New York: National Civil Service Reform League, 1884), p. 19. Hereinafter references to the League will be abbreviated as NCSRL.

[9] Eaton, *Civil Service in Great Britain*, p. 392.

[10] Schurz, *Harper's Weekly*, XXXVII, 614.

deteriorates." [11] Most of the reformers probably agreed with Charles J. Bonaparte who stated:

But I, at least, cannot imagine a good man who has thought on the subject and who knows enough about it to think to any purpose, and who yet fails to see that to promise or confer public office as a bait or reward for personal or party service is always and everywhere immoral.[12]

The reformers generally compared the morality of civil service reform with that of the abolition of slavery,[13] and, in short, sought "to lift all parties up to a higher conception of public duty and to restore the Government to the principles and practices of its founders." [14] They therefore joined the Jacksonians in attempting to make a fundamental change in the political system by altering the nature of the civil service.

Although the reformers' proposals were diverse, at the foundation of most of them was a distinction between the business-like or administrative, and the political components of the civil service. The reformers believed that of the great

[11] U.S., Civil Service Commission (CSC), "Reform of the Civil Service: A Report to the President, December 18, 1871," in Charles Eliot Norton (ed.), *Orations and Addresses of George William Curtis* (New York: Harper and Bros., 1894), II, 37. The report was written by Curtis. Paul P. Van Riper, *History of the United States Civil Service* (Evanston: Row, Peterson and Co., 1958), did a symbol analysis of civil service reform literature, and found quantitative differentiation between the symbols of "morality" and "efficiency" to be in greater than 2:1 ratio in the *Proceedings of the League* between 1882 and 1892 (p. 86n.).

[12] Charles J. Bonaparte, *Civil Service Reform as a Moral Question* (New York: NCSRL, 1889), p. 4.

[13] For example, see George William Curtis, "The Administration and Reform," in Norton (ed.), *Orations*, II, 359, and *Civil Service Reform Under the Present National Administration* (New York: NCSRL, 1885), p. 23; and Foulke, *Spoilsmen*, p. 3.

[14] Edward O. Graves, *The Meaning of Civil Service Reform* (Geneva, N.Y.: Geneva Civil Service Reform Association, 1885), p. 3.

number of "places [in the civil service] very few are political. Political offices are those which are concerned with devising and enforcing a policy which the people have approved at the polls." [15] They were aware of the fact that "it may be difficult to determine precisely the limits of the offices which in this sense may be called political," [16] but nevertheless certain that the distinction was tenable. The specific measures of reform were designed to apply almost entirely to the nonpolitical component: "What civil service reform demands, is simply that the business part of the government shall be carried on in a sound businesslike manner." [17]

The reformers often made analogies to the business world to demonstrate what they believed was the nonsensical nature of the spoils system as it applied to the administrative part of the civil service. For example, Schurz said,

imagine a merchant discharging his sales men and bookkeepers, a manufacturer discharging his foreman and artisans, a railroad corporation discharging its engineers and switchmen, a bank discharging its cashiers and tellers every four years on the ground that they have been in their places long enough and somebody else ought to have them now.[18]

In later years the belief that the practices of public personnel administration should be equated with those of the private sphere tended to encourage extension of the range of discrimination by minimizing constitutional limitations on the government's authority to act upon the rights of its employees. For

[15] Civil Service Reform Association, *A Primer of Civil Service Reform* (n.p.: no publisher, n.d.), p. 1.

[16] CSC, "Report to the President, 1871," p. 76.

[17] Carl Schurz, *The Necessity and Progress of Civil Service Reform* (Washington: Good Government, 1894), p. 3.

[18] Carl Schurz, *Civil Service Reform and Democracy* (Washington: Good Government, 1893), p. 21.

the reformers, however, it meant that it was possible "to take the whole non-political public service out of politics." [19]

The reformers believed that the most effective method of achieving their overall goals was to depoliticize the civil service by terminating recruitment based on political opinion, affiliation, and services. Political appointment was at the foundation of the spoils system, and it was important before that, but the reformers rejected it for the administrative part of the civil service. Curtis argued that it was as illogical to appoint to a nonpolitical post on the basis of politics as to make "a man surveyor of highways because he played sweetly upon the French horn." [20] After the enactment of the Civil Service Act [21] the desire to exclude politics from personnel actions became the basis of an important decrease in the range of discrimination. In 1884, Civil Service Rule VIII provided that

no question in any examination, or proceeding by, or under, the Commission or examiners, shall call for the expression or disclosure of any political or religious opinion or affiliation, and if such opinion or affiliation be known, no discrimination shall be made by reason thereof by the examiners, the commission or the appointive power.[22]

Although interference with religious freedom and equality with regard to public employment was largely prohibited by Article VI of the Constitution, the rule did establish a greater degree of equality of access to civil service positions in the competitive service and partially protected the First Amendment rights of applicants for these positions.

[19] George William Curtis, *The Situation* (New York: NCSRL, 1886), p. 17.
[20] George William Curtis, "Civil Service Reform," in Norton (ed.), *Orations,* II, 3–4.
[21] U.S., *Statutes at Large,* XX, 403 (January 16, 1883).
[22] U.S., CSC, *Annual Report,* I (1884), 47.

The reformers wanted to substitute merit ascertained through open competitive examination for politics in the selection of civil servants in the administrative part of the service.[23] It has been said, "indeed, merit appointment with merit tenure comprehends the whole program of Civil Service Reform." [24] Some of the reformers argued that merit appointment was not only a reform, but a part of "the great law which nature applies in every gradation of organic life—the survival of the fittest." [25] They believed that only through open competitive examination could favoritism be eliminated, the best civil servants be obtained, and justice prevail. The idea was not original; it had been tried elsewhere, notably in England, and could be presented "not merely as a fine theory or as a high, ideal conception of purity and justice in politics, but as an embodiment of principles and methods matured during a century." [26] From the English example it was concluded that

open competition presents at once the most just and practicable means of supplying fit persons for appointment. It is proved to have given the best public servants; it makes an end of patronage; and, besides being based on equal rights and common justice, it has been found to be the surest safeguard against both partisan coercion and official favoritism.[27]

[23] To be more accurate, the reformers sought merit and fitness. The latter element, however, was not indigenous to reform, although they stressed it more than the spoilsmen. See chap. 5, *infra.*

[24] Carl Schurz, *Congress and the Spoils System* (New York: George G. Peck, 1895), p. 30.

[25] William D. Foulke, *The Theory and Practice of Civil Service Reform* (Washington: NCSRL, 1884), p. 11. See also Eaton, *Civil Service in Great Britain,* p. 419.

[26] *Ibid.,* pp. 370–71.

[27] *Ibid.,* p. 365. The reformers agreed with John Stuart Mill that competitive exams were desirable because "a mere pass examination never, in the long run, does more than to exclude absolute dunces";

While the choice of open examinations tended to increase the degree of equality of access, the exams themselves, depending on their content, could, in an age in which the opportunity for higher education was highly correlated with wealth, create significant inequalities. Throughout the long debate over reform, it was argued by some that exams would provide an "opening wedge to aristocracy in this country," by excluding the common people from the civil service.[28] In 1872, Senator Carpenter of Wisconsin, an opponent of reform, made the following argument against exams:

So, sir, it comes to this at last, that . . . the dunce who has been crammed up to a diploma at Yale, and comes fresh from his cramming, will be preferred in all civil appointments to the ablest, most successful, and most upright businessman in the country, who either did not enjoy the benefit of early education, or from whose mind, long engrossed in practical pursuits, the details and niceties of academic knowledge have faded away.[29]

The central issue was, therefore, whether exams should be of a practical or a literary character.

Some of the reformers, along with Schurz, ridiculed "the idea of a great American aristocracy consisting of Treasury clerks, or letter carriers, or custom inspectors, or even such

---

quoted in U.S., CSC, *Report to the President* (Washington: U.S. Government Printing Office, 1874), p. 79. This belief was generally demonstrated to be correct by the United States by experience with pass exams instituted in 1853. U.S., *Statutes at Large*, X, 211 (March 3, 1853). A person taking these exams was required to add 2 and 2 and to answer such questions as, What is the capital of the Union? Schurz, *Democracy of the Merit System*, p. 20. Moreover, pass exams, even when open, do not exclude favoritism and therefore would be of little utility in undermining the professional politician.

[28] Statement of Representative John A. Logan, U.S., *Congressional Globe*, 40th Cong., 2d Sess., Part 1, p. 265 (January 8, 1869).

[29] *Ibid.*, 42d Cong., 2d Sess., Part 1, p. 458 (January 18, 1872).

magnates as revenue collectors or presidential postmasters or Indian agents," [30] but most were in favor of, or at least willing to accept, practical exams. They believed that "the essential point is not to find coal-heavers who can scan Virgil correctly, but coal-heavers who, being properly qualified for heaving coal, are their own masters and not the tools of politicians." [31] In any case, practicability was necessary due to the political climate at the time, and a requirement that exams be practical was added to the reformers' civil service bill by the Senate in 1882. Moreover, the requirement was taken seriously by many, such as Theodore Roosevelt, who once suggested that marksmanship exams be given for the position of collector of customs at El Paso because that officer had to be "handy with his gun," [32] and the social class basis of the civil service did not, at least immediately, undergo any important changes due to the introduction of examinations.[33] Reform, therefore, on the whole, decreased the range of discrimination of the public employment relationship by decreasing the degree of discrimination concerning equality of access for those in the competitive civil service.

[30] Schurz, *Democracy of the Merit System*, p. 18.

[31] George William Curtis, *The Year's Work in Civil Service Reform* (New York: NCSRL, 1884), p. 16.

[32] Foulke, *Spoilsmen*, p. 92.

[33] The U.S., CSC. *Annual Report*, III (1886), 8, reported that out of 7,138 candidates in general examinations, 6,053 were from public schools, 327 were from business colleges which were similar to high schools, and 758 claimed a partial college education. In 1900–1901, out of 1,477 competitive appointments in Washington, 200 had more than secondary-school education, of whom 41 were physicians and 122 were engineers. See Leonard D. White, *The Republican Era* (New York: The Free Press, 1965), p. 349.

II

The reformers wanted to reorient the civil service on a formal legal basis, rather than by informal means. "What we want," Curtis said, "is to intrench the principle and practice of Washington in the law." [34] Another reformer explained that "it was on account of discretionary appointments that the spoils system crept in. To abolish the spoils system, appointments must cease to be discretionary. . . . We consider that fixed rules, however imperfect, are better than arbitrary power." [35]

The struggle to legislate reform was long, and at times bitter. Despite some earlier progress, it was not until 1881 that reform began to make permanent gains.[36] In that year Eaton asked Senator Pendleton, an Ohio Democrat, to allow the New York Civil Service Reform Association to substitute a bill for one Pendleton had previously submitted. Pendleton agreed and in January the bill, primarily the work of Eaton, was submitted to the Senate. There was little action taken at the time, but two events strongly influenced enactment of the bill. First, on July 2, 1881, President Garfield was shot by an office seeker, and popular hostility toward the spoils system increased. Second, and more important, the Republican party suffered a significant defeat in the midterm elec-

[34] Curtis, "Civil Service Reform," p. 19.

[35] Foulke, *Theory and Practice*, p. 9.

[36] For the legislative history of reform see Hoogenboom, *Spoils,* entire; White, *Republican Era*, pp. 279ff., *et passim;* U.S., CSC, *History of the Federal Civil Service 1789 to the Present* (Washington: U.S. Government Printing Office, 1941), pp. 38ff., *et passim*. The most notable early success came between 1871 and 1874 when a Civil Service Commission was established. See Lionel Murphy, "The First Civil Service Commission," *Public Personnel Review,* III (January and July, 1942), 29–39, 218–31.

tion of 1882, and wanted to protect itself against future Democratic spoils.[37] Moreover, several Republicans who were identified with the spoils system were defeated and the nation appeared to be in favor of reform. After a long debate and important amendment, the civil service bill became law when President Arthur, a spoilsman par excellence, signed it on January 16, 1883.[38]

The Civil Service Act still provides the legal foundation for the modern civil service, and has had a continuing influence on the development of the public employment relationship. The final form of the act was different from the reformers' bill in some respects. The most important change, aside from the requirement of practical exams, was one, supported by Pendleton himself, allowing entrance at all levels of the civil service rather than at the lowest level only. The act provided for a Civil Service Commission of three persons, no more than two of whom could be members of the same political party. The commissioners were to be appointed by the president with the advice and consent of the Senate, and were removable by the president.[39] The CSC was to draw up

[37] This is the primary thesis of Hoogenboom, *Spoils;* see pp. ix, 236ff., *et passim.*

[38] The bill was passed in the Senate by a vote of 38 to 5, and in the House by 155 to 47. The vote was bipartisan although Republicans were more unified in their support of the bill. See U.S., *Congressional Record,* 47th Cong., 2d Sess., XIV, Part 1, 467–68, 866–67. The constitutionality of the Act was upheld in *Butler* v. *White,* 83 F. 578 (1897), in which the Circuit Court for West Virginia said, "If the time should ever come . . . when Congress cannot regulate the administration of the civil service . . . it will be an untoward event which will strike at the very foundation of the existence of the government" (p. 582). The decision was based on the same ideas which were at the foundation of the doctrine of privilege.

[39] In 1956 the commissioners were given six-year overlapping terms. However, they could still be removed during their terms.

rules to aid the president and "for carrying this act into effect." It also had the authority to investigate and report on "all matters touching the enforcement and effects" of the rules and the act. The act specified that these rules should provide for, among other things, the following: open competitive examinations of a practical nature, selection from the highest scorers,[40] and a probationary period for all competitive appointees. The act further specified that the rules should provide that "no person in the public service is for that reason under any obligation to contribute to any political fund, or to render any political service, and that he will not be removed or otherwise prejudiced for refusing to do so," and "that no person in said [competitive civil] service has any right to use his official authority or influence to coerce the political action of any person or body."

The act contained several provisions which were more or less divorced from the reformers' main objectives but which affected the degree of equality of access to civil service positions. It provided that no more than two members of a family could be in the competitive civil service at the same time; instituted an apportionment rule, based on the populations of the states and territories, for appointment to positions in Washington; provided for the continuance of pre-existing veteran preference; and somewhat closer to the reformers' ideals, it provided that "no person habitually using intoxicating beverages to excess" should be in the competitive service.[41]

[40] In 1871 the attorney general ruled that it was unconstitutional to require the highest scorer to be appointed because the Constitution gave the appointing power to the president, courts, and department heads, and some discretion was necessary. The opinion eventually became the basis of the "rule of three" which is used at the present time. See U.S., *Opinions of the Attorneys General*, XIII, 510 (1871).

[41] See also chap. 5, *infra*.

The act placed about 10 per cent of the total number of positions in the competitive or classified service. Since that time several extensions and exclusions have been made by executive order and act of Congress. Since 1919 at least 70 per cent, and since 1947 at least 80 per cent, have generally been in the classified service.[42] The distinction between classified and nonclassified positions has sometimes been the basis of the domain of discriminations.

The last five sections of the act were intended to prevent political assessment. They strengthened already existing legislation for this purpose, and illegalized solicitation, assessment, subscription, or other contribution for any political purpose, from any United States employee or person paid by the United States, by any other civil or military employee or officer, or legislative, judicial, or territorial official. No one could engage in the prohibited activity in a place in which government employees worked. No employee was allowed to give political contributions to any other government employee, and employees could not be dismissed or demoted for refusing to contribute. Violations were punishable by removal from office, three years' imprisonment, and/or a $5,000 fine.

In attempting to abolish assessment the reformers were anxious to end an important source of partisan income and to protect employees. However, anti-assessment regulations can present constitutional problems. Some officials thought that such regulations interfered with a man's natural right to spend his money as he pleased and were therefore unconstitutional.[43] Curtis and other reformers saw the issue in a different

[42] See Herbert Kaufman, "The Growth of the Federal Personnel System," in Wallace Sayre (ed.), *The Federal Government Service* (Englewood Cliffs: Prentice-Hall, 1965), p. 41; and CSC *Annual Report,* since 1963.

[43] Hoogenboom, *Spoils,* p. 229.

light: "The question is not whether a government employee may not give if he chooses to give. . . . The question is whether he may decline to give, if he chooses, with the same freedom as a citizen who is not an employee." [44] The constitutional issue was, however, previously settled by the Supreme Court in 1882. Section six of an act of August 15, 1876 [45] provided that

all executive officers or employees of the United States not appointed by the President, with the advice and consent of the Senate, are prohibited from requesting, giving to, or receiving from, any other officer or employee of the government, any money, property, or other thing of value for political purposes.

The act was challenged in *Ex parte Curtis,* a case involving assessment by General Newton M. Curtis, a special Treasury Department agent. The Court upheld the constitutionality of the law because Congress could use its legislative power to promote the efficiency of the civil service and could legitimately place restrictions on public employees. Moreover, the restrictions in this instance appeared to be relatively minor:

The managers of political campaigns, not in the employ of the United States, are just as free now to call on those in office for money to be used for political purposes as they ever were, and those in office can contribute as liberally as they please, provided their payments are not made to any of the prohibited officers or employees.[46]

Although the law was constitutional, for the same reason it was not very effective.

Justice Bradley, in a dissenting opinion, found even these minor restrictions on employee freedom to be in violation of

[44] George William Curtis, "Should the Black-Mail be Paid," *Harper's Weekly,* XXVIII (September 20, 1884), 612.

[45] See *Ex parte Curtis,* 106 U.S. 371 (1882).   [46] *Ibid.,* p. 373.

the Constitution. Although the purpose of the law was legitimate, it made it

a condition of accepting any employment under the government that a man shall not, even voluntarily and of his own free will, contribute in any way through or by the hands of any other employee of the government to the political cause which he desired to aid and promote. I do not believe that Congress has the right to impose such a condition upon any citizen of the United States.[47]

The *Curtis* decision became an important precedent for the development of the doctrine of privilege, but assessments were not effectively abolished. In 1899, Schurz took note of the fact that "the levying of assessments upon persons in the Federal service has again assumed very formidable dimensions." [48]

The difficulty with anti-assessment and other legislation which seeks to protect employees from illegitimate coercion is that it can only be effective under two conditions, both of which may have undesirable side effects. First, it can be effective if the activity which is likely to be coerced is outlawed, rather than the coercion of it alone. In the case of assessment, although probably unenforceable, this would mean that employees, as was formally the situation under President William Henry Harrison,[49] could not contribute under any circumstances. Similarly, when it is feared that political activity

[47] *Ibid.*, p. 376. Bradley's dissent was an early expression of the principles of the doctrine of substantial interest.

[48] Carl Schurz, *Renewed Struggles* (n.p.: NCSRL, 1899), p. 24. Assessments, although still illegal, remain an important part of American politics. For example, on March 26, 1968, it was reported that "high civil service officials are being asked, in some cases with more pressure than usual even in an election year, to contribute sizable sums to a Democratic party dinner." The *New York Times*, March 26, 1968, p. 1.

[49] See chap. 2, *supra*.

might be coerced, the activity itself must be illegalized. This method, while often intended to protect civil servants, tends to extend rather than decrease the range of discrimination by increasing the degree and domain of discrimination in the negative direction—and from the employee's point of view may be a cure which is worse than the disease. Second, the civil servant can be provided with legal or constitutional job security which strictly limits the causes for which he may be legitimately removed and which establishes procedures designed to ascertain the validity of the charges against him. This method presents difficulties of administrative control and has a tendency to make superior officers reluctant to go through the removal process in instances of minor fault. The latter method also encourages a less negatively discriminatory relationship and the development of positive discriminations. The reform movement taken as a whole influenced both methods. On the one hand, it influenced legislation concerning political neutrality which forbids political activity on the part of civil servants. On the other hand, it eventually encouraged a few important limitations on the executive power of removal which were designed to protect civil servants against arbitrary dismissal and had the effect of decreasing the range of discrimination.

III

Many of the reformers were originally in favor of regulating the removal power, but reform as a whole did not support this position until the late 1890's. Before 1897, despite many attempts, important limitation on the executive removal power was only achieved under the Tenure of Office Act of 1867, which prohibited the removal of presidential officers without the consent of the Senate.[50] Curtis referred to the act as "both

[50] U.S., *Statutes at Large*, XIV, 430 (March 2, 1867). The act was

a wholesome and necessary restraint upon the Executive. . . . It tends, also, to make the whole system of offices more independent, and thus to remove one of the most demoralizing influences in our politics." [51] In actuality, however, it was outside the realm in which reform would later make its greatest gains because it pertained more to the political component of the civil service than to that part which the reformers considered to be administrative. The act reversed the Decision of 1789, but later Curtis became a leading proponent of the limited-access and unlimited-removal system favored by that decision.

Curtis and those reformers who were in agreement with him argued that if appointment was limited on the basis of merit, a superior officer would have nothing to gain by removing an employee for illegitimate reasons, because he could not freely choose a successor. This had the great advantage of establishing a qualified stable civil service without creating problems of insubordination or vested rights in office. As Curtis expressed it:

But to promote the efficiency of the Civil Service it is not enough to ascertain fitness by examination and to test aptitude by probation, unless there also be provided a reasonable security of tenure of the office. . . . It is undeniable, however, that such fixity of tenure tends to great perplexity and inconvenience in administration, and that the responsible head of a branch of the public service may justly complain if he has no immediate control of his subordinates. If it were necessary to establish unfitness or indolence, . . . by such proof as would be accepted in a court of law, sentence would seldom be pronounced, even against notorious

---

weakened by *ibid.,* XVI, 6 (April 5, 1869) and reepaled by *ibid.,* XXIV, 500 (March 3, 1887).

[51] George William Curtis, "Irresponsible Executive Power," *Harper's Weekly,* XII (May 19, 1868), 306.

delinquents. . . . A discretion of removal . . . if so guarded in its exercise that it be not liable to abuse, is most desirable in every office.

. . . . .

It seems to us . . . more desirable to afford this reasonable security of permanence in office by depriving the head of illegitimate motives for removal rather than by providing a fixed tenure, to be disturbed only upon conviction after formal accusation and trial.[52]

This position was incorporated into the Civil Service Act which prohibited only removals for failure to contribute money or render service for political purposes, and which established no procedural safeguards for the dismissed.

At first, the system seemed to prevent widespread removals. By 1886 the removal rate among 5,000 classified employees was 6.5 per cent per year, while in the unclassified service it ranged from 25 per cent in the Foreign Service to 71 per cent in the Department of the Interior.[53] By 1897, however, Schurz, who was originally in favor of restricted removals,[54] explained:

It was, indeed, thought at first by civil service reformers that arbitrary removals would cease whenever the competitive system made arbitrary appointments impossible. . . . But this sanguine expectation did not stand the test of experience, and Mr. Curtis himself, toward the end of his life, was inclined to abandon it.
. . . [Some appointing officers] would make arbitrary removals for the purpose of opening a chance for some trick by which, in

[52] CSC, "Report to the President, 1871," pp. 51, 55.

[53] White, *Republican Era,* pp. 340–41, from an investigation by the NCSRL.

[54] See Schurz's bill, S. 298, U.S., *Congressional Globe,* 41st Cong., 3d Sess., Part 1, p. 779 (January 27, 1871), which contemplated removal after charges and trial by a civil service board.

spite of the competitive system, they might put the favorites of power into vacated places.[55]

Moreover, unchecked removal power could not prevent specific removals based on the individual civil servant's political or religious opinions and affiliations, and was of little utility in preventing coercion of political activity and assessment.[56]

On July 27, 1897, action was taken to remedy the situation. President McKinley provided by executive order that

no removal shall be made from any position subject to competitive examination except for just cause and upon written charges filed with the head of the Department, or other appointing officer, and of which the accused shall have full notice and an opportunity to make defense.[57]

The rule underwent several changes, but in essence, it was incorporated into law by the Lloyd–La Follette Act of 1912,[58] which stated, in part, that

no person in the classified Civil Service of the United States shall be removed therefrom except for such cause as will promote the

[55] Schurz, *Democracy of the Merit System,* p. 29; see White, *Republican Era,* pp. 341–42, for evidence that Schurz's summary of the situation was correct.

[56] Civil Service Rule II, sect. 3 (May 6, 1896), prohibited personnel actions made on the basis of politics or religion. See U.S., CSC, *Civil Service Act and the Rules Promulgated by the President* (Washington: U.S. Government Printing Office, 1899).

[57] U.S., CSC, *Annual Report,* XVIII (1901), 282. Previously, President Cleveland had declined to approve a similar civil service rule. See White, *Republican Era,* p. 343.

[58] U.S., *Statutes at Large,* XXXVII, 555 (August 24, 1912). The real issue involved in this act was the prohibition of "gag orders." These orders hampered postal workers from effectively unionizing, by preventing them from presenting political and other grievances to Congress except through their department head. This was a negative discrimination abridging the employees' First Amendment rights which was outlawed before the courts ruled on it.

efficiency of said service and for reasons given in writing, and the person whose removal is sought shall have notice of the same and of any charges preferred against him, and be furnished with a copy thereof, and also be allowed a reasonable time for personally answering the same in writing, and affidavits in support thereof; but no examination of witnesses nor any trial or hearing be required except in the discretion of the officer making the removal; and copies of charges, notice of hearing, answer, reasons for removal, and of the order of removal shall be made a part of the records of the proper department or office, as shall also the reasons for reduction in rank or compensation; and copies of the same shall be furnished to the person affected upon request, and the Civil Service Commission shall, upon request, be furnished copies of the same.

The act is still in force, although in recent years civil servants have been given greater job security through more procedural safeguards including the right to hearings, representation, and in some instances cross-examination.

The provisions of the Lloyd–La Follette Act are of significance for the public employment relationship. In *Taylor* v. *Taft*,[59] an important case in the doctrine of privilege, it was held that "the courts have no . . . jurisdiction" to review executive removals and that "this power of removal, therefore, would seem to be unrestricted, except as controlled by legislation of Congress." [60] However, once Congress required removals to be for such cause as would promote the efficiency of the service,[61] and civil servants were to be provided with a

[59] 24 App. D.C. 95 (1904).

[60] *Ibid.*, p. 98. It is significant that the court found no constitutional restrictions on removal, but only legislative ones.

[61] "Efficiency of the service," while somewhat ambiguous, was a meaningful phrase because there was a provision for rating efficiency. See U.S., *Statutes at Large*, XXXVII, 413 (August 23, 1912).

description of the cause, they had a greater opportunity for judicial recourse. If an employee were dismissed for an arbitrary or invalid reason, and was so informed, he could attempt to demonstrate, in court, that his removal was illegal because it would not promote the efficiency of the service. If he were removed because of his religious or political beliefs, or exercise of some other constitutionally or legally protected right, he legally had to be so informed and therefore might be able to plead his case successfully in court. If the employee suspected he was removed for political or religious reasons, but was told it was for inefficiency, he had the opportunity to try to prove, in court, that the superior officer acted in bad faith and removed him for illegitimate cause. While the right to know why one was removed might not have afforded extensive job security, it did provide somewhat greater protection than the system of removals unaccompanied by explanation and tended toward a decrease in informal negative discrimination. Moreover, it had the effect of providing the courts with a more important role in civil service removals and in defining the public employment relationship.

IV

The reform movement and its legislative outcomes established the fundamental basis of the present-day United States civil service and the framework for the modern public employment relationship. It had important long- and short-run effects on the development of the relationship. Reform was designed to be "but another successive step in the development of liberty under law," [62] and to a considerable extent it was immediately intended to increase the liberty of civil servants and

[62] George William Curtis, *Party and Patronage* (New York: NCSRL, 1892), p. 10.

to decrease the range of discrimination. The Civil Service Rules prohibited personnel actions based on politics or religion, and eventually the reformers encouraged the adoption of procedural and substantive restrictions on removal which were designed to protect the individual civil servant against arbitrary dismissal. The reformers' efforts at creating greater equality of access were inadequate, however, and it was necessary for more comprehensive action to be taken in the future. Moreover, the attempt to prohibit coercion was unsuccessful, and the reformers' concepts of public employment, especially the distinction between politics and administration and their desire for a nonpolitical civil service, encouraged the prohibition of voluntary political activity which abridged civil servants' First Amendment rights and constituted an important increase in the range of discrimination.

Reform also had important indirect effects on the development of the public employment relationship. It placed the public personnel system, and especially removals, on a more uniform and formalized legal basis. The distinction between the classified and nonclassified civil service, established by the Civil Service Act, has been used to define the domain of specific discriminations. Furthermore, the reformers' equation of the private and public spheres with regard to employment practices ignored constitutional limitations on governmental authority over citizens and encouraged the acceptance of negative discriminations.

Civil service reform marked a turning point in the development of the public employment relationship. It was the last successful attempt to reorient entirely the civil service and the public employment relationship. Therefore, since its decline as an important political movement, the relationship has tended to center on specific issues and regulations rather than comprehensive attempts, such as were made during the founding period, the time of the spoils system, and the reform movement, to redefine the civil service's relationship with other elements of the political system.

4 | Political Neutrality

In the United States political neutrality, or restrictions on the political activity of civil servants, has been an important negative discrimination of the public employment relationship, and one which has been of great consequence to the development of judicial doctrines concerning the relationship. Political neutrality clearly indicates the extent to which the roles of citizen and civil servant may be considered to be incompatible. It abridges the First Amendment rights of civil servants, despite the fact that these rights are generally considered fundamental to democracy. Restrictions on political activity have been one of the most important controls on the gross characteristics of the United States bureaucracy, and have been intended to insure its partisan impartiality, and to eliminate the possibility that the civil service, either voluntarily or under coercion, could use partisan political activity to subvert the democratic process.[1] Although Presidents Jefferson, William H. Harrison, and Tyler, and several members of Congress, attempted to establish a politically neutral civil service before the reform movement became an important factor in American political life, these efforts, perhaps with

[1] The latter aim is clearly a legacy of the spoils system and is of special importance in the United States. See Leon Epstein, "Political Sterilization of Civil Servants: The United States and Great Britain," *Public Administration Review*, X (Autumn 1950), 282, 284; and Fritz Morstein Marx, *The Administrative State* (Chicago: University of Chicago Press, 1957), p. 144.

the exception of Jefferson's, were out of phase with the political system and were uniformly unsuccessful.[2] Political neutrality had to follow the depoliticizing of public personnel administration and was only successfully instituted after the adoption of the merit system.

The civil service reformers rejected the spoils concept of a political civil service. They wanted to disassociate the civil service from politics and politics from the civil service. They sought a relatively permanent and competent service which would serve all administrations equally well. As George William Curtis expressed it, "the tap root of the evils and abuses which reform would destroy is the partisan prostitution of the civil service. Offensive partisanship is a phrase which fitly describes it."[3] Reformer Dorman B. Eaton believed that "it must be regarded as one of the greatest anomalies of our politics . . . that we have had no prevailing public opinion which has fixed any well-defined limits to the use of official authority for political or even for partisan ends."[4] The concepts of reform directly and indirectly influenced the development of such limits.

A minor, but effective, step toward divorcing the civil service from partisan politics occurred in 1873 when President Grant issued an executive order forbidding federal civil ser-

[2] For Jefferson's attempt see chap. 1, *supra*. For Harrison's and Tyler's see James D. Richardson (ed.), *Messages and Papers of the Presidents of the United States, 1789–1897* (Washington: U.S. Government Printing Office, 1898), IV, 38, 52. The most important congressional attempt was made in 1839, see U.S., *Congressional Globe,* 25th Cong., 3d Sess., Part 1, pp. 59, 189.

[3] George William Curtis, *Civil Service Reform Under the Present National Administration* (New York: National Civil Service Reform League, 1885), p. 14.

[4] Dorman B. Eaton, *The Civil Service in Great Britain* (New York: Harper and Bros., 1880), pp. 409–410.

vants from holding state, territorial, or local offices.[5] The order was aimed at carpetbaggers rather than reform. Although it did not prevent civil servants from campaigning, it tended to limit the civil servant's political activity in his own behalf, and to disassociate federal civil servants from state politics. It was also a step in the direction of limiting obvious partisan identification within the civil service.

In 1877, President Hayes issued the first political neutrality order to be based on the concepts of reform. The order provided, in part, that

no officer should be required or permitted to take part in the management of political organizations, caucuses, conventions, or election campaigns. Their right to vote and to express their views on public questions, either orally or through the press is not denied, provided it does not interfere with the discharge of their official duties.[6]

Despite Hayes's favorable attitude toward reform, his department heads failed to take the order seriously or enforce it.[7] The next important attempt to depoliticize the civil service was the Civil Service Act, which, as previously discussed,[8] contained some clauses which were designed to prevent coerced political activity.

Three years after the enactment of the Civil Service Act, President Cleveland issued an order for political neutrality which stated:

[5] Richardson, *Messages,* VII, 218 (January 17, 1873). The order was revoked by Executive Order 11408, U.S., *Federal Register,* XXXIII, Part 4, 6459 (April 25, 1968). This was done in conjunction with a recent trend toward decreasing negative discrimination. See chap. 8, *infra.*

[6] Richardson, *Messages,* VII, 450–51.

[7] Leonard D. White, *The Republican Era* (New York: The Free Press, 1965), p. 330.

[8] See chap. 3, *supra.*

Officeholders are the agents of the people, not their masters . . . they should scrupulously avoid in their political action, as well as in the discharge of their official duty, offending by a display of obtrusive partisanship. . . .

They have no right as officeholders to dictate the political action of their party associates or to throttle freedom of action within party lines by methods and practices which pervert every useful and justifiable purpose of party organization.

The influence of Federal officeholders should not be felt in the manipulation of political primary meetings and nominating conventions. The use by these officials of their positions to compass their selection as delegates to political conventions is indecent and unfair: and proper regard for the proprieties and requirements of official place will also prevent their assuming the active conduct of political campaigns.[9]

Although Cleveland clearly understood the root of the problem and its significance, and was a firm supporter of reform, he apparently found Republican partisan activity more "indecent and unfair" and made removals accordingly.[10] Nevertheless, Cleveland's order, and to a lesser extent, that of President Hayes, were of importance because they set precedents for prohibiting civil servants from taking active part in political parties as well as political campaigns and electioneering activities.

The first successful system of political neutrality was established by President Theodore Roosevelt. Roosevelt was actively involved in the quest for civil service reform and tended to place greater emphasis on the impartiality aspect

[9] Richardson, *Messages,* VIII, 494 (July 14, 1886).

[10] See A. B. Sageser, *The First Two Decades of the Pendleton Act* (Lincoln: University of Nebraska Press, 1935), p. 121. It should be noted that Cleveland was the first president since William H. Harrison to succeed an opposition administration without being able, for political reasons, to justify removals on the basis of the theory of rotation.

of political neutrality than did earlier presidents. In 1893, as a civil service commissioner, he personally wrote the Commission's statement on neutrality: [11]

A man in the classified service has an entire right to vote as he pleases and to express privately his opinions on all political subjects; but he should not take any active part in political management or in political campaigns, for precisely the same reasons that a judge, an army officer, a regular soldier, or a policeman is debarred from taking such active part. . . . It leaves him free to vote, think, and speak privately as he chooses, but it prevents him while in the service of the whole public, from turning his official position to the benefit of one of the parties into which the whole public is divided; and in no other way can this be prevented.[12]

Roosevelt thought that a distinction between the degree of discrimination applied to classified and nonclassified civil servants was desirable. He criticized Cleveland for being "led into absolutely hypocritical professions and conduct both because he made sweeping promises and issued sweeping orders applying to everybody, classified and unclassified alike, and then did not live up to them even as regards the classified ,places." [13] In June 1902, President Roosevelt wrote the CSC a letter stating that

after my experience under two Presidents, . . . I had become convinced that it was undesirable and impossible to lay down a rule for public officers not in the classified service which should limit their political activity as strictly as we could rightly and properly limit activity of those in whose choice and retention . . . political considerations did not enter.[14]

Civil servants in the nonclassified domain were placed under the following restriction: *"Office-holders must not use their*

[11] White, *Republican Era,* pp. 330–31.
[12] U.S., Civil Service Commission, *Annual Report,* XI (1894), 21.
[13] Quoted in White, *Republican Era,* p. 330.
[14] U.S., CSC, *Annual Report,* XX (1903), 126.

offices to control political movement, must not neglect their public duties, must not cause public scandal by their activity." [15] The degree of discrimination for those in the classified service was to be much greater.

Shortly after writing the above letter to the CSC, Roosevelt instructed his department heads to issue orders for political neutrality.[16] These orders were enforced unevenly by the department heads and demonstrated the need for independent and uniform enforcement. Therefore, on June 3, 1907, Roosevelt issued an executive order to amend Civil Service Rule I, section one, to include the following:

persons who by the provisions of these rules are in the competitive classified service, while retaining the right to vote as they please and to express privately their opinions on all political subjects, shall take no active part in political management or in political campaigns.[17]

Because the Civil Service Act, however ineffectively, specifically prohibited the coercion of political activity, and the merit system reduced the likelihood of widespread coercion in the classified service, and because the domain of discrimination under the order was the entire classified service, the order was an important extension of the range of discrimination. The extent of this increase, however, largely depended on how the CSC defined "privately" and "active part."

The CSC strictly interpreted Roosevelt's order and developed what are among the most highly restrictive prohibitions on political activity of any in modern democratic political systems. The CSC has striven for clarity and comprehensiveness, but it has conceded that "it is impossible to give a complete list of the particular activities in which an employee

[15] *Ibid.* Italics in original.
[16] See *ibid.;* and XXIII (1906), 50ff.
[17] *Ibid.*, XXIV (1907), 9.

may not engage." [18] The most complete lists of such activities are found in the Commission's Form 1236 and "Pamphlet 20." [19] The exact content, and therefore the degree and range of discrimination, of these lists has varied over time as political issues and civil service rules have changed. For example, Form 1236 (1939) said that "activity in campaigns concerning the regulation or suppression of the liquor traffic is prohibited," [20] but this prohibition has since been deleted. Nevertheless, it is possible to list, in general terms, their basic provisions.

Although originally prohibited by Roosevelt's order, civil servants are presently allowed to express themselves publicly, unless it is "in such a way as to constitute taking an active part in political management or in political campaigns." [21] A civil servant cannot take any part in a political convention other than that of spectator. He can attend primary meetings, mass conventions, caucuses, and the like, and vote on any question presented, "but he may not pass this point in participating in its deliberations." [22] He cannot take any part in a political meeting. He cannot hold such offices as precinct committeeman and ward committeeman, or serve on any committee of a political party. Employees can join political clubs, but cannot be active in organizing them, become officers in them, or address them on any partisan political matters. They cannot distribute campaign literature, badges, or buttons, although they can wear badges and buttons and display politi-

---

[18] U.S., CSC, *Political Activity and Political Assessment of Federal Officeholders and Employees* (Washington: U.S. Government Printing Office, 1939), p. 2. Hereinafter this publication will be referred to as Form 1236 with the year of publication following.

[19] U.S., CSC, *Political Activity of Federal Officers and Employees* (Washington: U.S. Government Printing Office, periodically).

[20] CSC, Form 1236, p. 8, No. 23.

[21] CSC, Pamphlet 20 (May 1966), p. 13.   [22] *Ibid.,* p. 10.

cal posters or pictures in their homes and on their automobiles. They cannot publish or be connected editorially or managerially with a partisan newspaper and cannot write, for publication, signed or unsigned letters or articles soliciting votes for a candidate or a faction. An employee can vote, but he cannot be a watcher, checker, or challenger, or engage in any other partisan political activity at the polls. He cannot be in a political parade, except as a member of a musical organization that is generally available for such purposes.[23] Civil servants cannot initiate nominating petitions in behalf of partisan candidates, or canvass for signatures. They may, however, sign petitions. An employee cannot, with some exceptions, be a candidate for public office.[24] Today, a civil servant can accept a local office if he is elected "without being a candidate, his name not appearing on the ballot but being written in by voters . . . [as] a spontaneous action"![25] Civil servants can be active "in organizations having for their primary object the promotion of good government or the local civic welfare."[26] They cannot indirectly engage in any of the prohibited activities and are held responsible for the political activity of their spouses or others acting in collusion with them: the domain of discrimination therefore includes not only civil servants themselves, but, in practice, their families as well.

These prohibitions are enforced by the CSC, which until 1938 did not have the authority to remove employees, although it could recommend such action to the department

[23] Even this was prohibited for a time. See CSC, Form 1236 (1939), p. 8, No. 26.

[24] These exceptions are for local offices in certain communities having large concentrations of federal employees. See CSC, Pamphlet 20 (May 1966), pp. 16–18, for a full explanation and listing.

[25] *Ibid.*, p. 15.   [26] *Ibid.*, p. 12.

heads.[27] Although under Roosevelt's executive order civil servants had no legal right to hearings, the CSC could grant
them at its discretion, and a case law was developed in over
3,000 decisions by 1940.[28] The restrictions on civil servants'
political activity represent a high degree of discrimination in
the negative direction. Moreover, their inherent ambiguity can
remove almost entirely a cautious employee and his family
from that part of the political process which is unrelated to his
functions as a civil servant. It is impossible to anticipate
exactly what the CSC will consider a partisan issue as opposed to a "good government" issue, or what constitutes
collusion with one's spouse in many instances.

The interpretations by the CSC under the Roosevelt order
were incorporated into law by the First Hatch Act,[29] which
extended the domain of discrimination to nonclassified civil
servants. It in no way increased the degree of negative discrimination concerning political activity; in fact, it encouraged its
reduction. The legislative history of the act demonstrates that
it was primarily justified as a means to prevent partisan political activity on the part of the civil service from undermining
the democratic process by creating a one-party system, or
at least the tendency toward one. The origin and successful
enactment of the act was directly related to some of the
important and far-reaching changes in American politics and
governmental structure which took place during the depression
and the New Deal.

During President Franklin D. Roosevelt's first two adminis-

[27] Civil Service Rule XV of that year allowed the CSC to order
the salaries of classified employees to be withheld. See U.S., CSC,
*Civil Service Act and Rules, Statutes, Executive Orders, and Regula-
tions* (Washington: U.S. Government Printing Office, 1941), p. 114.

[28] Henry Rose, "A Critical Look at the Hatch Act," *Harvard Law
Review*, LXXV (January 1962), 511.

[29] U.S., *Statutes at Large*, LIII, Part 2, 1147 (August 2, 1939).

trations the role of the bureaucracy in the United States political system underwent important changes. Rather than being a mere tool to administer the laws, such as the civil service reformers envisioned, it became more and more obviously involved in the policy-making process. The concept of the welfare state required that the government fulfill more functions, and the administration of these functions required changes in the bureaucracy. By the end of 1934 there were some sixty new agencies, only five of which had been placed under the jurisdiction of the CSC.[30] These exemptions were made primarily so that Roosevelt could staff the agencies on a patronage basis rather than through merit procedures. His use of patronage, however, was more ideological than traditional, and because of the economic crisis the civil service was more attractive than usual to intellectuals and other members of the college-bred middle class whom Roosevelt sought.[31] The outcome of these and other changes was that the bureaucracy became more powerful and more central to the political life of the nation. It also became much larger and, as Table 4 indicates, the proportion of civil servants in classified positions rapidly declined.

During Roosevelt's second term, Congress became increasingly antagonistic toward the expanding executive power. This hostility often centered on the changes which took place in the bureaucracy. Congressman Rees, a Kansas Republican, warned:

We have created bureaus and commissions in the name of emergency, and have given them power and authority beyond all expectations. We have added group after group of employees. The policy of this Congress is to increase these bureaus as well as the

[30] Paul P. Van Riper, *History of the United States Civil Service* (Evanston: Row, Peterson and Co., 1958), p. 320.

[31] *Ibid.*, pp. 324–29.

Table 4. The percentage of civil
servants in the classified civil
service, 1930–1940

Year ending June 30	Percentage in the classified service
1930	79.6
1931	79.6
1932	80.1
1933	79.7
1934	66.9
1935	63.3
1936	60.5
1937	63.2
1938	66.1
1939	67.7
1940	72.5

Source: Commission on Organization of the Executive Branch of the
Government, *Report on Personnel
and Civil Service* (Washington: U.S.
Government Printing Office, February 1955), pp. 97–98.

number of employees, rather than to decrease them. . . . Today
we have approximately 900,000 Federal employees, 300,000 of
whom secured their positions because of political patronage. . . .
If this Congress continues its present practice, we are going to
foster and approve the most gigantic political machine that is
known in any nation anywhere.[32]

The fear of such a machine, or at least the use of federal
employees for partisan purposes, and hostility toward the
administration and the bureaucracy were instrumental in moti-
vating Congress to bring nonclassified employees under the

[32] U.S., *Congressional Record,* 76th Cong., 1st Sess., LXXXIV,
Part 9, 9603 (July 20, 1939).

already existing political activity restrictions on classified civil servants.

In 1938, political factors combined to make political neutrality an important political issue. Roosevelt attempted his "purge," in which the Works Progress Administration and other New Deal agencies were thought to be important tools,[33] and James Garner and his allies sought political neutrality as a means of preventing Roosevelt from controlling the next Democratic National Convention.[34] Senator Hatch, a Democrat from New Mexico, who had previously introduced political neutrality bills in 1935 and 1937, attempted to take advantage of the growing sentiment in favor of such legislation. Hatch introduced a bill "to prevent the use of Federal official patronage in elections and to prohibit Federal officeholders from misuse of positions of public trust for private and partisan ends." [35] He argued that there was a potential danger in the existing system:

When I look out over the country, and observe the vast, vast numbers of Federal employees who reach out and extend to every county and to every precinct in the United States, I realize that some

[33] For WPA see U.S. Congress, Senate, *Report of the Special Committee to Investigate Campaign Expenditures and Use of Government Funds in 1938* (Washington: U.S. Government Printing Office, 1939), p. 39. A historian, David A. Shannon, *Twentieth Century America* (Chicago: Rand McNally and Co., 1963), has concluded that although the "charge is difficult to assess . . . there were same real cases of local WPA offices using their power for corrupt political purposes in Pennsylvania, Kentucky, and Tennessee" (p. 344). In Tennessee one WPA superintendent was convicted for misappropriating funds and levying assessment on relief workers. U.S., *Congressional Record,* LXXXIV, Part 9, 9598.

[34] Samuel Lubell, *The Future of American Politics* (Garden City: Doubleday and Co., 1956), p. 14.

[35] U.S., *Congressional Record,* 75th Cong., 3d Sess., LXXXIII, Part 4, 4458 (March 31, 1938), S. 847.

other administration . . . could absolutely control any political convention in which Representatives, Senators, or even a President were to be nominated.[36]

He expressed the fear that even in the absence of coercion, the political activity of civil servants, if motivated toward uniform ends, could subvert the democratic process:

The conventions I have seen, and I think all conventions in the United States which select delegates, are those which begin in the precinct, with the precinct chairman calling a little convention at which, 99 times out of 100, no one but employees are present. The precinct convention selects delegates to the county convention. The county convention from a similar group selects delegates to a State convention, and the State convention likewise selects similar delegates to the national convention. The people never express their choice.[37]

Hatch said his objective was "good party government," as opposed to "pure" politics.[38]

The administration was opposed to the bill. Senate majority leader Alben Barkley argued that there should be no negative discrimination along these lines, because, in his words, "I am not prepared to admit, nor do I believe, that the thousands of Federal employees in the United States are any worse than the rest of our citizens." [39] Some Senators, along with McAdoo of California, argued that the bill "is fundamentally a violation of that right [free speech] guaranteed to every citizen of the United States." [40] and at least one Senator thought that "if the bill should become a law there would be nobody left in the party to attend conventions." [41] The bill lost by a vote of 19 to 39.[42]

---

[36] *Ibid.*, p. 4459.   [37] *Ibid.*, p. 5219.   [38] *Ibid.*, p. 5400.
[39] *Ibid.*, p. 5406.   [40] *Ibid.*, p. 5404.
[41] *Ibid.*, p. 5220, Senator Reames.
[42] *Ibid.*, p. 5409. The vote was as follows: Republicans, 8 for,

Shortly after this bill was defeated, Hatch introduced an amendment to a relief and work appropriation bill which would have extended the application of the political activity restrictions on classified employees to all persons who received any compensation from it.[43] He said that since 1935 he had

realized how perfectly natural it would be for men with the best motives in the world to try to keep their own party in power, and to use their influence as county chairman or foremen over those receiving the bounties and benefits from our [work-relief] program, and in some instances perhaps corruptly to influence and control votes.[44]

It was his "firm judgment and belief that if we build up a system by which we can use funds from the Public Treasury to control the votes of the people of the Nation it is no exaggeration to say that the moment that is done democracy in America is dead." [45] The amendment lost 37 to 40.[46]

Hatch tried again in 1939 and this time was successful. The Senate passed what became known as the First Hatch Act on a call of the calendar on the assumption that the bill would be weakened by the House Judiciary Committee.[47] Although the Committee did weaken it, amendments from the floor restored most of its strength. Opponents of the bill made arguments similar to those presented earlier in the Senate. Representative Parsons announced that "this House is about

---

0 against, 7 not voting; Democrats 8, 39, and 30; Independent Republicans, 1 for; Farmer-Labor, 1 for and 1 not voting; Progressive, 1 for.

[43] *Ibid.*, p. 7962 (June 2, 1938).   [44] *Ibid.*, p. 7963.

[45] *Ibid.*, p. 7964.

[46] *Ibid.*, p. 8000. The vote was: Republicans, 12 for, 0 against, 3 not voting; Democrats, 22, 40, 15; Independent Republican and Progressive each, 1 for; Farmer-Labor, 1, 0, 1.

[47] See *ibid.*, 76th Cong., 3d Sess., LXXXVI, Part 15, 2434 (March 5, 1940).

to witness the demise of political parties in this country," [48] and another Representative attacked the bill on the grounds that it would

take away from the American people that inherent right that was handed down to them by our founding fathers. . . . If enacted into law, it will deprive the American people of the right to express their opinion on Government, the right to take part in politics, and is beyond a doubt the furthest step that has been taken in the history of this Nation toward dictatorship.[49]

Those in support of the bill continued to argue that it was necessary for the maintenance of democratic government. As Representative Ramspeck of Georgia expressed it, "I believe if we are going to maintain good government in this country and have a democratic form of government that is to survive, we have to remove the rank and file employees from being pawns in the political game." [50] The bill was passed in the House by a vote of 241 to 134.[51]

The most important section of the act was section 9(a), which basically incorporated the already existing civil service political neutrality rule into law and extended it to non-classified employees in the executive branch.[52] While the act extended the domain of discrimination, in one respect it encouraged a decrease in the degree of discrimination. It allowed public employees to express their views on all "political sub-

[48] *Ibid.*, LXXXIV, Part 9, 9594.
[49] *Ibid.*, p. 9609. Representative Hook.   [50] *Ibid.*, p. 9616.
[51] *Ibid.*, p. 9639. A previous motion to recommit lost 146 to 232 (p. 9638). The final vote was: Republicans, 156 for, 0 against, 9 not voting; Democrats, 83, 133, 42; Farmer-Labor, 1 not voting; Progressives, 2 for; American Labor, 1 not voting.
[52] The president, vice-president, office of the president, department heads and assistant heads, and presidential officers engaged in the making or execution of foreign policy or nationwide administration of the laws were excepted.

jects," rather than only to express them "privately." This
change was deliberate,[53] and in 1941 the civil service rule was
altered accordingly.[54] The change was equivocal, however,
because the right of public expression was still qualified by
the prohibition against taking active part in political management or campaigns. It was later qualified by section 15,
which provided that the act "shall be deemed to prohibit the
same activities . . . as the United States Civil Service Commission has heretofore determined are at the time this section
takes effect prohibited" on the part of classified employees.
The CSC's determinations were based on the rule with the
word "privately" in it, and the situation has been somewhat
ambiguous.[55] Another decrease in the degree of discrimination occurred in 1940 when the Second Hatch Act also allowed civil servants to express their views on "candidates" as
well as on political subjects.[56]

[53] *Ibid.,* pp. 9622–25, 9630, 9637–40; see also *ibid.,* LXXXIII, Part
7, p. 8000.
[54] Executive Order 8705, U.S., *Federal Register,* VI, Part 1, 1313
(March 5, 1941). Until the issuance of this order the CSC maintained
the old standard for classified civil servants. See U.S., CSC, *Annual
Report,* LVII (1940), 19.
[55] For a full criticism of the act from this standpoint see Rose,
Harvard Law Review, LXXV, entire; and Joseph M. Friedman and
Tobias Klinger, "The Hatch Act: Regulation by Administrative Action of the Political Activity of Government Employees: I," *Federal
Bar Journal,* VII (October 1945), 8–9.
[56] U.S., *Statutes at Large,* LIV, Part 1, p. 767 (July 19, 1940).
This act extended the domain of discrimination to state employees
whose compensation was made possible by federal funds. It also made
minor amendments to the First Hatch Act. During debate on it, the
Senate rejected an amendment to strike out section 9(a) of the First
Hatch Act by a vote of 41 to 44. See *Congressional Record,* LXXXVI,
Part 15, 2439 (March 5, 1940). The first eight sections of the First
Hatch Act were aimed at prohibiting coercion, assessments, and racial
and religious discrimination in hiring or providing relief. They were
punishable by a year imprisonment and/or $1,000 fine, and enforced

The CSC continued to be the enforcing agency for classified employees. Hearings remained discretionary until 1955 when they were made mandatory for veteran preference eligibles and available to other employees.[57] Under the original act removal was mandatory if the civil servant had engaged in prohibited activities, but in 1950 it was amended to allow suspension for ninety days or more if the CSC voted unanimously against removal.[58] In 1962 the minimum period of suspension was reduced to thirty days.[59] Enforcement for nonclassified civil servants was through their departments or agencies. Nonclassified employees, however, have the right of appeal to the CSC for final determination. Between August 2, 1939, and June 30, 1967, the CSC received 3,938 complaints, 3,299 of which were closed without action; in 237, removals were made, and in 352, suspensions were ordered.[60]

---

by the Department of Justice. Section 9A was directed at excluding disloyal persons from positions in the federal bureaucracy and will be further discussed in chap. 6, *infra.*

[57] See *Flanagan* v. *Young,* 228 F. 2d 466 (1955); and U.S., CSC, *Annual Report,* LXXIII (1956), 125–26. Previously, the CSC's general rule was that "a hearing will not be granted if the respondent has admitted an alleged violation or if it is established by indisputable record proof. But if the respondent admits the facts alleged . . . he is entitled to be heard upon the issue of whether such facts constitute a violation." See James W. Irwin, *Hatch Act Decisions* (Washington: U.S. Government Printing Office, 1949), p. 33. The civil servant could be represented by an attorney if he so desired.

[58] U.S., *Statutes at Large,* LXIV, Part 1, 475 (August 25, 1950).

[59] Public Law 87-753 (October 5, 1962).

[60] U.S., CSC, *Annual Report,* LXXXIV (1967), 68. The remainder of cases were either reopened (13) or pending (37). In fiscal 1968 there were two removals and sixteen suspensions, but the Commission failed to report the number of complaints received. See *ibid.,* LXXXV (1968), 82–83.

II

Political neutrality has been the center of a great deal of controversy. Almost all the arguments against it, except those dealing with its constitutionality, are in one way or another dependent upon the attitudes of civil servants toward the restrictions. However, to consider all negative discriminations as automatically undesirable from the point of view of the civil servant would be a serious error. The reasons why civil servants might oppose political neutrality are obvious, but there are important reasons why many of them might favor it. Although the rights abridged are of great overall significance for democratic political systems, many citizens, probably most, seldom exercise them. Moreover, the inability to take part in the restricted political activities is the most complete and effective method of protecting civil servants from coercion. Tables 5 and 6 present the results of a recent survey of the attitudes of federal civil servants toward restrictions on political activity.

Table 5. General attitudes of federal employees toward allowing more or less political activity

Attitude	Percentage [a]
Should allow more participation	47
Should remain the same	48
Should allow less	1
Don't know	3

Source: U.S., Commission on Political Activity of Government Personnel, *Report* (Washington: U.S. Government Printing Office, 1968), II, 20, Table 26.

[a] Percentage total is less than 100 due to rounding.

Table 6. Federal employee attitudes toward changes in
the Hatch Act [a]

Attitude	Percentage [b]
Should remain as is; do not favor changes	35
Should be changed to allow more participation in political activity	19
Should allow federal employees to campaign or work for a political party or candidates of his choice	13
Should allow federal employees to hold local or nonpartisan office	6
Should allow federal employees to hold political or partisan office	6
Should allow freedom to speak on political matters, discuss politics when they want	4
Repeal the Hatch Act	3
Should allow local participation of all kinds (except holding office)	3
Should lessen or decrease penalties	2
Should tighten the restrictions, clarify the restrictions	1
Should allow federal workers to drive people to the polls	1
Don't know what changes should be made	12
Should be changed (not ascertained how)	5
All other responses	3

Source: U.S., Commission on Political Activity of Government Personnel, *Report* (Washington: U.S. Government Printing Office, 1968), II, 20, Table 27.

[a] Asked of 62 per cent of sample who had heard of the Hatch Act.
[b] Includes multiple responses.

The division of civil servants with regard to restrictions on political activity negates some of the criticism of the Hatch acts. It does not, however, at least directly, affect arguments concerning their constitutionality. The courts have generally been favorable toward political neutrality, as they have been, until recently, toward almost all negative discriminations. The issue of constitutionality was not decided by the Supreme Court until 1947 in the case of *United Public Workers* v. *Mitchell* [61] in which it upheld political neutrality by a four-to-three margin.[62] By that time, however, there had been several opinions on the issue which influenced the development of the doctrine of privilege.

One of the first judicial statements on political neutrality occurred well before it was successfully adopted. Justice Bradley, in his dissent in *Ex parte Curtis*,[63] argued:

Congress might just as well, so far as the power is concerned, impose, as a condition of taking any employment under the government, entire silence on political subjects. . . . The whole thing seems to me absurd. Neither men's mouths nor their purses can be constitutionally tied up in that way.

One of the earliest cases, *Louthan* v. *Commonwealth* [64] was decided in agreement with Bradley's conclusion. The Virginia Supreme Court declared a statute for political neutrality unconstitutional because

the officer in question is a constitutional officer, and while he may be removed from office for malfeasance, misfeasance, or gross neglect of official duty, or for sufficient cause, he cannot be removed for exercising any right guaranteed to him by the [Virginia] Constitution without violating that instrument. . . . These rights are guaranteed to all the citizens of the state, not to any portion or class of citizens.[65]

This decision is in striking contrast to the general body of law which later developed and often has been overlooked as a precedent, although at the present time similar lines of reasoning are becoming more common.

[61] 330 U.S. 75 (1947).
[62] Justices Jackson and Murphy took no part.
[63] 106 U.S. 371, 377–78 (1882). See chap. 3, *supra*.
[64] 79 Va. Repts. 197 (1884).   [65] *Ibid.*, p. 206.

In 1892, Oliver Wendell Holmes, then a judge on the Massachusetts Supreme Court, rejected the *Louthan* conclusion and replaced it with a doctrine which was for many years much more appealing to the courts and members of the political system in general. In *McAuliffe* v. *New Bedford* [66] he upheld the dismissal of a policeman who violated a regulation for political neutrality on the ground that

there is nothing in the Constitution or the statute to prevent the city from attaching obedience to this rule as a condition to the office of policeman, and making it a part of the good conduct required. The petitioner may have a constitutional right to talk politics, but he has no constitutional right to be a policeman. . . . The servant cannot complain, as he takes the employment on terms which are offered him. On the same principle, the city may impose any reasonable condition upon holding office within its control. This condition seems to us reasonable, if that be a question open to revision here.[67]

This decision has been one of the most influential in the doctrine of privilege. Because there was no right to office, the government could legitimately interfere with an employee's constitutional rights if it appeared reasonable to do so. But Holmes expressed some doubt as to whether the court could legitimately assess the reasonableness of the restrictions, and other courts have tended to ignore or uncritically accept the reasonableness of similar enactments. For example, in a Pennsylvania case it was held that

if in the judgment of the legislature, political activity on the part clerks and employees of a city *is likely* to interfere with efficient public service, there would appear to be no legal reason why such activity should not be restrained or prohibited, so long as the individual elects to continue in the public service. If such restric-

[66] 155 Mass. 216 (1892).   [67] *Ibid.,* p. 220.

tion is distasteful to him, he has the alternative of seeking other employment.[68]

The tendency not to examine the reasonableness of restrictions reduced Holmes's decision to the statement that "the petitioner may have a constitutional right to talk politics, but he has no constitutional right to be a policeman." [69] In other words, because there was no constitutional right to office, the constitutional rights of citizens in public employment could be abridged; due process did not apply to civil service removals.

The Supreme Court's decision in the *United Public Workers* case accepted Holmes's conclusion, but at the same time limited some of its implications. The case involved a classified civil servant who held the position of roller in the mint at Philadelphia. He was removed for holding a party office and for political activity. Justice Reed, speaking for the Court, reasoned that

we have a measure of interference by the Hatch Act and the Rules with what otherwise would be the freedom of the civil servant under the First, Ninth and Tenth Amendments. And, if we look upon due process as a guarantee of freedom in those fields, there is a corresponding impairment of that right under the Fifth Amendment.[70]

But the case involved a civil servant and "for regulation of employees it is not necessary that the act regulated be any-

[68] *Commonwealth ex rel. Rotan* v. *Hasskarl* 21 Pa. Dist. R. 119, 123 (1912). Emphasis added.

[69] Probably no other single sentence has been quoted so often in cases of this sort and discussions of the issues involved. Although it no longer represents valid law, it still carries a logical appeal for many. For example, see the *New York Times,* June 12, 1968, p. 42, "Waivers of Immunity."

[70] 330 U.S. 75, 94–95.

thing more than an act reasonably deemed by Congress to interfere with the efficiency of the public service," [71] and "the argument that political neutrality is not indispensable to a merit system for federal employees may be accepted. But because it is not indispensable does not mean that it is not desirable or permissible." [72] In other words, civil servants were in a special constitutional position and the clear and present danger test did not apply to them.

Justice Douglas in a partial dissent rejected the Court's reasoning as it applied to industrial workers. He thought that those rights are too basic "in our democratic political society to be sacrificed or qualified for anything short of a clear and present danger to the civil service system." [73] Justice Black, joined by Justice Rutledge, entirely rejected the Court's reasoning: "There is nothing about federal and state employees as a class which justifies depriving them or society of the benefits of their participation in public affairs." [74]

Although the majority accepted the constitutionality of negative discrimination, it also accepted limitations on its extent. Justice Reed stated:

Appellants urge that federal employees are protected by the Bill of Rights and that Congress may not "enact a regulation providing that no Republican, Jew or Negro shall be appointed to federal office, or that no federal employee shall attend Mass or take any active part in missionary work." None would deny such limitations on Congressional power.[75]

These limitations however, were less obvious than the Court implied. For example, "active part in missionary work," in

---

[71] *Ibid.,* p. 101.   [72] *Ibid.,* p. 100.
[73] *Ibid.,* p. 126. Douglas distinguished between industrial and administrative civil servants and would have allowed a greater degree of discrimination for the latter.
[74] *Ibid.,* p. 111.   [75] *Ibid.,* p. 100.

some instances might bring the civil servant into the sphere of prohibited political activity. In fact, there was such a case on record at the time, and its decision was presumably incorporated into the Hatch Act by section 15. In 1932, Archie B. Cole's removal was recommended by the CSC because his "participation in meetings, circulation of literature and other activities in connection with a society antagonistic to Governmental policy [Jehovah's Witnesses] is sufficient evidence of his unfitness for Government employment" on the grounds of political activity.[76] Moreover, in practice, Republicans have been, wherever possible, excluded by Democratic administrations, and Jews and Negroes have at times been excluded by informal means and/or by law from civil service positions.[77]

Although the Court's reasoning concerning these limitations was ambiguous, it nevertheless had an important bearing on judicial doctrines concerning the public employment relationship. By declaring that negative discrimination could be unconstitutional, the Court required the judicial branch to play a greater role in overseeing the relationship, and tended to restore the importance of examining the reasonableness of discriminations. The limitations set by the decision made it a precedent for future decisions seeking to disallow negative discriminations.

III

In the United States political neutrality has probably been of greater importance to the political system than any other discrimination of the public employment relationship. In accordance with the reformers' ideas, it changed the role of the

[76] Quoted in Rose, *Harvard Law Review,* LXXV, 515–16.
[77] See chap. 5, *infra.* For some recent developments concerning political neutrality, see chap. 8, *infra.*

civil service from that of an overtly partisan force to that of a relatively neutral one. The development of regulations concerning political neutrality has been based on a desire for impartial administration and a desire to prevent the civil service from becoming a partisan political force which might subvert the democratic process. The degree and domain of discrimination under provisions for political neutrality at the present time are very extensive and therefore these regulations represent one of the most important elements in the range of discrimination.

Judicial decisions on the constitutionality of political neutrality have had a large impact on the development of the public employment relationship. Holmes's decision in the *McAuliffe* case was very influential in the development of the doctrine of privilege which encouraged a negatively discriminatory relationship, and the Supreme Court's decision in the *United Public Workers* case weakened that doctrine and provided a precedent for abandoning it. In retrospect, the latter decision can be seen as a transitional one between the doctrine of privilege and that of substantial interest. Political neutrality therefore played a crucial role in the development of the public employment relationship. It established an extensive range of discrimination, and made it a central part of the political system. It was also central to the development of the doctrine of privilege, and at the same time related to its decline.

5 | Equality of Access to Civil Service Positions

I

The degree of equality of access to civil service positions [1] is an important element of the public employment relationship and one which has been fundamental to the decline of the doctrine of privilege. It has also been of great significance for political systems generally, and in systems providing for the basic equality of citizens, restrictions on equality of access have often been among the most important discriminations of the relationship. Although inequalities of access in the United States based upon social class status have been of great importance in the past,[2] these inequalities have been less important in more recent years, and efforts to influence the degree of equality have been made along other lines

The United States Constitution provides for the basic equality of all citizens. The due process clause of the Fifth Amendment has been interpreted to provide citizens with equality in the face of federal action.[3] In the case of religious and political equality this interpretation can be reinforced by the First Amendment. Political norms, such as the assertion

---

[1] Access to civil service positions is intended to mean access to all positions in the bureaucracy rather than only some positions. The term is also intended to include conditions within the service, such as unequal pay for equal work, which tend to make public employment more attractive to one group than to another.

[2] See chaps. 1–2, *supra*.

[3] *Bolling* v. *Sharpe,* 347 U.S. 497 (1954).

in the Declaration of Independence that "all men are created equal," although violated in many instances, also tend to support the principle of equality. Furthermore, with specific reference to public employment, Article VI of the Constitution prohibits religious tests as a qualification for office.

Nevertheless, the constitutional right of equality is relative and impossible to define comprehensively, except on an *ex post facto* basis. The requirement of equality has varied in its application to different subjects. For example, equality with regard to voting differs constitutionally from equality involving public employment. Moreover, there has been no comprehensive definition of the constitutional right of equality with respect to access to civil service positions. Although the Supreme Court indicated that a proscription based upon race, politics, or religion would be unconstitutional in *United Public Workers* v. *Mitchell*,[4] it is not clear that this statement would apply in all individual cases. For instance, it has been held that "a public employee still assumes the risk, as far as the Constitution is concerned, of being discharged for personal or political reasons," [5] and abridgment of equality on the basis of political affiliation continues to be very common in the nonclassified civil service. Furthermore, one of the most important qualifications of equality has applied to all those citizens who have not been entitled to veteran preference. But whether this has suspended the constitutional right of equality, and constituted a negative discrimination, is difficult to determine because veterans have been granted other special privileges as well. These characteristics of the constitutional provision concerning equality make it difficult to analyze the public employment relationship concerning equality. In some instances, such as exclusions based upon race and religion, negative

[4] 330 U.S. 75 (1947). See chap. 4, *supra*.
[5] *Norton* v. *Blaylock,* 285 F. Supp. 659, 662 (1968).

discrimination is in general easily identified; in others, however, such as exclusions based upon place of residence, it is
not. It is useful therefore to review all the major modifications
of citizen equality of access to civil service positions rather
than only those which are clearly negative discriminations or
have been declared unconstitutional by the courts.

The systemic importance of equality of access lies less in
its restriction of individual rights than in its effect on political,
social, and other groups. The composition of public bureaucracies is often one of the most significant characteristics of
a political system. The importance of racial, ethnic, religious,
geographical, social class, and similar bases of a civil service
is difficult to overestimate. The concept of "representative
bureaucracy" has been used to elaborate upon this importance.[6]
The concept includes the proposition, especially for democratic political systems, that if all major social and interest
groups are given sociological and/or functional representation
in public bureaucracies, these bureaucracies will be better
integrated with the other features of the system and will perform more satisfactorily. It also includes the idea that

bureaucracies . . . symbolize values and power realities and are
thus representational in both a political and an analytical sense.
Therefore, . . . social conduct and future behavior in a society
may be channelized and encouraged through the mere constitution
of the bureaucracy.[7]

[6] See, among others, J. Donald Kingsley, *Representative Bureaucracy* (Yellow Springs: Antioch Press, 1944), with special reference
to Great Britain; Paul P. Van Riper, *History of the United States
Civil Service* (Evanston: Row, Peterson and Co., 1958), especially
pp. 7–8, 551–53; Samuel Krislov, *The Negro in Federal Employment*
(Minneapolis: University of Minnesota Press, 1967), especially pp.
46–65; and V. Subramaniam, "Representative Bureaucracy: A reassessment," *American Political Science Review*, LXI (December
1967), 1010–19.

[7] Krislov, *The Negro*, p. 64.

Throughout history, therefore, "restriction on the opportunity to hold public office has been an effective instrument of social control" because bureaucratic representation is crucial to any group interested in political power or greater social status.[8]

The United States experience concerning equality of access to civil service positions demonstrates the importance of bureaucratic representation. From 1789 until 1829 every president sought characteristics in appointees which resulted in an upper social class bureaucratic composition, thereby maintaining political power within that group. In the expectation of increasing his party's political power, Jefferson sought, at one time, to make the civil service reflective of the nation's partisan distribution. Jackson perceived a connection between the rule of gentlemen and their control of the bureaucracy, and sought to limit their political importance by decreasing their bureaucratic representation. The reformers overtly sought a civil service which would be more efficient and encourage a higher morality in the nation, and more covertly sought to alter its composition in order to restore political leadership to men of higher social status. Some of the opponents of reform argued that the reform program would encourage the development of aristocracy in the United States. In more recent years, Negroes and women, both of whom have faced formal inequalities of access at various times, have sought and have been afforded greater bureaucratic representation as part of an overall drive to abolish societal inequalities concerning them.

The symbolic value of governmental personnel policy is easily imagined and often readily identifiable. One of the most striking examples of this value was demonstrated when some federal agencies became racially segregated under Presidents Taft and Wilson, and "with the government setting the

[8] *Ibid.*, pp. 46–47.

example for the community, Negroes lost what rights they had previously enjoyed in Washington theaters and restaurants, and were systematically segregated in housing and private employment." [9]

Under the United States Constitution, public personnel actions based upon race, color, religion, ethnicity, and in many instances sex as well, generally constitute discrimination of the public employment relationship. Negative discrimination in this area has been continually decreasing since the early 1940's. This decrease began as an attempt to unify the nation and make it more productive in preparation for World War II. Since the war it has been an integral part of the overall civil rights movement and has been due to the same political, economic, and social forces which have led to that movement. Symbolically, although not materially, the most important statement of this decrease has been the 1964 Civil Rights Act, which provides that

it shall be the policy of the United States to insure equal employment opportunities for Federal employees without discrimination because of race, color, religion, sex, or national origin, and the President shall utilize his existing authority to effectuate this policy.[10]

While there has been formal or informal inequality on all of these grounds at one time or another, and such inequality will undoubtedly continue into the future, abridgment of the equality of Negroes and women has been most extensive.[11]

[9] National Committee on Segregation in the Nation's Capitol (NCSNC), *Segregation in Washington* (Chicago: NCSNC, 1948), p. 62.

[10] U.S., *Statutes at Large,* LXXVIII, Part 1, 241, Title VII (July 2, 1964).

[11] Data on religious and ethnic inequality are scarce. Undoubtedly it has existed informally and there is some evidence to this effect. Re-

In 1802, Postmaster General Gideon Granger warned that if Negroes were allowed to carry the mail it would pose a threat to security because they might coordinate insurrectionary activities and acquire subversive ideas. For example, they might learn "that a man's rights do not depend on his color." [12] A man's legal rights did depend on his color in 1810 when Congress enacted a law providing that "no other than a free white person shall be employed in conveying the mail." [13] The law was re-enacted in 1825,[14] and modified by departmental order in 1828 to allow Negroes to carry mailbags from stage coaches to post offices under white supervision.[15] It was finally repealed after several efforts in 1865.[16]

Although the statute applied only to postal employees, it is believed that there were no Negroes in the bureaucracy until 1869 when Ebenezer Basset became minister to Haiti.[17] After that date, Negroes made slow but generally steady inroads and by 1928 achieved a proportion in the civil service roughly equal to their proportion in the nation.[18] There was some evidence of racial inequality in reductions in force in 1894,[19] but the most important setbacks for Negroes came

---

cent policies attempting to eradicate inequalities on these grounds are "spillovers" from the civil rights movement.

[12] Leon F. Litwack, *North of Slavery* (Chicago: University of Chicago Press, 1961), p. 57.

[13] U.S., *Statutes at Large,* II, 594 (April 30, 1810). The provision applied to contractors as well as actual postal department employees.

[14] *Ibid.,* IV, 104 (March 3, 1825).

[15] Litwack, *North of Slavery,* p. 58.

[16] U.S., *Statutes at Large,* XIII, 515 (March 3, 1865). Repeal was attempted in 1862 and was successful in the Senate but tabled in the House. In 1863 re-enactment of general mail statutes did not repeat it but did not repeal it either. *Ibid.,* XII, 701 (March 3, 1863). See Litwack, *North of Slavery,* pp. 58–59; and Krislov, *The Negro,* p. 10.

[17] Krislov, *The Negro,* p. 12.   [18] Van Riper, *History,* p. 194.

[19] Theodore Roosevelt wrote: "In the War Department they have turned out about two-thirds of the young colored men who came in

under the Taft and Wilson administrations. President Taft believed that Negroes should not hold office where whites complained [20] and he accordingly minimized Negro appointments in the south.[21] Furthermore, he began segregation in the civil service by segregating census takers in Washington, restricting white workers to whites, and Negroes to Negroes.[22]

The Wilson administration, which "shared the southern view of race relations," [23] treated Negroes with still more inequality. Segregation was introduced in the Postal and Treasury departments.[24] In 1914 every Negro clerk, with two exceptions, in the auditor's office and post office was reduced in rank [25] and photographs were, for the first time, required by the Civil Service Commission before appointments could be made.[26] Partially because of Wilson and partially because of the Senate, presidential appointment of Negroes also

---

through our examinations during the past three or four years." Quoted in Leonard D. White, *The Republican Era* (New York: The Free Press, 1965), p. 342.

[20] NCSNC, *Segregation,* p. 60; W. E. B. DuBois, *Dusk of Dawn* (New York: Harcourt, Brace, and Co., 1940), p. 233, "[Taft] began his reactionary administration by promising the South that he would appoint no Federal official to whom the southern people were opposed."

[21] Krislov, *The Negro,* pp. 18–19.

[22] NCSNC, *Segregation,* p. 60.

[23] Arthur S. Link, *Wilson: The New Freedom* (Princeton: Princeton University Press, 1956), p. 246.

[24] *Ibid.,* p. 247; Krislov, *The Negro,* p. 20. Wilson believed segregation was "distinctly to the advantage of the colored people themselves," Link, *Wilson,* p. 251.

[25] NCSNC, *Segregation,* p. 61.

[26] Krislov, *The Negro,* p. 21. Photographs may have legitimate uses but they certainly afford the appointing officer an opportunity to abridge equality easily, without having to interview the person. In the context of Wilson's administration they were undoubtedly used against Negroes. In 1942 photographs were dropped by CSC order.

lagged.[27] Even the traditionally "Negro" posts of minister to Haiti and Register of the Treasury went to whites, although Negroes did remain in some other posts.[28]

The administrations following Wilson's were more favorable to Negro appointments, although some segregation continued until after World War II, and the vast majority of Negroes in the service occupied low status positions.[29] However, toward the beginning of Franklin D. Roosevelt's third term positive formal action was taken to ensure Negroes and other groups a greater degree of equality of access. The First Hatch Act (1939) [30] contained a limited prohibition against interference with equality on racial or religious grounds. In 1940 this provision was reinforced by the Ramspeck Act which prohibited the abridgment of equality on the basis of race, color, and creed in fixing salaries, in allocating positions to grades, and in making transfers, promotions, and other personnel decisions.[31] Previously, Roosevelt had changed Civil Service Rule I to include a prohibition against qualifica-

[27] Wilson was under constant pressure with regard to Negroes in the civil service from Southern members of Congress who organized the "National Democratic Fair Play Association," which according to Link, *Wilson,* p. 246, was made up of "demagogic rabid racists."

[28] See Kathleen L. Wolgemuth, "Woodrow Wilson's Appointment Policy and the Negro," *Journal of Southern History,* XXIV (November 1958), 457–71 for greater detail. It should be remembered that, at the time, most Negroes were Republicans.

[29] John A. Davis, "Non-Discrimination in the Federal Services," *The Annals of the American Academy of Political and Social Science,* CCXXIV (March 1946), 72. Segregation remained in the cafeterias of the Federal Reserve Board and the Bureau of Internal Revenue. Previously, it was most prevalent in the Census Bureau, Government Printing Office, Bureau of Printing and Engraving, and other factory-type work situations. See NCSNC, *Segregation,* pp. 62–63; Krislov, *The Negro,* pp. 137–38.

[30] See chap. 4, *supra.*

[31] U.S., *Statutes at Large,* LIV, 1214 (November 26, 1940).

tions of racial equality.[32] In 1941, Roosevelt went further in creating, by executive order, the first Fair Employment Practice Committee under the pressures of A. Philip Randolph's threatened march on Washington and the necessities of increased defense production.[33] The order applied to the government and to defense industries and was specifically justified as a means to counteract the tendency to deny employment to needed workers because of their race, color, creed, or national origin. Its most important feature was the establishment of an agency to investigate and attempt to redress grievances and to make recommendations to further equality of access. The order marked the beginning of positive administrative action to decrease negative discrimination concerning equality of access to civil service positions. Although Negro employment rose during the war, this was probably less because of the order and previous legislation than because of the laws of supply and demand.[34] The order was nevertheless important because it provided a precedent which has been reaffirmed by successive administrations although changes in investigatory and enforcement agencies have been made.[35]

The most important advances for Negroes have been, of course, in the 1960's as a part of the civil rights movement

[32] Executive Order 8587, U.S., *Federal Register,* V, Part 4, 4445 (November 7, 1940).

[33] Executive Order 8802, *ibid.,* VI, Part 2, 3109 (June 25, 1941).

[34] Krislov, *The Negro,* p. 30.

[35] Truman, Executive Order 9980, U.S., *Federal Register,* XIII, Part 1, 431 (July 26, 1948); Eisenhower, Executive Order 10590, *ibid.,* XX, Part 1, 409 (January 18, 1955); Kennedy, Executive Order 10925, *ibid.,* XXVI, Part 3, 1977 (March 6, 1961); Johnson, Executive Order 11246, *ibid.,* XXX, Part 10, 12319 (September 24, 1965); Nixon, Executive Order 11478, *ibid.,* XXXIV, Part 8, 12985 (August 12, 1969). See Krislov, *The Negro,* pp. 34–45, *et passim;* Louis Ruchames, *Race, Jobs, and Politics: The Story of FEPC* (New York: Columbia University Press, 1953).

and related governmental efforts to improve the condition of Negroes in American society. Between 1961 and 1962, Negroes constituted 17 per cent of all net hiring,[36] and several agencies have made positive efforts to increase the number of Negroes and Spanish-speaking minority members appearing on the federal registers through recruitment drives at high schools and colleges attended by these groups.[37] In some instances, efforts to recruit Negroes have amounted to benevolent inequality. For example, in 1963, Congressional hearings were held on technical violations of postal regulations in the promotion of Negro post office workers in Dallas, Texas,[38] and the Foreign Service has instituted an experiment to enable Negroes to by-pass written examinations.[39] As a result of these efforts to increase Negro representation in the bureaucracy, they are proportionally overrepresented at the present time. They are unevenly distributed among the departments and agencies, however, and they are primarily in the lower status positions.[40]

Equality of access to civil service positions for women has been a related but more complex problem because the differences between the sexes have obvious implications for the specialization of function, and the social repercussions of feminine equality have been extremely far-reaching. The

[36] Frederick C. Mosher, "Features and Problems of the Federal Civil Service," in Wallace Sayre (ed.), *The Federal Government Service* (Englewood Cliffs: Prentice-Hall, 1965), p. 171.

[37] U.S., President's Committee on Equal Employment Opportunity, *Report* (Washington: U.S. Government Printing Office, 1963), p. 30.

[38] See Krislov, *The Negro*, p. 77.

[39] See the *New York Times*, March 23, 1968, p. 22.

[40] See U.S., CSC, *Study of Minority Group Employment in the Federal Government, 1967* (Washington: U.S. Government Printing Office, 1968), pp. 3–44. See also CSC, *Annual Report*, LXXXV (1968), 15–20. By 1966, Negroes constituted 14.9 per cent of the civil service, but only 1.2 per cent of the top three grades in the General Schedule. *Ibid.*, pp. 15–16.

formal basis of inequality on the basis of sex was derived from an 1870 statue which paradoxically had been intended to give women greater equality: "Women may, in the discretion of the head of any department, be appointed to any of the clerkships therein authorized by law, upon the same requisites and conditions and with the same compensations, as are prescribed for men." [41] The law was interpreted to allow an appointing officer to exclude women for reasons unrelated to their capacity or the efficiency of the service, and until 1919 women were excluded from about 60 per cent of the civil service examinations.[42] Unequal compensation had originally been provided for by law,[43] and despite the 1870 statute it continued in some agencies until 1923, when the Classification Act provided that "in determining the rate of compensation which an employee shall receive the principle of equal compensation for equal work irrespective of sex shall be followed." [44]

Equality was sometimes abridged with regard to married women, rather than women per se. In 1913, postal regulations provided that "no married woman will be appointed to a classified position" and that women in such positions would not be reappointed after marrying.[45] The Economy Act of June 30, 1932, provided that in reductions in force, an em-

---

[41] U.S., *Revised Statutes*, No. 165, U.S., *Code* (1964 ed.), V, 33 (July 12, 1870). Originally U.S., *Statutes at Large*, XVI, 250.

[42] Van Riper, *History*, p. 261.

[43] U.S., CSC, *History of the Federal Civil Service 1789 to the Present* (Washington: U.S. Government Printing Office, 1941), p. 35.

[44] U.S., *Statutes at Large*, XLII, 1488 (March 4, 1923). Reaffirmed by the Classification Act of 1949, *ibid.*, LXIII, Part 1, 954 (October 28, 1949).

[45] Section 157. Quoted in Lucille Foster McMillin, *Women in the Federal Service* (Washington: U.S. Government Printing Office, 1941), p. 26. The provision was amended in 1918 to allow the appointment of married women whose husbands or sons were in the military service. It was revoked in 1921.

ployee whose spouse was also in the service should be dismissed before other civil servants. The provision led to three times more dismissals of women than of men.[46] Marital status was, however, made an illegal basis for interference with equality in 1937.[47]

During World War II and after, women made significant proportional gains, but it was not until the 1960's in relation to new drives for equality that important positive steps were taken to ensure feminine equality. In 1961, President Kennedy established, by executive order, a President's Commission on the Status of Women.[48] The order was based on the premise that "women's basic rights . . . should be respected and fostered as part of our nation's commitment to human dignity, freedom, and democracy." Its object with regard to federal personnel policies was "to assure non-discrimination on the basis of sex and to enhance constructive employment opportunities for women." Since 1962 the abridgment of equality on the basis of sex has been allowed only in "unusual situations" in which the CSC finds it justified "on the basis of objective standards." [49] As a result of these efforts, the CSC concluded in 1964 that "instances of overt discrimination against women are now rare." [50] The proportion of women in the higher civil service positions is low however, and this

[46] See *ibid.*, pp. 21–22.

[47] U.S., *Statutes at Large*, L, 533 (July 26, 1937).

[48] Executive Order 10980, U.S., *Federal Register*, XXVI, Part 12, 12059 (December 14, 1961).

[49] Memo for Heads of Departments and Agencies, July 24, 1962; quoted in U.S., President's Commission on the Status of Women, *Report* (Washington: U.S. Government Printing Office, 1963), p. 15. Law enforcement positions requiring the bearing of firearms are an example of positions which can be reserved for men under the CSC's interpretation. See also Executive Order 11375, U.S., *Federal Register*, XXXII, Part 10, 14303 (October 13, 1967).

[50] U.S., CSC, *Annual Report*, LXXXII (1965), 8.

is probably due in part to inequality with regard to promotions.[51]

Modifications of citizen equality of access to civil service positions based upon race, color, religion, sex, and ethnicity are now, as a matter of policy, illegitimate, but other important inequality in this area remains. In the past, and in nonclassified positions at the present, the abridgment of equality on political grounds has been important. At the present time, however, the most important qualifications of equality are based upon merit, fitness, veteran preference, and "unorthodox" political opinions.

The merit system interferes with the equality of citizens on the basis of their ability, or supposed ability, to perform given functions. It is by no means value free—that is, it is not without differential social significance—as the struggle to introduce it clearly demonstrated. As late as 1928 its basic assumption was challenged by the president of the United States Chamber of Commerce, who stated that "the best public servant is the worst one. A really efficient public servant is corrosive. He eats holes in our liberties." [52] Moreover, when merit is based largely on qualities that some groups in society are prevented from attaining equally, it abridges equality in its application rather than in its principle with regard to those groups. For example, if Negroes are denied equal public school education and treated with inequity by a large proportion of

[51] See President's Commission on the Status of Women, *Report,* pp. 2, 3, 14, for the employment of women and their grade allocations. Appointments of women in the classified service increased from about 15 per cent in 1961 to 33 per cent in 1967. Nevertheless, they constitute only about 1 to 2 per cent of the top four grades in the General Schedule. See U.S., CSC, *Annual Report,* LXXXV, 20–21.

[52] Quoted in Committee on Employee Relations in the Public Service, *Employee Relations in the Public Service* (Chicago: Civil Service Assembly, 1942), pp. 49–50.

colleges and universities, the merit system can become a major obstacle to their equality of access to civil service positions. Within its value framework, however, merit tends to discourage other interferences with equality, and is an important factor supporting equality of access.

An important exception to equality of access and merit, although one generally supported by the advocates of the merit system, has been exclusion on the basis of unfitness. When lack of fitness indicates inability to perform assigned functions, it is relatively value free. Sometimes, however, exclusion has been based upon characteristics which do not necessarily have a detrimental effect on job performance. In the latter case the symbolic character of public employment is often the basis for exclusion. For example, the Civil Service Act provided that "no person habitually using intoxicating beverages to excess shall be appointed to, or retained in, any office, appointment, or employment to which the provisions of this act are applicable." [53] Previous misconduct or delinquency, and "criminal, infamous, dishonest, immoral, or notoriously disgraceful conduct" have also been the basis of exclusions.[54] Fitness has led to character investigations, fingerprinting, and invasions of privacy, as well as to some definitions of immorality which cannot be considered to be entirely in accord with prevailing social norms.[55]

[53] U.S., *Statutes at Large,* XX, 403 (January 16, 1883).

[54] Civil Service Rule V, sec. 3. See U.S., CSC, *Civil Service Act, Rules, Statutes, Executive Orders, and Regulations* (Washington: U.S. Government Printing Office, 1941), p. 37.

[55] An example of a dismissal for immorality for an act which would probably not be considered immoral by a large segment of society was that of a New York policeman for living with an unmarried woman. See the *New York Times,* August 1, 1968, p. 27. Federal dismissals for homosexuality, where security is not at issue, raise a similar issue.

The Civil Service Act created and encouraged some important exceptions to the principles of merit and fitness. It provided "that whenever there are already two or more members of a family in the public service in grades covered by this act, no other member of such family shall be eligible to any of said grades." [56] The act also provided that appointments in the classified civil service in Washington were to be apportioned among the states, territories, and District of Columbia on the basis of population.[57] These provisions could prevent the appointment of the most meritorious applicants on the basis of their place of residence and kinship. A more important exception to the merit system was the act's provison that nothing therein should be construed to negate preference for veterans.

Veteran preference has been a consistent modification of citizen equality of access to civil service positions. From Washington's first administration until 1865 it was practiced on an informal, but nevertheless real basis. Since 1865 it has been formalized through a myriad of statutes, executive orders, and administrative regulations.[58] The most recent exten-

[56] A family was defined by an opinion of an attorney general as "those who live under the same roof with the head of the family and form his fireside." U.S., *Opinions of the Attorneys General*, XVIII, 83 (1884), and XXVI, 303 (1907). In this connection it should be noted that the Postal Revenue and Federal Salary Act of 1967, Public Law 90-206, prohibits nepotism in all three branches of the federal government. See U.S., CSC, *Annual Report*, LXXXIV (1967), 21.

[57] Apportionment began under the spoils system, but has not worked well, and there have usually been large disparities. See William C. Deming, *Application of the Merit System in the United States Civil Service* (Washington: U.S. Government Printing Office, 1928), pp. 23–28.

[58] For the history of veteran preference in the United States up to 1935 see John F. Miller, "Veteran Preference in the Public Service" in Carl J. Friedrich *et al., Problems of the American Public Service* (New York: McGraw-Hill, 1935), pp. 243–336.

sive revision of veteran preference was in 1944. The CSC identified the basic ideas behind this revision as

(1) to recognize the economic loss suffered by citizens who have served their country in uniform, (2) to restore veterans to a favorable competitive position for government employment, and (3) to recognize that a larger obligation is owed to disabled veterans.[59]

It was also due to a desire to reintegrate veterans into American society, and to political pressure from the veterans' lobbies. The provisions of the Veteran Preference Act of 1944 [60] are comprehensive and clearly demonstrate how veteran preference interferes with basic citizen equality of access and the merit system. Briefly, the major provisions of the act have granted preference in federal employment to honorably discharged veterans who served in wartime or in peacetime expeditions for which campaign badges have been issued. Greater preference has been given to those with disabilities contracted in service. Under certain circumstances the wives, mothers, or widows of veterans have been given preference as well. Disabled veterans, their wives, and eligible widows and mothers have been given ten additional points to their earned ratings on civil service examinations. They have also been placed at the head of the eligible register in the order of their augmented ratings.[61] This kind of preference, sometimes referred to as "absolute preference," can go far to undermine the merit system. When a similar preference was granted between 1919 and 1922, in one instance the highest ranking

[59] U.S., CSC, *Veteran Preference in Federal Employment* (Washington: U.S. Government Printing Office, 1957), p. ii.

[60] U.S., *Statutes at Large*, LVIII, Part 1, 387 (June 27, 1944).

[61] Originally, scientific and professional positions with a salary of $3,000 were excepted. Under the Classification Act of 1949 grades 9 and higher were excluded. See CSC, *Veteran Preference,* p. 11.

veteran scored 68 on an exam and was appointed over seventy nonveterans, of whom at least one scored 95.[62] Other eligible veterans have received a five-point preference and have been placed on the register in the order of their augmented ratings.

The act further provided that examinations for guard, elevator operator, messenger, and custodian were to be closed to nonpreference eligibles, and that additional positions could be similarly restricted by order of the president.[63] The act also provided for the waiver of the family and apportionment rules, and health, age, and educational requirements under certain circumstances. The act required an appointing officer passing over a preference eligible to file his reasons for so doing with the CSC, which could request more information and delay the actual appointment. In 1947 the CSC was given the authority to force the officer to comply with its determination.[64] Eligibles have also been given preference in reductions in force and in other personnel actions. Their military service time has been added to their civil service employment in determining seniority. The act provided that eligibles with a "good" efficiency rating were not to be dismissed before nonpreference eligibles in similar positions with equal or lower ratings. In removals, suspensions, demotions, and other personnel actions, eligibles have been given thirty days' advance written notice, the right to answer and furnish affidavits, and the right to appeal adverse decisions to the CSC.[65]

The effect of veteran preference on equality and its sub-

[62] Miller, "Veteran Preference," p. 281.

[63] The positions of veteran relations adviser in the Office of Price Administration, and a number of offices in the Veterans Administration were soon added by Executive Order 9589, U.S., *Federal Register*, X, Part 7, 9063 (July 16, 1945). Later orders have restricted other positions.

[64] U.S., *Statutes at Large*, LXI, Part 1, 723 (August 4, 1947).

[65] Section 14.

version of the merit system are far-reaching. The 1944 legislation clearly interferes with the citizen equality of those who did not serve in the armed forces in wartime, those who are unfit for military service, and persons whose religious beliefs prevent their participation in war. It especially discriminates against women who as a group do not seek military employment in large numbers. For example, in 1961 women constituted only about 1.1 per cent of the military services, but about 24 per cent of the federal civil service.[66] It can also discriminate against minorities who are reluctant to serve voluntarily in the military if formal or informal inequality is common in these services. In the early 1960's about 29 per cent of the labor force, but 51 per cent of the federal civil service, were war veterans, as were nearly two-thirds of the male civil servants.[67]

There have been other formal preferences which have been of less importance. Since 1947 handicapped persons have received special treatment. In 1957, six out of every thousand federal employees had a physical disability, and by 1963 the figure was up to nineteen per thousand.[68] A system of preference was established for positions in the Railroad Retirement Board in 1937. Railroad employees were given preference over all other applicants, including veterans.[69] This preference has not been functional, because the Board's "work is not railroading, but merely record keeping and actuarial work like that of any insurance organization." [70]

A final important basis for modifying equality of access to

[66] President's Commission on the Status of Women, *Report*, p. 2.
[67] Mosher, "Features," p. 202.
[68] *Ibid.*, p. 170. See Executive Order 10640, U.S., *Federal Register*, XX, Part 10, 7717 (October 10, 1955); and U.S., *Statutes at Large*, LXIII, Part 1, 409 (July 11, 1949) and LXVIII, Part 1, 659 (August 3, 1954).
[69] CSC, *History*, p. 125.   [70] *Ibid.*

civil service positions has been the exclusion of persons whose opinions and associations are believed to indicate that they might use official position to subvert the authority of the government. These exclusions often constitute important negative discrimination because they interfere with rights generally protected by the First Amendment. The most important exclusion on this basis has been due to regulations concerning loyalty-security, which are given broader treatment in the following chapter. Another important instance of this was the exclusion of those who asserted, or belonged to organizations which asserted, a right to strike against the government.

This exclusion was first applied to postal workers, and by implication to other civil servants as well, by the Lloyd–La Follette Act, which otherwise granted the right to unionize.[71] In 1946, Congress began passing riders to appropriations bills providing that

no part of the funds of . . . this Act shall be used to pay the salary or wages of any person who engages in a strike against the Government . . . or who is a member of an organization of Government employees that asserts the right to strike against the Government.[72]

Civil servants were also required to sign the following affidavit:

I . . . do hereby swear (or affirm) that I am not engaged in any strike against the Government . . . and that I will not so engage while an employee of the Government; . . . that I am not a member of an organization of Government employees that asserts the right to strike against the Government . . . and that I will not become a member of such an organization.[73]

[71] U.S., *Statutes at Large*, XXXVII, 555 (August 24, 1912). There has, however, been no formal right to establish a union shop.

[72] For example, see *ibid.*, LX, Part 1, 595 (July 20, 1946).

[73] Quoted in Morton R. Godine, *The Labor Problem in the Public Service* (Cambridge: Harvard University Press, 1951), p. 168n.

The Labor Management Relations Act of 1947 placed anti-strike provisions on a more permanent basis:

It shall be unlawful for any individual employed by the United States or any ageny thereof including wholly owned Government corporations to participate in any strike. Any individual . . . who strikes shall be discharged immediately, . . . and shall not be eligible for reemployment for three years by the United States or any such agency.[74]

In 1955, membership in an organization of government employees asserting the right to strike against the government was made a felony punishable by imprisonment of a year and a day and/or a fine of $1,000, but by 1969 this provision was held to be unconstitutionally vague.[75]

II

Although several of the foregoing modifications of citizen equality of access clearly interfere with the constitutional right of citizen equality, few have been directly overturned on constitutional grounds by the federal courts. The most significant judicial opinions for the public employment relationship in this area have indicated that the abridgment of equality on the basis of race, color, ethnicity, religion, and perhaps sex, which were illegalized in the federal civil service as a matter

[74] U.S., *Statutes at Large*, LXI, Part 1, 136 (June 23, 1947).

[75] *Ibid.*, LXIX, Part 1, 624 (August 9, 1955). See also U.S., *Code* (1964 ed.), V, 118p, 118q, 118r. Although the Supreme Court has never ruled directly upon civil service strikes, in *U.S.* v. *United Mine Workers,* 330 U.S. 258 (1946), it indicated that there was no constitutional right to strike against the government. See chap. 8, *infra,* for other aspects of federal labor relations of importance to the public employment relationship. The 1955 provision was invalidated in *National Association of Letter Carriers* v. *Blount,* 305 F. Supp. 546. The decision came after a long series of state employment oaths were found to be unconstitutional. See chap. 7, *infra.*

of policy, would, at the present time, be considered unconstitutional. These opinions are of importance because they have undermined the basis of the doctrine of privilege and applied due process to public personnel actions.

In one sense, the issue of equality of access was logically outside the doctrine of privilege when it involved characteristics, such as race, which could not be surrendered voluntarily. Nevertheless, that doctrine was sometimes used as a basis for justifying exclusions on the assumption that because there was no right to government employment, personnel actions could not violate a citizen's constitutional rights. This position was adopted in an influential Illinois Supreme Court decision of 1917:

The [school] board has the absolute right to decline to employ or reemploy any applicant for any reason whatever, or for no reason at all. . . . It is no infringement upon the constitutional rights of anyone for the board to decline to employ him . . . and it is immaterial whether the reason for the refusal . . . is because the applicant is married or unmarried, is of fair complexion or dark, is or is not a member of a trades union, or whether no reason is given for such refusal.[76]

The *Fursman* position and the doctrine of privilege were rejected in a series of cases involving unequal salary scales for white and Negro teachers in segregated southern school systems. In *Mills* v. *Lownes*[77] the Federal District Court of Maryland accepted the doctrine of privilege: "The right of the state to prescribe the qualifications for and the salary annexed to a public office . . . is ordinarily free from restriction, and it would not seem that a state employee who has accepted employment . . . could complain."[78] However, the

[76] *Fursman* v. *Chicago*, 278 Ill. 318 (1917). Two justices concurred but did not think the board's right was "absolute."

[77] 26 F. Supp. 792 (1939).   [78] *Ibid.*, p. 801.

Court found the doctrine to be irrelevant because a citizen who is "a qualified school teacher . . . has the civil right as such to pursue his occupation without discriminatory legislation on account of his race or color." [79] A year later the Circuit Court of Appeals for the Fourth Circuit ignored this alternative and directly rejected the doctrine of privilege. In *Alston* v. *School Board* [80] it agreed that government employment was not a right, but reasoned that

even in the granting of privilege, the state may not impose conditions which require the relinquishment of constitutional rights. If the state may compel the surrender of one constitutional right as a condition of its favor, it may, in like manner, compel a surrender of all. It is inconceivable that guarantees embedded in the Constitution . . . may thus be manipulated out of existence.[81]

The court held that the unequal pay scales were unconstitutional.[82]

A related issue was raised in *Brooks* v. *School District*.[83] The city of Moberly, Missouri, desegregated its school system but failed to re-employ any Negro teachers. The court stated that "any rule, practice or custom of denying plaintiffs re-employment because of race or color would be discriminatory

[79] *Ibid.* The Court avoided a constitutional ruling in this case, but in its sequel, *Mills* v. *Board of Education*, 30 F. Supp. 245 (1939), held unequal salaries based on race unconstitutional.

[80] 112 F. 2d 992 (1940).

[81] *Ibid.,* p. 997. The Court was quoting the Supreme Court's decision in *Frost Trucking* v. *Railroad Commission,* 271 U.S. 583, 594 (1925), which was evidently never applied to public employment previously, although it logically included it.

[82] The same result was reached in *Thomas* v. *Hibbits,* 46 F. Supp. 368 (1942), although the reasoning was less explicit, and in *McDaniel* v. *Board of Public Instruction,* 39 F. Supp. 638 (1941), which relied on the *Alston* precedent.

[83] 267 F. 2d 733 (1959).

and in violation of plaintiffs' constitutional rights." [84] The court found, however, that although "the result is unusual and somewhat startling," [85] there was no positive evidence of the abridgment of equality on the basis of race. The decision, nevertheless, clearly rejected the doctrine of privilege and the reasoning expressed in *Fursman.*

The Supreme Court indicated that it accepted the *Alston* reasoning as it applied to equality of access in the *United Public Workers* case. Jumping ahead of judicial developments, however, it was not until 1961 that the Court applied this reasoning directly to an equality-of-access case. *Torcaso* v. *Watkins* [86] involved a Maryland statute requiring individuals to declare their belief in God as a condition of holding public office, in this case the position of notary public. The Maryland Court relied on the doctrine of privilege in ruling that "the petitioner is not compelled to believe or disbelieve, under the threat of punishment of other compulsion. True, unless he makes the declaration of [this] belief he cannot hold public office, . . . but he is not compelled to hold office." [87] The Supreme Court, per Justice Black, held that "the fact, however, that a person is not compelled to hold public office cannot possibly be an excuse for barring him from office by state-imposed criteria forbidden by the Constitution." [88]

Judicial decisions on the issue of equality of access therefore played an important role in the evolution of constitutional doctrines concerning the public employment relationship because they undermined the reasoning of the doctrine of privilege and provided the basis for the doctrine of sub-

[84] *Ibid.,* p. 735.　　[85] *Ibid.,* p. 739.

[86] 367 U.S. 488 (1961).　[87] *Ibid.,* p. 495.

[88] *Ibid.* Black based his opinion on the First Amendment rather than Article VI, and relied on *Weiman* v. *Updegraff,* 344 U.S. 183 (1953), a loyalty-security case, which in turn relied on the *United Public Workers* case. See chap. 7, *infra.*

stantial interest. Under the *Alston* rule, which was partially reaffirmed by the Supreme Court in *United Public Workers* and *Torcaso,* there was no right to public employment, but there were constitutional rights which could not be abridged in it or in application for it. This rule applied due process to certain public personnel actions and, after being more fully accepted in a series of loyalty-security cases, made negative discrimination of the public employment relationship more difficult and more easily challenged in the courts.

III

The degree of citizen equality of access to civil service positions is an important element in the public employment relationship, and one which was influential in the alteration of judicial doctrines affecting it. At one time or another, abridgments of equal access have involved, to a greater or lesser extent, social class status, kinship, race, color, religion, sex, ethnicity, merit, fitness, veteran status, place of residence, and political and other beliefs. At the present time, interferences with equality based on race, color, religion, ethnicity, probably sex, and political views can be considered to be negative discriminations of the public employment relationship. Although other practices abridge equality, it is uncertain whether they interfere with the constitutional requirement of it. Since the early 1940's important efforts have been made to eliminate inequality based on race, color, religion, ethnicity, and sex, with special attention being given to Negroes and women. At the same time, greater efforts have been made to exclude persons whose beliefs indicate that they may be predisposed to attempt to disrupt the functioning of the bureaucracy or overthrow the government. The domain of the former discriminations has usually been informally regulated, while that of the latter has generally been determined by law.

The judicial decisions concerning equality of access having the greatest effect on the public employment relationship have been those involving inequalities based on race and religion. These decisions undermined the reasoning of the doctrine of privilege and provided the groundwork for the emergence of the doctrine of substantial interest.

6 | Loyalty and Security

Throughout the history of the United States there have been several extensive attempts to ensure the loyalty of the bureaucracy and to reduce the likelihood of civil servants using their official positions for subversive purposes. These attempts, or regulations concerning loyalty-security,[1] have often constituted an important element in the range of discrimination of the public employment relationship by creating a high degree and a large domain of discrimination in the negative

[1] In theory, loyalty and security are distinct. Loyalty is a state of mind, and while security includes this element, it also includes character traits such as reliability and trustworthiness. Security also involves an official estimation of the civil servant's susceptibility to coercion from subversives, which, for example, might be greater in the case of sexual deviants than in the case of other individuals. In theory, loyalty regulations can be based on the moral proposition that "no person who is not satisfied with our form of government should be permitted to draw compensation from that Government." U.S., *Congressional Record,* 76th Cong., 1st Sess., LXXXIV, Part 9, 9635 (July 20, 1939), statement of Representative Nichols. Such regulations can also be based on the general belief that disloyal persons will be less effective or efficient in performing their duties. Security regulations, on the other hand, theoretically require a determination that all or some positions are sensitive, i.e., they provide their occupants with extraordinary opportunities to engage in meaningful subversion. The Oppenheimer case represented an attempt to distinguish between loyalty and security in practice. See U.S., Atomic Energy Commission, *In the Matter of J. Robert Oppenheimer* (Washington: U.S. Government Printing Office, 1954). However, in most instances these theoretical distinctions have been largely obscured.

direction. More specifically, these regulations have tended to infringe upon the civil servant's First Amendment rights of free speech, thought, press, and association, and their constitutional right of privacy.[2] Unlike most other negative discriminations they have also raised the constitutional questions whether civil service removals for reasons such as disloyalty, which may seriously stigmatize the individual and impair his chances of obtaining other suitable employment, constitute punishment and therefore require Sixth Amendment procedures; and whether such removals can be otherwise procedurally invalid under the due process clause of the Fifth Amendment. The extensive negative discrimination created by loyalty-security regulations introduced during the last three decades was, as Chapter 7 indicates, influential in the decline of the judicial doctrine of privilege and in the emergence of the doctrine of substantial interest.

In the United States the introduction of loyalty-security regulations has tended to coincide with periods of war or intense international tension during which the security of the nation has been believed to be endangered. Although comprehensive regulations of this nature had been introduced during the Revolutionary War, the Civil War, and World War I, it was not until 1939 that they became a continuing feature of the civil service and an important part of the public employment relationship.[3] In general, the evolution of modern

[2] Invasion of the civil servant's privacy generally is discussed in chap. 8, *infra*.

[3] Descriptions of Revolutionary War, Civil War, and World War I regulations can be found in Harold M. Hyman, *To Try Men's Souls* (Berkeley: University of California Press, 1959), chaps. iii, vi, xi, and *Era of the Oath* (Philadelphia: University of Pennsylvania Press, 1954), entire; and in Paul P. Van Riper, *History of the United States Civil Service* (Evanston: Row, Peterson and Co., 1958), pp. 265ff. Revolutionary War regulations have been mentioned in chap. 1, *supra*.

regulations concerning loyalty-security was largely influenced by a perceived danger to the nation which resulted primarily from World War II, the Cold War, the "loss" of China,[4] the widespread belief that the bureaucracy had been extensively infiltrated by Communists and Communist sympathizers who were pursuing subversive ends,[5] the Korean War, and the development of the political and social phenomenon of "McCarthyism" generally.[6] The evolution of these regula-

While some of these earlier regulations created extensive negative discrimination, they generally existed only for short periods and have had little lasting impact on the public employment relationship. The largest increase in the range of discrimination under these regulations was probably introduced by the Sedition Act of 1918, which provided that "any employee or official of the United States Government who commits any disloyal act or utters any unpatriotic or disloyal language, or who, in any abusive and violent manner criticizes the Army or Navy or the flag of the United States shall be . . . dismissed" from the civil service. U.S., *Statutes at Large,* XL, 554 (May 16, 1918). The act was repealed in 1921. Van Riper, *History,* p. 267.

[4] Many believed, and United States Ambassador to China Patrick Hurley charged, that subversive State Department officials were responsible for the failure of United States policy in China. Eventually, John Service, John Vincent, and John Davies, all of whom were involved in formulating China policy, were dismissed on loyalty-security grounds. See Bert Andrews, *Washington Witch Hunt* (New York: Random House, 1948), p. 9; and Ralph S. Brown, Jr., *Loyalty and Security* (New Haven: Yale University Press, 1958), pp. 366–69.

[5] This view was especially widespread after the 1948 House Un-American Activities Committee (HUAC) held its *Hearings Regarding Communist Espionage in the United States Government* at which Elizabeth Bentley and Whittaker Chambers gave testimony to this effect. See U.S., Congress, House, Hearings Before HUAC, 80th Cong., 2d Sess. (1948). Hereinafter, HUAC Hearings.

[6] During the "McCarthy Era" loyalty-security testing was widespread, sometimes extending to wrestlers, boxers, piano dealers, and sport fishermen. Brown, *Loyalty and Security,* pp. viii, 18, 377. Similar proliferations of loyalty-security testing took place during the Revolutionary War, the Civil War, and to a somewhat lesser extent during World Wars I and II. See Hyman, *Men's Souls,* chaps. iii, vi,

tions, however, was also largely influenced by partisan politics, especially during the decade following World War II. For example, in 1952 the Republican party platform charged that "by the administration's appeasement of communism at home and abroad it has permitted communists and fellow travelers to serve in many key agencies and to infiltrate our American life" and promised that "a Republican President will only appoint persons of unquestioned loyalty. We will overhaul loyalty and security programs." [7]

The actual development of a comprehensive system of loyalty-security regulations consisted of a myriad of statutes, executive orders, and administrative regulations, only some of which were of major importance to the public employment relationship.[8] The first major regulation concerning loyalty-

---

xi–xiii, and Hyman, *Era,* entire. Loyalty-security regulations pertaining to the civil service are nevertheless based on a perceived incompatibility between the roles of citizen and civil servant because the scope of regulations concerning the latter has generally been far more extensive. For modern loyalty-security regulations pertaining to noncivil servants see Brown, *Loyalty and Security,* chaps. iii–vii, *et passim.* There has been an important dispute over the causes and roots of McCarthyism. See Michael Rogin, *The Intellectuals and McCarthy* (Cambridge: M.I.T. Press, 1967); Edward Shils, *The Torment of Secrecy* (Glencoe: The Free Press, 1956); and Daniel Bell (ed.), *The Radical Right* (New York: Doubleday and Co., 1964).

[7] The *New York Times,* July 11, 1952, p. 8.

[8] For a more complete analysis of the development and legislative history of loyalty-security regulations see Thomas I. Emerson and David M. Helfeld, "Loyalty Among Government Employees," *Yale Law Journal,* LVIII (December 1948), 1–143; Eleanor Bontecou, *The Federal Loyalty-Security Program* (Ithaca: Cornell University Press, 1953), entire; Brown, *Loyalty and Security,* entire; U.S., Commission on Government Security, *Report* (Washington: U.S. Government Printing Office, 1957), pp. 5–39 (hereinafter *Wright Report*). Several statutes, administrative regulations, and judicial decisions concerning loyalty-security are reprinted in Clinton Rossiter *et al., Digest of the Public Record of Communism in the United States* (New York: Fund for the Republic, 1955), Part I, sec. G.

security to be adopted after World War I was section 9A of the First Hatch Act.[9] During the House debate on the act, Representative Nichols of Oklahoma introduced an amendment making it

unlawful for any person employed in any capacity by any agency of the Federal Government, whose compensation, or any part thereof, is paid from funds authorized or appropriated by any act of Congress, to have membership in any political party or organization which advocates the overthrow of our constitutional form of government in the United States.[10]

He warned that "the time is here when we of this body had better begin to give a little concern to the cankerous infection within the vitals of this Government which is being nurtured and fed by those of foreign birth who advocate European "isms" as a substitute for our form of government." [11] Although Nichols said that "there is not a man or a woman here who would dare vote against the amendment," [12] it was originally defeated, but eventually passed 151 to 96 on a teller vote.[13]

Section 9A was to be enforced by removal or by denial of appointment, and in November 1940 the Civil Service Commission modified its rules prohibiting the abridgment of equality on the basis of politics in the classified civil service by refusing "to certify to any department or agency the name of any person when it had been established that he was a member of the Communist Party, the German-American Bund, or any other Communist, Nazi or Fascist organization." [14] The CSC also required all classified employees to

[9] U.S., *Statutes at Large*, LIII, Part 1, 1148 (August 2, 1939), not to be confused with section 9(a) which was the political neutrality section, see chap. 4, *supra*.

[10] *Congressional Record*, LXXXIV, Part 9, 9635.

[11] *Ibid.*   [12] *Ibid.*   [13] *Ibid.*, p. 9636.

[14] U.S., CSC, *Annual Report*, LVII (1940), 21.

state whether they were members of any organization within the section's purview.[15] The Hatch Act's provision and the CSC's related regulations constituted an important negative discrimination because they abridged the civil servant's constitutional right to join political organizatons which, although unpopular and unorthodox, were legal.

After the United States entered World War II a large scale loyalty-security program was introduced. In 1942 the CSC adopted its War Service Regulations, which provided that an applicant could be denied examination and an eligible person denied appointment if there was "a reasonable doubt as to his loyalty to the Government of the United States." [16] In practice, however, the CSC primarily investigated conditional employees, that is, employees whose appointments were approved subject to subsequent investigation, in positions, with the exception of those in the Departments of War, Treasury, and Agriculture, "in which persons disloyal to the United States, or persons not actively disloyal but of weak character, would have the opportunity to do serious damage to the war program." [17] Under the CSC regulations an employee could appeal an adverse determination to its Board of Appeals and Review, after which a final appearance could be made before the commissioners.[18] By June 30, 1946, the Commission had rated 1,297 persons unsuitable for reasons related to disloyalty.[19] The major proportion were allegedly Communists. The degree of negative discrimination established under the CSC's regulations is difficult to estimate. The Commission expressed concern for the rights of those investigated and prohibited its investigators from inquiring about race, color, reli-

[15] *Ibid.*
[16] U.S., *Federal Register,* VII, Part 9, 7723 (September 30, 1942).
[17] U.S., CSC, *Annual Report,* LX (1943), 9.
[18] *Ibid.,* pp. 13–14.   [19] *Ibid.,* p. 12, and LXIII (1946), 20.

gion, union membership, or an individual's reading preferences.[20] Investigation of political affiliation was permissible
only in cases in which a civil servant was suspected of violating regulations concerning political neutrality or of being a
member of a political organization which advocated overthrow of the government.[21] There is some evidence, however,
that these limitations were not enforced and it has been reported that investigators were more interested in Communist
sympathies than in pro-Japanese, Nazi, or Fascist leanings.[22]

The removal of disloyal and similarly unsuitable incumbent
civil servants was primarily the responsibility of the various
departments and agencies. In February 1943, President Roosevelt issued Executive Order 9300 which created an Inter-
departmental Committee on Employee Loyalty Investigations.[23] The Committee recommended that an employee whose
removal for loyalty-security reasons was proposed be afforded
a formal hearing, the right to be represented by counsel, and
the right to present witnesses. The exact number of civil
servants dismissed is not available, but it is believed that out
of some 6,000 investigated by the Federal Bureau of Investigation between July 1942 and June 1946, somewhere
between 100 and 200 were removed for loyalty-security reasons.[24]

Although most of the World War II loyalty-security investigations were made by the executive branch, Congress did
engage in one investigation which had an important influence

[20] *Ibid.*, LX, 14–15.   [21] *Ibid.*, p. 14.

[22] Gladys M. Kammerer, *Impact of War on Federal Personnel Administration, 1939–1945* (Lexington: University of Kentucky Press,
1951), pp. 121–22.

[23] U.S., *Federal Register*, VIII, Part 2, 1701 (February 5, 1943).
The Committee replaced a similar one established by the attorney general in 1942.

[24] Van Riper, *History,* p. 397.

on judicial doctrines concerning the public employment relationship. Briefly, in 1943, Representative Martin Dies, a Texas Democrat and HUAC Chairman, accused thirty-nine "irresponsible, unrepresentative, crackpot, radical bureaucrats" of disloyalty.[25] The accused were subsequently afforded secret hearings at which they were denied the opportunity to have counsel and to confront and cross-examine witnesses, and the time to adequately prepare their defense.[26] As a result of the hearings, a rider was successfully attached, despite the opposition of the Senate and the President, to the Urgent Deficiency Appropriations Act for 1943,[27] barring the payment of any compensation to three of the thirty-nine civil servants. In 1946 the rider was declared unconstitutional as a bill of attainder by the Supreme Court in *United States* v. *Lovett*,[28] a decision which influenced the decline of the doctrine of privilege.[29]

In March 1947, under considerable pressure from the Republican-dominated Congress, President Truman issued Executive Order 9835, or the Loyalty Order, which extensively modified the system of regulations concerning loyalty-security which had developed during World War II.[30] The order was

[25] U.S., *Congressional Record,* 78th Cong., 1st Sess., LXXXIX, Part 1, 479 (February 1, 1943).

[26] Kammerer, *Personnel Administration,* pp. 129–30; Robert E. Cushman, "The Purge of Federal Employees Accused of Disloyalty," *Public Administration Review,* III (Autumn 1943), 306–307. See, generally, Frederick L. Schuman, "Bill of Attainder in the Seventy-Eighth Congress," *American Political Science Review,* XXXVII (October 1943), 819–29.

[27] U.S., *Statutes at Large,* LVII, Part 1, 450 (July 12, 1943).

[28] 328 U.S. 303.   [29] See chap. 7, *infra.*

[30] U.S., *Federal Register,* XII, Part 3, 1935 (March 21, 1947). The order revoked Executive Order 9300, but did not limit any pre-existing statutes. The Atomic Energy Commission, military services, and the Mutual Security Administration maintained separate programs. See

based on the assumption that "maximum protection must be afforded the United States against infiltration of disloyal persons into the ranks of its employees, and equal protection from unfounded accusations of disloyalty must be afforded to the loyal employees of the Government." The order required "a loyalty investigation of every person entering the civilian employment of any department or agency in the executive branch of the federal government," and provided that "the head of each department and agency . . . shall be personally responsible for an effective program to assure that disloyal civilian officers or employees are not retained in employment in his department or agency." [31] The order further provided for the establishment of a Loyalty Review Board (LRB) within the CSC to review cases and generally oversee loyalty-security matters, and for the appointment of agency and departmental loyalty boards.

A civil servant charged with being disloyal had the right to a hearing before an agency or departmental loyalty board. He also had the right to appeal an adverse decision to the department or agency head and then to the LRB.[32] At these

---

Bontecou, *Loyalty-Security*, p. 39, and Brown, *Loyalty and Security*, chap. iii. For a detailed analysis of the events leading up to the issuance of this order and Truman's probable motives, see David H. Rosenbloom, "Individual Liberty Versus National Security" (unpublished Master's dissertation, Department of Political Science, University of Chicago, 1966), chap. ii.

[31] The loyalty investigations originally were to be made by the CSC or by the various departments and agencies, depending upon the circumstances and the status of the individual involved, but Congress, through its control of appropriations, required the transfer of a major part of this function to the FBI. See Van Riper, *History,* pp. 447–48; Bontecou, *Loyalty-Security*, pp. 75–76. Eventually Public Law 298, 82d Cong., 2d Sess., U.S., *Statutes at Large*, LXVI, Part 1, 43 (April 5, 1952) made the CSC the principal investigative agency.

[32] The LRB's decisions were mandatory in the case of veteran preference eligibles, and the CSC suggested that its decisions should be

hearings, which were not open, the civil servant was granted the right to have counsel and to present supporting witnesses and evidence. The charges were to be "stated specifically and as completely as, in the discretion of the employing department or agency, security considerations permit." [33] Although the Loyalty Order did not prohibit the confrontation and cross-examination of adverse witnesses, it did not guarantee these procedures, and at the program's inception, LRB Chairman Seth Richardson stated that "disclosure of evidential sources to the employee, and the resulting opportunity of cross-examination of such sources by him will probably not be practicable." [34] Richardson later defended this procedure on the basis of a perceived incompatibility between the roles of citizen and civil servant:

It has been vigorously and forcefully contended that this procedure is injurious to the employee in that it deprives him of the right to confrontation and cross-examination of the undisclosed informants. The Board has never been oblivious to the pertinency and force of this contention and agrees that such a procedure could and should not be sustained with regard to a citizen non-employee in a controversy with the Government. Such practice certainly smacks of unfairness and does not jibe with what is usually done in court.[35]

The Loyalty Order was less explicit concerning individuals who were entering the civil service, but eventually fourteen

---

followed in other cases as well. See U.S., CSC, *Annual Report,* LXV (1948), 14.

[33] The courts have at times invalidated removals under similar regulations because the charges were too vague. See *Deak* v. *Pace,* 185 F. 2d 997 (1950), a loyalty-security case; and *Money* v. *Anderson,* 208 F. 2d 34 (1953).

[34] The *New York Times,* December 28, 1947, p. 28.

[35] Seth Richardson, "The Federal Employee Loyalty Program," *Columbia Law Review,* LI (May 1951), 549.

Regional Loyalty Boards were established to hear their cases.

The original standard for removal or refusal of civil service employment under the Loyalty Order was that, "on all the evidence, reasonable grounds exist for belief that the person involved is disloyal to the government of the United States." In 1951 the burden of proof was transferred to the individual when the standard became "a reasonable *doubt* as to the loyalty of the person involved." [36] The order did not define disloyalty, but it did specify several grounds which might provide the basis of an adverse determination:

a. Sabotage, espionage, or attempts or preparations therefor, or knowingly associating with spies or saboteurs;

b. Treason or sedition or advocacy thereof;

c. Advocacy of revolution or force or violence to alter the constitutional form of government of the United States;

d. Intentional unauthorized disclosure to any person, under circumstances which may indicate disloyalty, . . . of documents or information of a confidential or non-public character obtained by the person making the disclosure as a result of his employment by the Government . . . ;

e. Performing or attempting to perform his duties, or otherwise acting so as to serve the interests of another government in preference to the interests of the United States;

f. Membership in, affiliation with or sympathetic association with any foreign or domestic organization, association, movement, group or combination of persons, designated by the Attorney

---

[36] Executive Order 10241, U.S., *Federal Register*, XVI, Part 5, 3690 (April 28, 1951), emphasis added. The change was really a reintroduction of the War Service Regulations standard. It led to the rehearing of some civil servants previously cleared under the original standard. This practice was upheld in *Jason* v. *Summerfield*, 214 F. 2d 273 (1954). The reopening of cases on this and other grounds was a common practice under loyalty-security regulations. See David Fellman, "The Loyalty Defendants," *Wisconsin Law Review*, CMLVII (January 1957), 29.

General as totalitarian, fascist, communist, or subversive, or as having adopted a policy of advocating or approving the commission of acts of force or violence to deny other persons their rights under the Constitution, . . . or as seeking to alter the form of government . . . by unconstitutional means.[37]

In November 1947, Truman clarified his intention concerning the last section by stating: "Membership in an organization is simply one piece of evidence which may or may not be helpful at arriving at a conclusion as to the action which is to be taken in a particular case." [38] The final section, however, was apparently the most important in the processing of cases,[39] and it was the most significant negative discrimination directly established by the order. A much greater degree of discrimination was achieved in the enforcement of the Loyalty Order, but before examining this aspect, it is useful to review two other major loyalty-security regulations which led to similar negative discrimination of the public employment relationship.

In 1950, regulations concerning loyalty-security were extensively modified by Public Law 733.[40] It provided that notwithstanding "the provisions of any other law," the Secretaries

---

[37] These grounds were not meant to be exhaustive. The activities proscribed by the first three sections were largely illegal, see *Wright Report*, pp. 616–22. The first public listing of organizations within the purview of section (f) was on March 20, 1948, in U.S., *Federal Register*, XIII, Part 3, 1473. See Bontecou, *Loyalty-Security*, pp. 166–74, for an analysis.

[38] CSC, *Annual Report*, LXV, 15. In *Kutcher* v. *Gray*, 199 F. 2d 783 (1952) it was held that membership in the Socialist Workers party, an organization designated as subversive, was not, in the absence of a determination of disloyalty, adequate grounds for removal under the Loyalty Order of section 9A of the Hatch Act.

[39] Richardson, *Columbia Law Review*, LI, 547.

[40] Eighty-First Congress, 2d Sess., U.S., *Statutes at Large*, LXIV, Part 1, 476 (August 26, 1950).

of State, Commerce, Defense, Army, Navy, and Air Force, the Attorney General, the Atomic Energy Commission, the Chairman of the National Security Resources Board, the Director of the National Advisory Committee for Aeronautics, and the Secretary of the Treasury with regard to the Coast Guard could each suspend or remove any civilian officer or employee under his jurisdiction when he determined that it was "necessary or advisable in the interest of the national security of the United States." [41] If the civil servant involved was a citizen, had a permanent or indefinite appointment, and had completed his probationary or trial period, he had the right to a hearing before "a duly constituted agency authority for this purpose," and a review of the case by the agency head or his designee. A civil servant removed under P.L. 733 could obtain other federal civil service employment only after the approval of the CSC. It further provided that its provisions could be extended to "such other departments or agencies of the Government as the President may, from time to time, deem necessary in the best interests of national security." P.L. 733 did not limit the application of the Loyalty Order, but rather placed civil servants in the various departments and agencies to which it applied under the jurisdiction of both regulations. It was therefore possible for a civil servant to be found loyal under the Loyalty Order and dismissed in the interests of national security under P.L. 733.

In April 1953, President Eisenhower fulfilled the Republicans' 1952 campaign promise by issuing Executive Order

[41] Under earlier statutes, the secretaries of war, navy, coast guard, the secretary of state, and the director of the Central Intelligence Agency had similar authority. See *ibid.*, LVI, Part 1, 1053 (December 17, 1942); LXIII, Part 1, 498 (July 20, 1949), first enacted LX, Part 1, 458 (July 5, 1946); and LXI, Part 1, 498 (July 2, 1947). P.L. 733 did not define the attitudes and behavior which it proscribed.

10450, generally known as the Security Order.[42] This order revoked the Loyalty Order, and basically extended the provisions of P.L. 733 to all government departments and agencies. The Security Order also abolished the LRB, the Regional Loyalty Boards, and the system of centralized loyalty hearings. It made the department and agency heads "responsible for establishing and maintaining . . . an effective program to insure that the employment and retention in employment of any civilian officer or employee within the department or agency is clearly consistent with the interests of the national security." The Security Order required that the appointment of new civil servants be subject to investigation and created a distinction between sensitive and nonsensitive positions by providing that the scope of investigation was to be determined "according to the degree of adverse effect the occupant of the position sought to be filled could bring about, by virtue of the nature of the position, on the national security." The primary responsibility for investigation was vested in the CSC for classified positions and the various departments and agencies for excepted positions.[43] All incumbent civil servants in sensi-

[42] U.S., *Federal Register,* XVIII, Part 4, 2489 (April 27, 1953). It should be noted that the order was overtly based on the doctrine of privilege. Its preamble stated that individuals were "privileged to be employed in the departments and agencies of the Government." During Eisenhower's campaign he declared that "to work for the United States government is a privilege, not a right. And it is the prerogative of the Government to set the strictest test upon the loyalty and patriotism of those entrusted with our nation's safety." the *New York Times,* October 4, 1952, p. 8.

[43] The CSC conducts two basic types of investigations, a "national agency check and inquiry" and a "full field investigation." The former consists of written inquiries to previous employers, references, neighbors, school authorities, and local law enforcement agencies, and a check of the FBI, HUAC, Armed Forces intelligence, and CSC files for information regarding the person involved. A full field investiga-

tive positions were to be fully investigated, as were any employees previously investigated extensively under the Loyalty Order. Any civil servant might be investigated if there were reason to believe that his continued employment was not consistent with the interests of national security. The procedures prescribed by P.L. 733 were to be followed in dismissing incumbent civil servants, but the Security Order established no system of hearings for applicants.

The Security Order was similar to the Loyalty Order and P.L. 733 in that it did not define the specific behavior or attitudes which it proscribed. It did, however, indicate some activities which could be used to provide the basis of adverse decisions. These activities more or less consisted of the CSC's fitness or suitability standards and the indicators of disloyalty invoked by the Loyalty Order. Therefore, a determination that a civil servant's employment was not clearly consistent with the interests of the national security might be made on the basis of disloyalty, as well as on that of drunkenness, immoral or disgraceful conduct, unreliability, and similar reasons. The Security Order created a somewhat higher degree of negative discrimination because it made association with an advocate of forceful overthrow of the government and "any facts which furnish reason to believe that the individual may be subjected to coercion, influence, or pressure which may cause

---

tion consists of the same procedure, substituting interviews for written inquiries. See U.S., CSC, *Annual Report*, LXXI (1954), 53. On October 10, 1968, the author happened to be interviewed by a CSC investigator engaged in a full field Security Order investigation of a former neighbor. The interview included the following questions: "What kind of a person is she?" "Does she belong to any organizations that you know of?" "How are her morals?" "It there any reason to believe that she is not loyal to the United States?" "Does she drink?" and several others concerning her previous employment, her reasons for dropping out of college, her husband, and her family.

him to act contrary to the best interests of the national security," grounds for removal. The degree of negative discrimination was further increased in October 1953, when Eisenhower added the following ground for removal: "Refusal by the individual, upon the ground of constitutional privilege against self-incrimination, to testify before a congressional committee regarding charges of his alleged disloyalty or other misconduct." [44]

In 1955, loyalty-security regulations were further modified by Public Law 330,[45] which replaced section 9A of the Hatch Act. It prohibited membership in organizations advocating "the overthrow of our Constitutional form of government" and required civil servants to sign affidavits to the effect that their employment did not transgress this proscription. It was punishable by a one-thousand-dollar fine and/or a year and a day imprisonment, rather than by removal alone. A year later, the Security Order was modified by the Supreme Court's decision in *Cole* v. *Young* [46] that the order's extension of the more summary procedures of P.L. 733 to all civil service positions was invalid because these procedures were intended to apply to sensitive positions only. The decision did not foreclose the introduction of new loyalty-security regulations for civil servants in nonsensitive positions, but by that time the partisan political importance of loyalty-security had de-

[44] Executive Order 10491, U.S., *Federal Register,* XVIII, Part 6, 6583 (October 13, 1953). Civil service regulations also make refusal to "give to the Commission or its authorized representatives all information and testimony in regard to matters inquired of arising under laws, rules, and regulations administered by the Commission" grounds for removal or denial of appointment. See U.S., *Code of Federal Regulations* (January 1968), V, secs. 5.3, 731.201 (d).

[45] U.S., *Statutes at Large,* LXIX, Part 1, 624 (August 9, 1955). This law was indirectly found to be unconstitutional in *Stewart* v. *Washington.* See note 82, *infra.*

[46] 351 U.S. 536 (1956).

clined and no major action has yet been taken along these lines. The Security Order and Public Law 733, therefore, currently provide the primary basis for loyalty-security actions. It should be noted, however, that the civil service regulations continue to make a "reasonable doubt as to the loyalty of the person involved to the Government" a legitimate basis for the denial of examination of applicants, appointment of eligibles, and for the removal of civil servants in classified positions.[47]

II

The degree of negative discrimination of the public employment relationship created by the Loyalty Order, P.L. 733, and the Security Order has been largely established in their enforcement. The charges and information against an applicant or a civil servant, the questions he was asked, and statements serving as indicators of the attitudes of some loyalty-security board members demonstrate that this degree, at times, has been extremely high. Some of the charges and information against individuals were:

That you were a member of the American Labor Party of New York . . . in 1938 and 1939, which was cited as a communist front organization by the Committee on Un-American Affairs *in 1946.*[48]

. . . You made statements to the effect that you believe "the House Un-American Activities hearings in Washington, D.C., are more of a threat to civil liberties than is the Communist Party

---

[47] *Code of Federal Regulations* (January 1968), V, secs. 731.201 (f), 752.104 (a). Removals for disloyalty have been held to be within the meaning of "efficiency of the service." See *Kutcher* v. *Gray,* 199 F. 2d 783, 786 (1952).

[48] Walter Gellhorn, *Security, Loyalty, and Science* (Ithaca: Cornell University Press, 1950), p. 146. Emphasis added; under the Loyalty Order.

because they infringe upon free speech and if this sort of thing is continued there is more danger of fascism in this country than communism." Further, you have argued that "as long as the Communist Party is legal it is the duty of everyone to protect the Party's rights." [49]

[That the employee] . . . advocated the Communist Party line, such as favoring peace and civil liberties when those subjects were being advocated by the Communist Party.[50]

[That informants had referred to the employee] . . . as "Red" and "Pink." Included in this group are those . . . who have been extremely critical of the American Legion and of American laws and institutions.[51]

[That the employee stated that] . . . public power projects are designed for the benefit of politicians.[52]

In 1946 your father, with whom you resided, was a member of the International Workers Order. . . . Your parents . . . signed a Communist Party nominating petition in . . . 1940, with knowledge of the nature and the purposes of the petition.[53]

[That the employee's brother] . . . was a signer of a letter urging defeat of the Mundt Bill, an avowed purpose of the Communist Party.[54]

In 1950, Communist literature was observed in the bookshelves and Communist art was seen on the walls of your residence.[55]

[49] *Ibid.,* p. 151; Loyalty Order.   [50] *Ibid.,* p. 153; Loyalty Order.
[51] Adam Yarmolinsky, *Case Studies in Personnel Security* (Washington: Bureau of National Affairs, 1955), p. 3, case 4; Security Order, employee retained.
[52] *Ibid.,* p. 16, case 16; Security Order, removed.
[53] *Ibid.,* p. 39, case 37; P.L. 733, removed.
[54] *Ibid.,* p. 110, case 75; Security Order, removed.
[55] *Ibid.,* p. 143, case 107; Security Order, removed.

You have continued sympathetic association with your husband —— who is presently *charged* under the provisions of the Administrative Order ——.[56]

[That the employee] . . . had cohabited for some time with a woman who was not his wife.[57]

[That the employee] . . . was reported to have "belittled the capitalist system," to have propounded anti-capitalistic theories and to have read literature of a subversive nature.[58]

[That the employee stated he] . . . knew communists and respected them.[59]

Several of the questions individuals were asked indicate a similar degree of negative discrimination:

The [Civil Service] Commission has information to the effect that after you came to Washington you took a course in the Russian language. . . . Did you have any reason for taking this course? [60]

Do you have books in your library describing communism? [61]

[56] *Ibid.*, p. 154, case 112; Security Order, employee resigned prior to decision. Emphasis added.

[57] *Ibid.*, p. 177, case 146; Security Order, retained.   [58] *Ibid.*

[59] *Ibid.*, p. 181, case 175; Security Order, removed. Others include the following: "We have a confidential informant who says he visited your house and listened in your apartment for three hours to a recorded opera entitled 'The Cradle Will Rock.' He explained that this opera followed along the lines of a down-trodden laboring man and the evils of the capitalist system." Bontecou, *Loyalty-Security*, p. 142; Loyalty Order. "You maintain in your library books on communism, socialism, and Marxism." *Ibid.*, p. 110; Loyalty Order. "[The employee stated] . . . that most Americans have distorted ideas about communism and, hence, everyone should study that form of government in order to learn what it really is." *Ibid.*, p. 120; Loyalty Order.

[60] Francis Biddle, *The Fear of Freedom* (Garden City: Doubleday and Co., 1952), p. 222; Loyalty Order.

[61] *Ibid.*, p. 224; Loyalty Order.

What do you think of female chastity? [62]

What were your feelings at that time concerning race equality? [63]

How many times did you vote for him (Norman Thomas), if you care to say? . . . How about Henry Wallace? [64]

In your library at home, could you give me an idea of the type of literature or the books that you enjoy accumulating? . . . I would be interested also in knowing the types of periodicals.[65]

Do you have any favorite newspaper columnist of the day? . . . Any favorite radio or T.V. news commentators or news analysts? [66]

Were you a regular reader of *The New York Times?* [67]

Do you and your wife regularly attend any organized church services.[68]

Have you provided any sort of religious training for your children, sir? [69]

Do you believe in Government ownership of public utilities as a general proposition.[70]

Do you think communism, today, has any good features? [71]

Did you not state to other individuals that because you were opposed to the institution of marriage you did not marry your

[62] Yarmolinsky, *Personnel Security,* p. 12, case 10; Security Order, retained.
[63] *Ibid.,* p. 89, case 58; Security Order, removed.   [64] *Ibid.,* p. 91.
[65] *Ibid.,* p. 147, case 107; Security Order, removed.
[66] *Ibid.,* p. 206, case 224; Security Order, retained.   [67] *Ibid.*
[68] *Ibid.*   [69] *Ibid.*   [70] *Ibid.,* p. 209.   [71] *Ibid.,* p. 212.

wife at the time you assumed your marriage relation with her.[72]

Do you read Howard Fast? Tom Paine? Upton Sinclair? [73]

The statements of loyalty-security board members indicate that in some cases their attitudes may have made them predisposed to reach adverse decisions and to establish a high degree of negative discrimination:

Don't you think that any person is a security risk who at one time or another associated with a Communist . . . even though it was not a sympathetic association and even though he may not have known at the time the person was a Communist and even though the association terminated many years ago.[74]

Certainly everybody who is supported by the Communists is a Communist.[75]

What I mean is that in order for anybody to make some charges there was a basis for those charges.[76]

Of course, the fact that a person believes in racial equality doesn't prove that he is a Communist, but it certainly makes you look

[72] Bontecou, *Loyalty-Security*, p. 141; Loyalty Order.

[73] *Ibid.;* Loyalty Order. Others include the following: "I understand that you are a Protestant[?]" Emerson and Helfeld, *Yale Law Journal,* LVIII, 74; Loyalty Order. "Have you ever discussed the Truman Doctrine?" *Ibid.;* Loyalty Order. "Would you say that your wife has liberal political viewpoints?" *Ibid.,* p. 75; Loyalty Order. "Was your father native born?" L. A. Nikoloric, "The Government Loyalty Program," *American Scholar,* XIX (Autumn 1950), 293; Loyalty Order. "Have you ever had Negroes in your home?" *Ibid.,* p. 294; Loyalty Order. "There is a suspicion in the record that you are in sympathy with the under-privileged. Is this true?" *Ibid.;* Loyalty Order. "Are your friends and associates intelligent, clever?" *Ibid.;* Loyalty Order.

[74] Yarmolinsky, *Personnel Security,* p. 18, case 16; Security Order, removed.

[75] *Ibid.,* p. 26, case 18; P.L. 733, removed.

[76] *Ibid.,* p. 106, case 66; Security Order, retained.

twice, doesn't it? You can't get away from the fact that racial equality is part of the Communist line.[77]

It is rather unusual, you will have to admit, for persons born and raised in Texas to feel that [integrated meetings] would be a reason to join the Washington Bookshop.[78]

Whether charges, information, questions, and board member attitudes of this type were routine has been a matter of dispute.[79] However, it appears certain that they were not rare, and that the enforcement of the Loyalty Order, P.L. 733, and the Security Order created a high degree of negative discrimination because a civil servant might be removed for disloyalty or in the interests of national security on the basis of his speech, associations, reading preferences, and religious beliefs, the conduct and opinions of his parents and other relatives, his beliefs and activities concerning race relations, and even on the basis of his artistic preferences. Although only a small proportion of civil servants have been dismissed under these regulations,[80] it is probable that several curtailed

[77] Gellhorn, *Security*, p. 152; Loyalty Order.

[78] Biddle, *Fear of Freedom*, p. 221; Loyalty Order.

[79] See Nikoloric, *American Scholar*, XIX, 284; and Nathaniel Weyl, *The Battle Against Disloyalty* (New York: Thomas Y. Crowell, 1953), p. 194 for opposing viewpoints. On December 17, 1948, the LRB ordered lower loyalty boards to avoid irrelevancies and directed that "discrimination shall not be exercised because of an applicant's or an employee's religious opinions or affiliations, or because of his marital status or his race." CSC, Memo 33, quoted in Bontecou, *Loyalty-Security*, p. 66n. The effectiveness of this and similar formal requirements is questionable because there were no procedures for enforcement.

[80] Under the Loyalty Order, a total of 560 persons were removed, and a total of 1,192 left the service after receiving interrogatories or charges. U.S., CSC, *Annual Report*, LXX (1953), 32. Removals under P.L. 733 and the Security Order are still being made, and cumulative figures are not available. In 1953–1954 removal figures were heavily influenced by partisanship. See Brown, *Loyalty and Se-*

the exercise of their First Amendment rights in order to avoid possible proceedings. A study of civil servants in Washington in 1951, for example, indicated the existence of a code of behavior under which it was deemed, by some, that among other things,

you should not discuss the admission of Red China to the U.N.; you should not advocate interracial equality; you should not mix with people unless you know them very well; if you want to read the *Nation,* you should not take it to the office; . . . you should take certain books off your private bookshelves.[81]

Toward the end of the 1950's and especially during the 1960's, as the McCarthy Era began to fade further into the political background and as loyalty-security lost its appeal as a major political issue, the degree of negative discrimination created in the enforcement of regulations concerning loyalty-security apparently declined. For instance, the following Defense Department memorandum was issued in 1962:

Care must be taken not to inject improper matters into security inquiries whether in the course of security investigations or other phases of security proceedings. For example, religious beliefs and affiliations or beliefs and opinions regarding racial matters, political beliefs and affiliations of a non-subversive nature, opinions regarding the constitutionality of legislative policies, and affiliations with labor unions are not proper subjects for such inquiries.

Inquiries which have no relevance to a security determination should not be made. Questions regarding personal and domestic

curity, pp. 54–60. In Appendix A, Brown estimates that there were 500 removals under P.L. 733 between 1950 and 1953; and 1,500 removals between 1953 and 1956 under the Security Order.

[81] Marie Jahoda, "Morale in the Federal Civil Service," *Annals of the American Academy of Political and Social Science,* CCC (July 1955), 111. See also Marie Jahoda and Stuart Cook, "Security Measures and Freedom of Thought," *Yale Law Journal,* LXI (March 1952), 295–333.

affairs, financial matters, and the status of physical health fall in
this category unless evidence clearly indicates a reasonable basis
for believing there may be illegal or subversive activities, personal
or moral irresponsibility, or mental or emotional instability involved.[82]

However, these regulations still constitute an important part
of the public employment relationship and the degree of nega-

[82] The memo was for the under-secretaries of the Army, Navy, and
Air Force. See U.S., Congress, House, Committee on Government
Operations, *Hearings, Use of Polygraphs as Lie Detectors by the
Federal Government,* 89th Cong., 1st Sess., pp. 618–19 (August 19,
1965). Other examples of the declining importance of loyalty-security
as a political issue and greater leniency toward individuals include the
"rehabilitation" of Oppenheimer; the recent clearance of John Davies
(see the *New York Times,* January 15, 1969, p. 1); and a Defense
Department trial examiner's decision that it was "relatively easy to
understand" why a Negro seeking racial equality should have joined
the Communist party in 1933 (see *ibid.,* September 30, 1968, p. 1).
Moreover, the CSC has stated that loyalty-security proceedings have
been "altered by changing customs and points of view. Teenagers are
standing on street corners hawking underground tabloids containing
material which their parents would have been jailed for publishing at
that age. Inevitably, public service reflects the mores of the society
which produces public servants." See U.S., CSC., *Annual Report,*
LXXXV (1968), 38. Jumping ahead of judicial developments, it is
also significant that the government failed to appeal when Form 61
was declared unconstitutionally vague by a special federal court in
Stewart v. *Washington* (June 4, 1969). The form required an applicant to sign an affidavit stating that he was neither a Communist
nor a fascist nor one who sought to overthrow the government and
at the time it was found to be unconstitutional the CSC was engaged
in the process of rewording the form because there was a feeling
that it was too harsh. See the *New York Times,* January 7, 1970, pp.
1, 17. The recent Health, Education, and Welfare "blacklisting" epi-
sode is also indicative of changing attitudes toward loyalty-security.
Few officials, if any, rigorously defended the practices concerning
security clearances for consultants, and as a result of widespread
criticism, these practices have been liberalized. See *ibid.,* and also
January 3, 1970, pp. 1, 10.

tive discrimination involved in their application continues to be significant.[83]

III

Since 1939, regulations intended to ensure the loyalty of the bureaucracy generally, and to prohibit the employment of individual civil servants who are believed to be likely to engage in subversive activities have constituted an important part of the public employment relationship and have been a major feature of the United States civil service. These regulations re-established the widespread importance of political opinion and affiliation in appointment and removal, although in a realm which in comparison with that of the spoils system was rather circumscribed. This realm nevertheless has been extensive in the enforcement of the regulations, and civil servants have been removed for beliefs, associations, and behavior which severely limited their First Amendment rights. The enforcement of regulations concerning loyalty-security also tended to infringe the privacy rights of civil servants. Although there has apparently been some moderation in more recent years, these regulations considerably extended the range of discrimination by establishing a high degree and a large domain of discrimination in the negative direction. They have also been of great importance to the development of the public employment relationship because they were influential in the decline of the judicial doctrine of privilege and in the emergence of that of substantial interest.

[83] For example, at least until 1967, State Department applicants were asked questions such as: "Did he [an applicant's boyfriend] abuse you? Did he do anything unnatural with you? You didn't get pregnant, did you? There's kissing, petting, and intercourse, and after that did he force you to do anything to him, or did he do anything to you?" U.S., Congress, Senate, Committee on the Judiciary, *Protecting Privacy and the Rights of Federal Employees,* Report 519, 90th Cong., 1st Sess., pp. 19–20 (August 21, 1967).

7 | The Emergence of the Doctrine of Substantial Interest

I

The judicial doctrine which currently determines the constitutional acceptability of negative discrimination of the public employment relationship in the United States is the doctrine of substantial interest. The doctrine, which has replaced the doctrine of privilege, holds that conditions imposed by the state upon civil servants which interfere with their ordinary constitutional rights as citizens cannot be justified on the basis that there is no constitutional right to public employment and may therefore be unconstitutional abridgments of substantive constitutional rights. Civil service removals consequently can be in violation of the constitutional requirement of procedural due process. Whereas the doctrine of privilege tended to maximize the perceived incompatibility between the roles of citizen and civil servant, the newer doctrine has tended to minimize this incompatibility by bringing the constitutional rights of civil servants closer to those of other citizens. The doctrine of substantial interest is also important because it provides the judicial branch with a greater role in determining the nature of the public employment relationship.

Although the emergence of the doctrine of substantial interest was influenced by decisions in cases involving political neutrality and equality of access to civil service positions, the most important cases encouraging its adoption as the principal doctrine involved issues presented by regulations concerning loyalty-security. This emergence was not immediate, but rather the result of several decisions. The first important loyalty-security case to reach the courts was *United States* v. *Lovett*,[1] which involved the 1943 Urgent Deficiency Appropriations Act's prohibition of the payment of any future compensation to three civil servants because of their alleged disloyalty.[2] The Supreme Court, per Justice Black, reasoned that the "congressional action, aimed at three named individuals, . . . stigmatized their reputation and seriously impaired their chance to earn a living"[3] and that "this permanent proscription from any opportunity to serve the Government is punishment, and of a most severe type."[4] The Court, therefore, held the act to be a bill of attainder and unconstitutional because it was "punishment without the safeguards of a judicial trial and 'determined by no previous law or fixed rule.'"[5] The case was of importance to the public employment relationship and the emergence of the doctrine of substantial interest because it established the principle that although there was no constitutional right to public employment, the government was not free to proscribe anyone from such employment in the absence of Sixth Amendment procedures or a fixed rule.

In 1950 the constitutionality of the Loyalty Order was upheld in *Bailey* v. *Richardson*.[6] The case raised several constitutional issues and became one of the most important loyalty-

[1] 328 U.S. 303 (1946).   [2] See chap. 6, *supra*, for greater detail.
[3] *Ibid.*, p. 314.   [4] *Ibid.*, p. 316.

[5] *Ibid.*, p. 317. Justice Jackson took no part. Justice Frankfurter concurred in an opinion joined by Justice Reed arguing that the act was not a bill of attainder and that the case should have been decided on the ground that the three, who continued to work for the government but were not paid, were entitled to recover their back pay.

[6] 182 F. 2d 46. The constitutionality of the civil service War Service Regulations, allowing the denial of examination of applicants and appointment of eligibles on the basis of disloyalty, had previously been upheld without important discussion in *Friedman* v. *Swellenbach*, 159 F. 2d 22 (1946), which was decided shortly after *Lovett*.

security decisions. Dorothy Bailey was a former civil servant who was removed in a reduction in force and was subsequently reinstated in her previous position which was of a nonsensitive and non-policy-making nature.[7] She was suspected of being a member of the Communist party and of being sympathetic toward it. After a hearing before the Fourth Regional Loyalty Board (FRLB) and the Loyalty Review Board (LRB), it was determined that there were reasonable grounds for belief that she was disloyal and she was removed. Her eligibility for future civil service employment was also canceled for a period of three years. At the hearings before these boards she had no opportunity to confront or cross-examine the informants against her. The Chairman of the LRB, Seth Richardson, did not think that the statements of these informants had been sworn, and he commented, "I haven't the slightest knowledge of who they are or how active they have been in anything." [8] Richardson nevertheless considered the information in these statements to be "evidence," rather than "allegations." [9] Miss Bailey was questioned in detail about her political opinions, her views on several subjects, and her union membership and activities. During her hearing before the LRB she was asked, "Did you ever write a letter to the Red Cross about the segregation of blood?" [10] Although President Truman had

[7] The facts of the case can be found in 341 U.S. 918, Transcript of Record, Joint Appendix, pp. 9–45. For a more detailed analysis of the case see David H. Rosenbloom, "Individual Liberty Versus National Security" (unpublished master's dissertation, Department of Political Science, University of Chicago, 1966), chaps iii–iv.

[8] Transcript, p. 38. See also Alan Barth, *The Loyalty of Free Men* (New York: Viking Press, 1951), pp. 113–14 for excerpts of the transcript of the hearing before the LRB.

[9] Barth, *Loyalty,* p. 114.

[10] 182 F. 2d 46, 73. Bailey answered, "I do not recall," and the board member who asked the question then asked for her personal opinion on the subject. After the case had been decided in court, and his question had been publicized, the board member explained that he

directed that Loyalty Order proceedings be "preserved in strict confidence," [11] the adverse decision of the FRLB was allegedly released to the press by that Board or its staff,[12] and later the LRB publicly announced its decision as well.[13]

The constitutionality of Miss Bailey's removal was upheld by the Court of Appeals for the District of Columbia in a decision which was subsequently affirmed, without opinion, by the equally divided Supreme Court.[14] Judge Prettyman, writing for the Court of Appeals, based his opinion on the doctrine of privilege. He believed that "the question is not whether she had a trial. The question is whether she should

---

was attempting to ascertain whether Bailey had engaged in "party line" activities with which she personally did not agree. See the *Washington Post*, May 2, 1951, letter of Harry Blair; reprinted in Eleanor Bontecou, *The Federal Loyalty-Security Program* (Ithaca: Cornell University Press, 1953), p. 140n.

[11] Bontecou, *Loyalty-Security*, p. 64.   [12] Transcript, p. 8.

[13] Bontecou, *Loyalty-Security*, p. 64. The FRLB decision might have been released by Bailey. The results of the cases of John Service, John Vincent, and John Davies were also officially announced. For a while the LRB also directed that in the event of a future inquiry by a prospective employer about a civil servant removed for disloyalty, the employer should be told that employment had been terminated under the Loyalty Order. This was done with the understanding on the part of Chairman Richardson that it meant that "a man is ruined everywhere and forever. No reputable employer would be likely to take a chance in giving him a job." The practice was eventually modified by the President to prevent any discosure of a disloyalty removal unless the employee requested it. *Ibid.*, pp. 64–65. According to former Attorney General Francis Biddle, publicity always attended disloyalty removals because "knowledge of the cases inevitably gets around among other employees." See Francis Biddle, *The Fear of Freedom* (Garden City: Doubleday and Co., 1952), p. 230. Because security removals can be made for reasons other than disloyalty they carry a somewhat lesser stigma and do not present as acute a problem.

[14] 341 U.S. 918 (1951). Justice Clark, formerly Truman's attorney general, took no part.

have had one." [15] He argued that she should not because she had no constitutional right to public employment, and "due process of law is not applicable unless one is being deprived of something to which he has a right." [16] Similarly, her First Amendment rights were not violated because

the plain hard fact is that so far as the Constitution is concerned there is no prohibition against the dismissal of Government employees because of their political beliefs, activities or affiliations. . . . The First Amendment guarantees free speech and assembly, but it does not guarantee Government employ.[17]

In order to strengthen this argument, which could be questioned under the *United Public Workers* v. *Mitchell* [18] decision, Prettyman invoked the civil service reformers' analogy to private employment:

The situation of the Government employee is not different in this respect from that of private employees. A newspaper editor has a constitutional right to speak and write as he pleases. But the Constitution does not guarantee him a place in the columns of a publisher with whose political views he does not agree.[19]

The Court further held that any injury to her reputation was irrelevant from a constitutional point of view because "if Miss Bailey had no constitutional right to her office and the executive officers had power to dismiss her, the fact that she was injured in the process of dismissal neither invalidates her dismissal nor gives her right to redress." [20] Prettyman found, however, that, in the absence of a general rule, the three-year proscription from civil service employment was unconstitutional under the *Lovett* decision.

Judge Edgerton dissented in an opinion which was based

[15] 182 F. 2d 46, 51.   [16] *Ibid.*, p. 58.   [17] *Ibid.*, p. 59.
[18] 330 U.S. 75, especially p. 100 (1947); see chap. 4, *supra.*
[19] 182 F. 2d 46, 60.   [20] *Ibid.*, p. 63.

upon some of the concepts later incorporated into the doctrine of substantial interest. He stated that "most dismissals, including among others dismissals for colorless or undisclosed reasons and dismissals for incompetence, are plainly not punitive. They do not require a judicial trial or even a full administrative hearing." [21] However, he reasoned that *"dismissal for disloyalty is punishment and requires all the safeguards of a judicial trial"* [22] because "a person dismissed as disloyal can obtain no normal employment, public or private." [23] Edgerton also argued that Miss Bailey's dismissal unconstitutionally abridged her freedom of speech and assembly. He explicitly rejected the doctrine of privilege: "The premise that government employment is a privilege does not support the conclusion that it may be granted on condition that certain economic or political ideas not be entertained." [24] Edgerton concluded that in its operation, the Loyalty Order "puts government employees under economic and social pressure to protect their jobs and reputations by expressing in words and conduct only the most orthodox opinions on political, economic, and social questions," [25] and that it was unconstitutional, at least in its application to nonsensitive and non-policy-making positions, because "the loss of employment, reputation, and earning power here involved is on its face a very substantial clog on the free exercise of . . . protected freedoms." [26]

Although there were no opinions written in the *Bailey* case when it was decided by the Supreme Court, several justices expressed their views on the issues involved in *Joint Anti-Fascist Refugee Committee* v. *McGrath* [27] which was decided the same day. The case concerned the Attorney General's

[21] *Ibid.*, p. 69.   [22] *Ibid.* Italics in original.
[23] *Ibid.*, p. 70. Edgerton interpreted *Lovett* to compel this result.
[24] *Ibid.*, p. 72.   [25] *Ibid.*, p. 73.   [26] *Ibid.*, p. 74.
[27] 341 U.S. 123 (1951).

right to designate an organization as subversive under the provisions of the Loyalty Order, and the Court, without majority opinion, indicated that such a designation could not be made in the absence of some procedural safeguards for the organization involved. Two Justices explicitly rejected the doctrine of privilege. Justice Douglas, who had previously denied the validity of that doctrine with regard to substantive rights in *United Public Workers,* now discarded it in its procedural application:

Dorothy Bailey was not, to be sure, faced with a criminal charge and hence not technically entitled under the Sixth Amendment to be confronted with witnesses against her. But she was on trial for her reputation, her job, her professional standing. A disloyalty trial is the most crucial event in the life of a public servant. If condemned, he is branded for life as a person unworthy of trust or confidence. To make that condemnation without meticulous regard for the decencies of a fair trial is abhorrent to fundamental justice. . . Of course, no one has a constitutional right to a government job. But every citizen has a right to a fair trial when his government seeks to deprive him of the privileges of first class citizenship.[28]

Douglas concluded that the "dragnet system of loyalty trials" was unconstitutional.[29] Justice Jackson also rejected the doctrine of privilege. He argued that "to be deprived not only of

[28] *Ibid.,* p. 180, 182–83.

[29] *Ibid.,* p. 180. Douglas suggested that disloyal employees might be prosecuted constitutionally for perjury on the basis of their oath of office (p. 181). Since 1884 the oath has been: "I, A B, do solemnly swear (or affirm) that I will support and defend the Constitution against all enemies, foreign and domestic; that I will bear true faith and allegiance to the same; that I take this obligation freely, without any mental reservation or purpose of evasion; and that I will well and faithfully discharge the duties of the office on which I am about to enter. So help me God." See U.S., *Code* (1964 ed.), V, 1, sec. 16 (1884).

present government employment but of future opportunity for it is certainly no small injury when government employment so dominates the field of opportunity." [30] He concluded that "the fact that one may not have a legal right to get or keep a government job does not mean that he can be adjudged ineligible illegally," [31] and he indicated that he would have reversed in *Bailey*.[32]

A few months after the Supreme Court affirmed the lower court's decision in *Bailey*, similar issues came before it in *Garner* v. *Los Angeles*.[33] The case involved a Los Angeles loyalty regulation which required all city employees to take an oath to the effect that within the preceding five years they had not advised, advocated, or taught the desirability of the overthrow of the governments of the United States or California by force or violence, and had not been affiliated with any group which did so. Justice Clark, speaking for the Court, stated that

we think that a municipal employer is not disabled because it is an agency of the state from inquiring of its employees as to matters that may prove relevant to their fitness and suitability for the public service. Past conduct may well relate to present fitness; past loyalty may have a reasonable relationship to present and future trust.[34]

The Court did, however, take a minor verbal step away from the doctrine of privilege by indicating that "legislative action curtailing a privilege previously enjoyed" might constitute

[30] 341 U.S. 123, 185.   [31] *Ibid.*

[32] Justice Black, who had rejected the doctrine of privilege in *United Public Workers,* and Justice Frankfurter indicated that they would have reversed in *Bailey*. Chief Justice Vinson and Justices Reed, Minton, and Burton were in favor of upholding Prettyman's decision in *Bailey*. Burton, however, was with the majority of Justices in the *Refugee* case because the Attorney General's action had been taken in the absence of *any* procedural safguards.

[33] 341 U.S. 716 (1951).   [34] *Ibid.*, p. 720.

"punishment" depending "upon 'the circumstances attending and the causes of the deprivation.' " [35] Justice Frankfurter, who concurred in part and dissented in part, joined those Justices who previously had rejected explicitly the logic of the doctrine of privilege. He argued:

> But it does not at all follow that because the Constitution does not guarantee a right to public employment, a city or a state may resort to any scheme for keeping people out of such employment. . . . Surely, a government could not exclude from public employment members of a minority group merely because they are odious to the majority. . . . To describe public employment as a privilege does not meet the problem. [36]

The Court addressed itself to the question of the constitutional status of public employees again in *Adler* v. *Board of Education*. [37] The case involved New York civil service regulations which prohibited the civil service, including public school, employment of anyone who advocated, advised, or taught the desirability of overthrowing the governments of the United States or the states or any of their political subdivisions, by force or violence. The Court upheld these restrictions, as they applied to teachers, [38] on the basis of the doctrine of privilege. Justice Minton, speaking for the Court, stated:

[35] *Ibid.*, p. 722.

[36] *Ibid.*, p. 725. Justice Burton dissented in part and concurred in part. He believed that the oath was unreasonable because it reached backward for a period of five years and left no room for a change of heart. Justice Douglas dissented in an opinion joined by Justice Black which concluded, "deprivation of a man's means of livelihood by reason of past conduct, not subject to this penalty when committed, is punishment whether he is a professional man, a day laborer who works for private industry or a government employee" (p. 735).

[37] 342 U.S. 458 (1952).

[38] The decision raised the question of whether teachers are in a different constitutional position than other public employees. The Court stated that "a teacher works in a sensitive area in a schoolroom" (p. 493). However, teacher status has encouraged the opposite result

It is clear that such persons have the right under our law to assemble, speak, think and believe as they will. . . . It is equally clear that they have no right to work for the state in the school system on their own terms. They may work for the school system upon reasonable terms laid down by the proper authorities of New York. If they do not choose to work on such terms, they are at liberty to retain their beliefs and associations and go elsewhere. Has the State thus deprived them of any right to free speech or assembly? We think not. . . . If, under the procedure set up in the New York Law, a person is found to be unfit and is disqualified from employment in the public school system because of membership in a listed organization, he is not thereby denied the right of free speech and assembly. His freedom of choice between membership in the organization and employment in the school system might be limited, but not his freedom of speech or assembly, except in the remote sense that limitation is inherent in every choice.[39]

Justice Douglas, joined by Justice Black, again rejected the doctrine of privilege in dissent:

I have not been able to accept the recent doctrine that a citizen who enters the public service can be forced to sacrifice his civil rights. I cannot for example find in our constitutional scheme the power of a state to place its employees in the category of second-class citizens by denying them freedom of thought and expression. The Constitution guarantees freedom of thought and expression to everyone in our society.[40]

---

as well. In *Shelton* v. *Tucker,* 364 U.S. 479 (1960), the Court argued that "the vigilant protection of the constitutional freedoms is nowhere more vital than in the community of American schools" (p. 487). In most cases involving teachers the language used by the courts has been broad enough to include other public employees as well, and such cases have been used as precedents in cases not involving teachers. Therefore it appears that teacher status is not determinative.

[39] 342 U.S. 458, 492–93.

[40] *Ibid.,* p. 508. Justice Black dissented separately on the basis

In *Weiman* v. *Updegraff*,[41] decided shortly after *Adler,* the Court rejected the doctrine of privilege and largely adopted that of substantial interest. The case involved an Oklahoma loyalty oath for all state officers and employees, in this instance for the faculty and staff of a state college, which required them to swear that they did not belong to an organization seeking to overthrow the government by force or violence. The Court, per Justice Clark, reasoned that the interest at stake was substantial: "There can be no dispute about the consequences visited upon a person excluded from public employment on disloyalty grounds. In the view of the community, the stain is a deep one; indeed, it has become a badge of infamy." [42] Clark then relied on that part of the *United Public Workers* decision which indicated that a law prohibiting Republicans, Jews, or Negroes from holding civil service positions would be unconstitutional, in concluding that the absence of a constitutional right to public employment was not constitutionally determinative. He argued that

we need not pause to consider whether an abstract right to public employment exists. It is sufficient to say that constitutional protection does extend to the public servant whose exclusion pursuant to a statute is patently arbitrary or discriminatory.[43]

Moreover, unlike its action in the *United Public Workers* case, the Court made a substantive determination which invalidated the negative discrimination before it. The Court held that due process does not permit "a state, in attempting to bar disloyal individuals from its employ, to exclude persons

---

that the regulations violated the Fourteenth Amendment's incorporation of the First Amendment. Justice Frankfurter dissented on the grounds that the action had not yet been completed in New York, and that no one had standing to sue.

[41] 344 U.S. 183 (1952). [42] *Ibid.,* pp. 190–91.
[43] *Ibid.,* p. 192.

solely on the basis of organizational membership, regardless of their knowledge concerning the organizations to which they had belonged," because "membership may be innocent" [44] if an individual is unaware of an organization's goals.[45]

II

The *Weiman* decision rejected the absence of a constitutional right to public employment as the determinative factor influencing the constitutionality of negative discriminations of the public employment relationship. This principle of the doctrine of substantial interest has provided the basis for several judicial decisions which have declared unconstitutional abridgments of the substantive constitutional rights of citizens in public employment. Several of these decisions, like *Weiman,* involved loyalty oaths. For example, in *Cramp* v. *Board of Public Instruction* [46] the Supreme Court invalidated a Florida loyalty oath which required public employees to swear that they had never "knowingly lent their aid, support, advice, counsel, or influence to the Communist Party," [47] on the ground that the oath, which was enforceable through removal and prosecution for perjury, was too broad because it could be used to proscribe anyone "who had ever supported any cause with contemporaneous knowledge that the Communist Party also supported it." [48] In *Baggett* v. *Bullitt* [49] the Court found a Washington State loyalty oath scheme uncon-

[44] *Ibid.,* p. 190.

[45] Justice Jackson took no part; Justice Burton concurred without opinion; Justice Black concurred on the basis that the oath violated the Fourteenth and First Amendments; Justice Douglas concurred with Justice Black; and Justice Frankfurter concurred in an opinion joined by Douglas which stressed the importance of educational facilities for the United States political system.

[46] 368 U.S. 278 (1961).   [47] *Ibid.,* p. 285.   [48] *Ibid.,* p. 286.
[49] 377 U.S. 360 (1964).

stitutionally vague because its "indefinite language" encouraged public employees to restrict "their conduct to that which is unquestionably safe," and "free speech may not be so inhibited." [50] In *Elfbrandt* v. *Russell* [51] the Court held that an Arizona loyalty oath, which could be enforced through perjury prosecutions, was unconstitutional because it proscribed membership in any organization having for "one of its purposes" [52] the overthrow of the government despite the fact that "those who join an organization but do not share its unlawful purposes and . . . activities, surely pose no threat, either as citizens or as public employees." [53]

There have also been several decisions of this nature involving other issues. For instance, in *Shelton* v. *Tucker,* freedom of association of teachers, and probably other public employees, was generally guaranteed, and in *McLaughlin* v. *Tilendis* [54] their right to join unions, in the absence of legislation to the contrary, was upheld. In *Steck* v. *Connaly* [55] and *Swaaley* v. *United States* [56] the civil servant's right to petition the government was upheld. In *Torcaso* v. *Watkins* [57] their freedom of religion was guaranteed. In *Powell* v. *Zuckert* [58] and *Saylor* v. *United States* [59] the civil servant's protection against unconstitutional searches and seizures was guaranteed. In *Slochower* v. *Board of Higher Education* [60] the Supreme Court upheld the right of a public employee not to

[50] *Ibid.,* p. 372.   [51] 384 U.S. 11 (1966).   [52] *Ibid.,* p. 13.

[53] *Ibid.,* p. 17. These cases are not exhaustive, see also *Whitehill* v. *Elkins,* 389 U.S. 54 (1967), *Gilmore* v. *James,* 274 F. Supp. 75 (1967), and *Keyishian* v. *Board of Regents,* 385 U.S. 589 (1967), which is discussed *infra.*

[54] 398 F. 2d 278 (1968).   [55] 199 F. Supp. 105 (1961).

[56] 376 F. 2d 857 (1961).

[57] 367 U.S. 488 (1961), see chap. 5, *supra.*

[58] 366 F. 2d 634 (1966).   [59] 374 F. 2d 894 (1967).

[60] 350 U.S. 551 (1956).

testify before a congressional committee on the basis of his constitutional privilege against self-incrimination.[61] In *Garrity* v. *New Jersey* [62] the Court held that "the protection of the individual under the Fourteenth Amendment . . . prohibits use in subsequent criminal proceedings of statements obtained under threat of removal from office, and that it extends to all, whether they are policemen or other members of our body politic." [63] Finally, in *Gardner* v. *Broderick* [64] and *Uniformed Sanitation Men's Association* v. *Commissioner* [65] the Court held that public employees could not be removed constitutionally for refusing to waive their privilege against self-incrimination before grand juries investigating their activities.

Although judicial decisions declaring negative discriminations unconstitutional illustrate the change in constitutional doctrines which has taken place and are of general importance to the public employment relationship, there have been relatively few decisions which have dealt comprehensively with the theoretical aspects of the relationship. One of the most important decisions of the latter nature was *Keyishian* v. *Board of Regents*. The case involved New York regulations concerning loyalty-security which had been partially tested in *Adler*. Justice Brennan, speaking for the Supreme Court, attempted to destroy completely any remaining authority attached to the doctrine of privilege. He rejected *Adler,* which was clearly based upon that doctrine, as a precedent:

[61] But see *Beilan* v. *Board of Education,* 357 U.S. 339 (1958), *Lerner* v. *Casey,* 357 U.S. 468 (1958), and *Nelson* v. *Los Angeles,* 362 U.S. 1 (1960), in which the Court held that failure to answer questions before the employing agency or an investigative arm of the state, or before a congressional committee after having been instructed to answer by the employing agency, was constitutionally valid ground for removal.

[62] 385 U.S. 493 (1967).   [63] *Ibid.,* p. 500.

[64] 392 U.S. 273 (1968).   [65] 392 U.S. 280 (1968).

Constitutional doctrine which has emerged since that decision has rejected its major premise. That premise was that public employment, including academic employment, may be conditioned upon the surrender of constitutional rights which could not be abridged by direct government action. . . . The Court of Appeals for the Second Circuit correctly said in an earlier stage of this case, ". . . the theory that public employment which may be denied altogether may be subject to any conditions, regardless of how unreasonable, has been uniformly rejected." . . . Indeed, that theory was expressly rejected in a series of decisions following *Adler*.[66]

Brennan then cited *Sherbert* v. *Verner*,[67] a case which did not involve the public employment relationship, to indicate that despite the major premise of the doctrine of privilege, conditions imposed upon a privilege could be considered to abridge individual rights in a constitutional sense: "It is too late in the day to doubt that the liberties of religion and expression may be infringed by the denial of or placing of conditions upon a benefit or privilege." [68] The decision left no doubt that the absence of a constitutional right to public employment was no longer constitutionally determinative.[69]

[66] 385 U.S. 589, 605–606.   [67] 374 U.S. 398 (1963).

[68] 385 U.S. 589, 606.

[69] The Court found the specific conditions involved invalid because of vagueness; and insofar as membership in subversive organizations was concerned, Brennan broadened the *Elfbrandt* rule, at least with regard to teachers, to include instances where criminal punishment was not pertinent: "Mere knowing membership without specific intent to further unlawful aims of an organization is not a constitutionally adequate basis for exclusion from such positions" (p. 606). Justice Clark dissented in an opinion joined by Justices Harlan, Stewart, and White. He indicated that he did not think *Adler's* major premise had been overruled previously, but his opinion nevertheless did reflect the change in the degree of negative discrimination which was constitutionally acceptable: "The issue here is a narrow one. It is not freedom of speech, freedom of thought, freedom of press, freedom of

The theoretical aspects of the public employment relationship under the doctrine of substantial interest have also been comprehensively dealt with in two cases involving the civil servant's freedom of speech and press. In *Meehan* v. *Macy* [70] the Court of Appeals for the District of Columbia Circuit, which by virtue of its location is influential in matters concerning civil servants, was presented with the question of the constitutional legitimacy of the removal of a federal civil servant who had been a private on the Canal Zone police force. During the Panama riots of January 1964 he had published material which the Court called "contemptuous," "intemperate," and "defamatory." [71] He was removed for conduct unbecoming a police officer, failure to obey instructions, and for failure to obtain clearance for publications pertinent to the government of the Canal Zone. The Court held that the first ground had been sustained, but that the other two were not adequately supported by the record, and it consequently remanded the case. [72] In the course of decision, the Court addressed itself to the civil servant's right of free speech:

We do not approve the . . . premise . . . that an employee of the Government cannot claim the right to both a Government job and freedom of speech. One who enters the routine service of the

assembly, or of association, even in the Communist Party. It is simply this: May the State provide that one who, after a hearing with full judicial review, is found to have wilfully and deliberately advocated, advised, or taught that our Government should be overthrown by force or violence or other unlawful means; or to have wilfully and deliberately printed, published, etc., any book or paper that so advocated *and to have personally* advocated such doctrine himself; or to have wilfully and deliberately become a member of an organization that advocates such doctrine, is prima facie disqualified from teaching in its University?" (pp. 628–29). Italics in original.

[70] 392 F. 2d 822 (1968).   [71] *Ibid.,* p. 833.

[72] One judge dissented in part on the basis that all three charges had been sustained.

Government cannot be forced to cede all of his protections from governmental excesses. Whatever liberties a private employer might have or take, the Government cannot disregard the Bill of Rights merely by calling on its prerogative to hire and fire employees. The constitutional climate of today is different from that of 1892 when Justice Holmes struck off his oft quoted phrase. Government employees do, to some extent, have "lesser rights" than others have under the Constitution . . . when . . . activities are reasonably deemed inconsistent with their public status and duties. But in some aspects, at least, their constitutional rights are inviolable notwithstanding their status as Government employees.[73]

The Court did, therefore, perceive some degree of incompatibility between the roles of citizen and civil servant, and it attempted to define the conditions under which the public employee's freedom of speech might be curtailed:

While a free society values robust, vigorous and essentially uninhibited public speech by citizens, when such uninhibited public speech by Government employees produces intolerable disharmony, inefficiency, dissension and even chaos, it may be subject to reasonable limitations, at least concerning matters relating to the duties, discretion, and judgment entrusted to the employee involved. There is a reasonable difference between the kind of discipline and limitation on speech the government may impose on its employees and the kind it may impose on the public at large.[74]

The Court then established a general rule regarding the civil servant's right of free speech: "Since public employees have some rights of free speech, the Government is required to be reasonably specific in notifying its employees as to utterances that are prohibited before it can make those utterances a basis for discipline." [75] The decision was of importance because it

[73] *Ibid.*, p. 832.   [74] *Ibid.*, p. 833.   [75] *Ibid.*, p. 835.

clearly indicated that the doctrine of substantial interest does not require a non-negatively discriminatory public employment relationship, despite its recognition that there are negative discriminations which are unconstitutional.

In *Pickering* v. *Board of Education* [76] the Supreme Court was presented with a similar issue and it attempted to establish a general approach to be used in cases involving negative discriminations of the public employment relationship. An Illinois public-school teacher sent a letter to a local newspaper, in connection with a proposed tax increase, which was critical of the way in which the local Board of Education and the District Superintendent of Schools had dealt with past proposals to raise revenue for the schools. He was removed, after a hearing, because the board believed the letter was "detrimental to the efficient operation and administration of the schools of the district." [77] Furthermore, it appeared that some of the statements in Pickering's letter were false. The Court, per Justice Marshall, held that the removal violated the teacher's First Amendment rights. Although Marshall specifically limited his decision to the circumstances involved, he also indicated the proper approach to be taken in similar cases. He explicitly rejected the doctrine of privilege, and argued that although "the threat of dismissal from public employment is . . . a potent means of inhibiting speech," [78]

. . . it cannot be gainsaid that the State has interests as an employer in regulating the speech of its employees that differ significantly from those it possesses in connection with regulation of the speech of the citizenry in general. The problem in any case is to arrive at a balance between the interests of the teacher, as a citizen, in commenting upon matters of public concern and the interests of the State, as an employer, in promoting the efficiency of the public services it performs through its employees.[79]

[76] 391 U.S. 563 (1968).   [77] *Ibid.,* p. 564.   [78] *Ibid.,* p. 574.
[79] *Ibid.,* p. 568.

In applying this balancing approach to the specific circumstances involved, the Court reasoned that

free and open debate is vital to informed decision making by the electorate. Teachers are, as a class, the members of the community most likely to have informed and definite opinions as to how funds allotted to the operation of the schools should be spent. Accordingly, it is essential that they be able to speak out freely on such questions without fear of retaliatory dismissal.[80]

Marshall indicated that in determining the balance the nature of the position involved was of importance [81] and he formulated what may eventually become a general standard concerning public employees' constitutional rights:

In these circumstances we conclude that the interest of the school administration in limiting teachers' opportunities to contribute to public debate is not significantly greater than its interest in limiting a similar contribution by any member of the general public.[82]

It would appear, therefore, that a general incompatibility between the roles of citizen and civil servant can no longer provide a basis for constitutionally acceptable negative discrimination and that a satisfactory demonstration of a specific incompatibility is required at the present time. Moreover, even if such an incompatibility can be demonstrated, the balancing approach demands a weighing of the negative discrimination involved against the undesirable consequences which will allegedly result if it is not invoked. The "specific incompatibility" and balancing approaches, if they replace the "reasonably deemed to interfere with the efficiency of the public service" rule established by the *United Public Workers*

[80] *Ibid.*, pp. 571–72.

[81] Marshall seemed to rely less on the fact that the position was an academic one than on the fact that it did not require a close working relationship with superiors and was not one of confidence.

[82] 391 U.S. 563, 573.

decision will, like the *Meehan* rule requiring prior notification
of prohibited speech and the doctrine of substantial interest
itself, tend to decrease the constitutionally acceptable range of
discrimination in the negative direction by placing greater
importance than previously on the rights of the individual and
less importance on the desire for specific administrative and
political consequences.[83]

The doctrine of substantial interest is not simply a doctrine
of unconstitutional substantive conditions, it also requires
procedural due process under certain circumstances. The
procedural aspect of the doctrine, like its related substantive
aspect, largely developed in a series of loyalty-security decisions. In *Peters* v. *Hobby*,[84] a Loyalty Order case, the Supreme
Court avoided a decision on the constitutional issues, but it
indicated that procedural due process was relevant when "substantial rights affecting the lives and property of citizens are
at stake." [85] In *Greene* v. *McElroy*,[86] an industrial security
case, the Court held that in the absence of explicit authoriza-
tion from the President or Congress, the Defense Department
could not deny an aeronautical engineer employed by a private firm a security clearance without affording him the opportunity to confront and cross-examine individuals who had
supplied information against him. Chief Justice Warren,
speaking for the Court, seemed to indicate that similar pro-

[83] Justices Douglas and Black concurred; Justice White concurred
in part and dissented in part on the ground that Pickering could have
been removed because his statements were false. On this point, the
Court held that removals for false statements in the otherwise legitimate exercise of free speech could be valid only if the statements
were made "knowingly or recklessly." *Ibid.,* p. 574. In a somewhat
related area, the Court has created a positive discrimination by holding that civil servants are immune from libel suits in some circumstances, see chap. 8, *infra.*

[84] 349 U.S. 331 (1955).   [85] *Ibid.,* p. 347.
[86] 360 U.S. 474 (1959).

cedural due process might be required in comparable civil service removals:

Certain principles have remained relatively immutable in our jurisprudence. One of these is that where governmental action seriously injures an individual, and the reasonableness of the action depends on fact findings, the evidence used to prove the Government's case must be disclosed to the individual so that he has an opportunity to show that it is untrue. . . . We have formalized these protections in the requirements of confrontation and cross-examination.[87]

Procedural due process was clearly held to be relevant to civil service removals in *Cafeteria Workers* v. *McElroy*.[88] The case involved a private cafeteria worker at a naval gun factory. Her access to the base was revoked for security reasons, without a hearing, by the naval officer in charge. The Court, per Justice Stewart, upheld the revocation, which involved only "the opportunity to work at one isolated and specific military installation," [89] and which did not "bestow a badge of disloyalty or infamy, with attendant foreclosure from other employment opportunity." [90] The decision, how-

[87] *Ibid.*, p. 496. Justice Clark dissented, stating that the decision cast "a cloud over both the Employee Loyalty Program and the one here under attack." *Ibid.*, p. 534. Justices Frankfurter, Harlan, and Whittaker concurred specially on the ground that the procedures were not authorized. Previously, in *Parker* v. *Lester*, 227 F. 2d 708 (1955), it was held that the denial of officially validated documents to seamen on United States merchant vessels without affording them confrontation and cross-examination was a violation of due process. It should be noted that the Court specifically limited its decision in *Parker* by stating: "The liberty to follow their chosen employment is no doubt a right more clearly entitled to constitutional protection than the right of a government employee to obtain or retain his job" (p. 717). See also *United States* v. *Robel*, 389 U.S. 258 (1967), and *Schneider* v. *Smith*, 390 U.S. 171 (1968), on industrial security.

[88] 367 U.S. 886 (1961).   [89] *Ibid.*, p. 896.

[90] *Ibid.*, p. 898. The Court reasoned that because security dismissals

ever, was important for the public employment relationship because Stewart stated that the interest of a government employee in retaining his job was "closely analogous" to the interest involved in the case before the Court,[91] and he rejected the principles of the doctrine of privilege in arguing that procedural due process was relevant:

The question remains whether . . . summarily denying Rachel Brawner access to the site of her former employment violated the Due Process Clause of the Fifth Amendment. This question cannot be answered on the easy assertion that, because she had no right to be there in the first place, she was not deprived of liberty or property by the Superintendent's action. "One may not have a constitutional right to go to Baghdad, but the Government may not prohibit one from going there unless by means consonant with due process of law." [92]

Stewart, in fact, directly discussed the constitutional status of civil servants. He observed that "it has become a settled principle that government employment, in the absence of legislation can be revoked at the will of the appointing officer," [93] but he noted that it had been recognized nevertheless that "an individual's interest in government employment was entitled to constitutional protection." [94] He reasoned, however, that "the Fifth Amendment does not require a trial type hearing in every conceivable case of government impairment of private interest," [95] and therefore "to acknowledge that there exist constitutional restraints upon state and federal governments in dealing with their employees is not to say that all such employees have a constitutional right to notice and a hearing before they can be removed." [96] Although due process was

could be made for reasons other than disloyalty, they did not stigmatize the individual.

[91] *Ibid.*, p. 896.   [92] *Ibid.*, p. 894.   [93] *Ibid.*, p. 896.
[94] *Ibid.*, p. 897.   [95] *Ibid.*, p. 894.   [96] *Ibid.*, p. 898.

relevant to civil service removals, the circumstances under which civil servants had a right to procedural safeguards and the specific safeguards required remained to be determined in subsequent cases.[97]

In general, the courts have held that statutes concerning the removal of civil servants have afforded adequate procedural safeguards for the individual involved. There have, however, been some exceptions which indicate that the principle that procedural due process is relevant to civil service removals is not of a hypothetical character. In *United States* v. *Rasmussen,*[98] the District Court for the District of Montana held that the removal of a county office manager of an Agricultural Stabilization and Conservation Service office for fraud, in the absence of confrontation and cross-examination, was a denial of due process of law. In a similar case, *Kelly* v. *Herak,*[99] the same judge on the same court reasoned that a government employee has no "constitutional right to a hearing with all the requirements of due process. On the other hand, it is clear also that due process may require procedures in some circumstances different from that required in others."[100] The Court held that the circumstances, in which an employee was removed for violating regulations rather than for inefficiency or insubordination, were within the scope of the *Greene* decision and therefore that "due process requires the disclosure of the evidence in support of the Government's case, including the rights of confrontation and cross-examination."[101] On appeal the Court of Appeals for the

---

[97] Justice Brennan dissented in an opinion joined by Chief Justice Warren and Justices Black and Douglas. Brennan agreed that procedural due process was relevant, but thought that it required more. He believed that the term "security risk" implied communism or disloyalty and therefore was a badge of infamy.

[98] 222 F. Supp. 430 (1963).   [99] 252 F. Supp. 289 (1966).
[100] *Ibid.,* p. 297.   [101] *Ibid.*

Ninth Circuit upheld the lower court's decision on nonconstitutional grounds, and remarked that it could find "no constitutional right to disclosure *in this case.*" [102] In *Lucia* v. *Duggan,*[103] the District Court for the District of Massachusetts held that the removal of a public-school teacher for wearing a beard was constitutionally defective because he was not given notice of the charges against him and because the hearing which resulted in his dismissal combined legislative-type and judicial-type functions. The Court argued that "whatever the derivation and scope of the plaintiff's alleged freedom to wear a beard, it is at least an interest of his, especially in combination with his professional reputation as a school teacher, which may not be taken from him without due process of law." [104] In *Olson* v. *Regents,*[105] the District Court for the District of Minnesota found the dismissal of a maintenance worker by the University of Minnesota to be unconstitutional. The Court reasoned that, "In this case plaintiff was 59 years of age and had been employed by the University for over 14 years. His chances for employment elsewhere are therefore minimal after his discharge by the University." [106] University regulations prohibited removals except for "just cause," and the Court held that, at least under these circumstances, "an employee in the public sector . . . should be entitled to an advance notice in writing of his termination, a written statement of the reasons therefor, and a reasonable time allowed within which to respond thereto." [107]

One of the most important exceptions has been *Birnbaum* v. *Trussel,*[108] in which the Court of Appeals for the Second Circuit was presented with the issue of whether a medical doctor could be dismissed summarily from a New York City

---

[102] *Herak* v. *Kelly,* 391 F. 2d 216 (1968). Emphasis added.
[103] 303 F. Supp. 112 (1969).   [104] *Ibid.,* pp. 117–118.
[105] 301 F. Supp. 1356 (1969).   [106] *Ibid.,* pp. 1362–1363.
[107] *Ibid.,* p. 1361.   [108] 371 F. 2d 672 (1966).

hospital for being a racist. The Court recognized that "public employees, of course, have no absolute right to a hearing on discharge from public employment because government employment is a privilege and not a property right," [109] and asserted that in recent years "the courts have become more inclined to consider the causes of a discharge and the methods and procedures by which a dismissal is effected as it may bear upon reputation and the opportunity for employment thereafter." [110] It held that in the specific instance involved

the appellant could properly claim that by summarily discharging him in the midst of such accusations [of racism] and by advising the other City hospitals by letter not to employ him, the Department of Hospitals gave them a stamp of official authority, and not only deprived him of his employment, but seriously damaged his professional reputation in the community as a physician. In such circumstances, the due process clause guarantees one the right to have notice of the charges against him and to a hearing on these charges before being dismissed.[111]

Another important exception was *Camero* v. *United States.*[112] The case was probably less significant because of the issues involved than because it was decided by the Court of Claims, which is influential in determining the validity of civil service removals. The Court held that procedural due process prohibited the removal of a classified civil servant after the agency lawyer participating in the removal hearing, who was in an adversary position, had engaged in *ex parte* communications with those who made the ultimate decision.

The *Weiman* decision and several cases following it clearly

[109] *Ibid.,* p. 677.   [110] *Ibid.*

[111] *Ibid.* One judge concurred on the basis that Birnbaum was denied equal protection because he was dismissed for being a Caucasian. Birnbaum made this claim, but the Court rejected it because there was a lack of evidence to this effect, and "other white doctors were not discharged" (p. 676).

[112] 375 F. 2d 777 (1967).

indicate that negative discrimination of the public employment relationship can no longer be justified on the basis that there is no constitutional right to government employment. They also indicate that such discrimination can be in violation of the civil servant's substantive constitutional rights, and that civil service removals can be in violation of the requirements of procedural due process. From the various decisions previously reviewed it appears that generally the more substantial the interest at stake, the greater the possibility that negative discriminations will be substantively or procedurally defective. Substantively, of course, interference with any constitutional right could be considered to be a substantial interest and an unconstitutional negative discrimination.[113] Thus, in equal protection cases, illegal search and seizure cases, and others, little more than an infringement of the civil servant's ordinary constitutional rights as a citizen has been involved. However, the courts have often found more than just an abridgment of the civil servant's constitutional rights through removal to be at stake. In *Weiman,* and presumably in all loyalty decisions after it, the Court recognized that because a "badge of infamy" was attached to disloyalty removals more was at stake than a specific public service position. In *Cramp, Elfbrandt, Garrity, Gardner,* and *Sanitation Men,* criminal punishment rather than just the loss of public employment was, to a greater or lesser extent, involved. In *Pickering,* the Court indicated that an informed

---

[113] Logically, the employment itself cannot be the substantial interest unless removals for inefficiency and similar causes are to assume constitutional stature. However, because *United Public Workers, Torcaso,* and equal protection cases have indicated that the government cannot exclude anyone from civil service employment for arbitrary reasons, any removal or denial of employment potentially violates this constitutional right, which could therefore be considered to be the substantial interest involved.

electorate as well as public employment and the First Amendment was at stake. In *Lovett,* proscription from future employment, rather than only the loss of a specific civil service position, was at stake.

Procedurally, the same precept appears to prevail. In the *Camero* case it was held that due process had been violated in an otherwise ordinary removal. In other cases, however, more than public employment alone has been involved. In *Lovett* the Court found the government's action to be procedurally defective because reputation and future employment were at stake. In *Rasmussen,* a removal for fraud which, the Court reasoned, would have stigmatized the individual's reputation was involved. In the first *Kelly* case the Court reasoned that a removal for violation of regulations would have a similar effect on the individual. In *Birnbaum* the Court clearly considered the individual's reputation and opportunities for future employment, rather than the specific position involved, to be a substantial interest. In *Lucia* professional reputation and a significant element of personal freedom were involved, and in *Olson* future employment was a major concern. There has, however, been no general agreement concerning the specific circumstances in which the substantial interest involved outweighs the benefits which are believed to accrue from the particular negative discrimination at issue. Furthermore, the substantiality of the interest itself often has been disputed. There were dissents based, at least in part, on this ground in *Baggett, Elfbrandt, Keyishian, Pickering, Slochower, Garrity,* and other cases. In *Williams* v. *Zuckert,*[114] only Justices Douglas and Black believed that confrontation and cross-examination were constitutionally required in the removal of a civil servant "for misconduct involving charges of immorality." [115] It appears therefore that

[114] 371 U.S. 531 (1963).   [115] *Ibid.,* p. 534.

although the general principles of the doctrine of substantial interest currently determine the constitutionality of negative discrimination, the validity of specific negative discriminations will, barring a reversal of the doctrine, continue to be decided largely on a case-by-case basis.

III

The doctrine of substantial interest has replaced the doctrine of privilege as the primary constitutional doctrine concerning negative discrimination of the public employment relationship. Although the newer doctrine's emergence was influenced by judicial decisions involving political neutrality, equality of access to civil service positions, and other issues, it most clearly emerged in cases involving issues presented by loyalty-security regulations. The doctrine established the principles that the absence of a constitutional right to public employment does not connote the absence of constitutional rights while in such employment and that civil service removals can be in violation of procedural due process. These principles were not original to the doctrine, but rather were principles which first had been urged by some members of Congress during debate over the Decision of 1789, and which had provided the basis of such earlier judicial opinions as *Louthan* v. *Commonwealth* and Justice Bradley's dissent in *Ex parte Curtis*.[116] The doctrine therefore elevated a persistent undercurrent of thought concerning the constitutional aspects of the public employment relationship to a position of dominance. The doctrine is of great importance to the relationship because it tends to reduce the range of discrimination by decreasing the constitutional acceptability of negative discrimination. While the doctrine might be reversed in the future,

[116] See chap. 4, *supra.*

at the present time this appears unlikely because its emergence has coincided with a related general political trend toward increasing the legal and constitutional rights of civil servants.

8 | The Public Employment Relationship Today

I

Since the mid-1950's and especially during the 1960's there have been several indications that significant levels of dissatisfaction with negative discrimination of the public employment relationship have not been confined to the judiciary, and that the degree of perceived incompatibility between the roles of citizen and civil servant generally has probably declined. There have been important areas in which the President, Congress, and the courts, apart from their development of the doctrine of substantial interest, have afforded, or made important attempts to afford, civil servants greater rights affecting the relationship. Specifically, civil servants have been afforded greater organizational and collective bargaining rights; there have been attempts, some of which have been successful, to provide greater protections against invasions of privacy, coercion by supervisors, and big-brotherism within the federal bureaucracy; there have been important developments with regard to decreasing the degree of negative discrimination involved in regulations concerning political neutrality; and the Supreme Court first created a positive discrimination concerning the law of libel and then created a negative discrimination intended to balance it. The relevant political and societal conditions surrounding the change in attitudes toward the relationship and efforts to alter it, including the adoption of the doctrine of substantial interest are, of course, more difficult to identify.

One of these conditions has been the growth of public employment at all levels and the widespread belief that it will continue to grow at a high rate. In 1966, public employees made up about 17 per cent of the working force, and it has been estimated that between 1960 and 1975 their number will increase by nearly 50 per cent.[1] Many have argued that revision of the public employment relationship is desirable at the present time because "the expansion of government enterprise with its ever increasing number of employees marks this area of the law a crucial one."[2] A related condition has been an increase in the membership of employee organizations which has contributed to a general increase in their political power.[3] For example, between 1949 and 1960 there were six successful discharge petitions to force legislation to the floor of the House, and in each instance pay-raise bills were involved and postal unions were largely responsible for the discharge; and in 1960 a pay-raise bill was passed over President Eisenhower's veto by overwhelming margins.[4] Eisenhower stated that the bill's original approval in Congress "was attended by intensive and unconcealed political pressure exerted flagrantly and in concert on members of Congress by a number of postal field service employees, particularly their leadership."[5] Furthermore, there appears to have been a

[1] Robert B. Moberly, "The Strike and Its Alternatives in Public Employment," *University of Wisconsin Law Review*, CMLXVI (Spring 1966), 549.

[2] *Bagley* v. *Hospital District*, 421 P. 2d 409, 417 (1966).

[3] Willem B. Vosloo, *Collective Bargaining in the United States Federal Civil Service* (Chicago: Public Personnel Association, 1966), p. 2.

[4] *Ibid.*, p. 57. The votes were 345–69 in the House and 72–24 in the Senate.

[5] *Ibid.*, p. 206, n. 44; quoted from the *New York Times*, July 1, 1960, p. 6.

widespread realization that, because of the governmental system of separated and shared powers, for employee organizations "it is a hard fact that militant tactics alone seem to have a chance for success." [6]

Another condition has been the existence of a generally perceived need for, and a difficulty in obtaining, highly qualified personnel to staff the upper levels of the federal bureaucracy. For example, in 1960, Senator Henry Jackson stated, "The fact is, we have encountered disturbing difficulties in securing first rate talent at the very time when the national security calls for the country's 'best brains' to man key posts at home and abroad," [7] and the Civil Service Commission's *Annual Report* often contains such statements as, "The need of the Federal Government for career personnel of outstanding ability has never been greater" [8] and "Government's far-ranging programs require an enormous supply of top-quality talent." [9] The existence of negative discriminations, which in the opinion of some make civil servants "second-class citizens," has often been cited as a partial cause of the inability of the civil service to attract first-rate talent. Robert Ramspeck, former CSC Chairman, has argued that

today, the federal government affects the lives [sic] of every human being in the United States. Therefore we need better qualified people, more dedicated people, in the Federal Service

[6] Rollin B. Posey, "The New Militancy of Public Employees," *Public Administration Review*, XXVIII (March–April 1968), 117.

[7] Quoted in Franklin P. Kilpatrick, Milton C. Cummings, Jr., and M. Kent Jennings, *The Image of the Federal Service* (Washington: Brookings Institution, 1964), p. 4. Kilpatrick *et al.* indicated that "for some time there has been presumptive evidence that the United States government is facing serious difficulties in attracting the numbers of able people it needs to carry out its critical functions, both at home and abroad" (p. 1).

[8] U.S., CSC, *Annual Report*, LXXX (1963), 3.

[9] *Ibid.*, LXXXII (1965), 10.

than we ever needed before. And we cannot get them if you are going to deal with them on the basis of suspicion, and delve into their private lives, because if there is anything the average American cherishes it is his right of freedom of action, and his right to privacy.[10]

Finally, it should be noted that although sufficient empirical data are lacking, a general increase in the prestige of public employment may have been associated with or resulted in more favorable attitudes toward civil servants and decreasing societal support for a negatively discriminatory public employment relationship,[11] and that the increasing power and perhaps social status of higher civil servants may have enhanced their ability to forestall the adoption of negative discriminations to which they are opposed.[12]

[10] U.S., Congress, Senate, Committee on the Judiciary, *Protecting Privacy and the Rights of Federal Employees,* Report 519, 90th Cong., 1st Sess., p. 3 (August 21, 1967). Hereinafter *Ervin Report.* There is a lack of knowledge as to whether negative discriminations are important in determining the appeal of public employment. The data in Kilpatrick *et al., Federal Service,* imply that they are not; see chaps. v, vi, and ix. The *Ervin Report,* on the other hand, implies the opposite conclusion. In any case, there appears to be a widespread belief that such discriminations are important.

[11] See Morris Janowitz and Diel Wright, "The Prestige of Public Employment: 1929 and 1954," *Public Administration Review,* XVI (Winter 1956), 15–21. Kilpatrick *et al., Federal Service,* found that the major characteristic attributed to federal civil servants by the general employed public was "good personal character" and that the next three were "capable of doing the work because of ability, training, background, qualifications," "good worker," and "agreeable personality" (p. 213, Table 10-2). Only 5 per cent of those responding thought civil servants were "poor or mediocre workers" (*ibid.*). However, whether these attitudes differ from those in past years is unknown. Both studies found that the prestige of civil service employment increases with decreasing socioeconomic status. Therefore general increases in prestige may not necessarily make the civil service more attractive to "top-quality talent" (*ibid.,* chap. v).

[12] See W. Lloyd Warner *et al., The American Federal Executive*

II

An important realm in which the degree of perceived incompatibility between the roles of citizen and civil servant has declined in recent years is that of labor relations. Despite the existence of civil service unions during the nineteenth century and their recognition by the Lloyd–La Follette Act,[13]

(New Haven: Yale University Press, 1963). They found that although at elite levels "American society is not becoming more caste-like . . . there is strong evidence of the operation of rank and effects of high birth in the selection of the American business and government elites" (p. 22). They also argued that "these men who occupy high position in the great civilian and military hierarchies of the federal government . . . exercise increasing power. They are far more influential, now and potentially, than their nineteenth-century predecessors and even those of only three or four decades ago" (p. 1). Reinhard Bendix, *Higher Civil Servants in American Society* (Boulder: University of Colorado, 1949), concluded that as of 1940 higher civil servants, defined differently from the Warner *et al.* study, came predominantly from lower-middle and middle class backgrounds and did not constitute a homogeneous social group. See pp. 121–22 for a summary of findings. It appears probable that in the recent American context the ability of higher civil servants to affect the public employment relationship has been confined primarily to excluding themselves from the domain of discrimination. For example, New Jersey Democratic Congressman Cornelius Gallagher stated: "I often hear the argument that national security and the good of the public service demand the use of such practices as personality testing and polygraph examinations. But when I ask the top officials of Government agencies, their assistants, and the assistants to the assistants, whether they were ever required to take such tests, the answer is always, 'No.'" U.S., Congress, House, Subcommittee of the Committee on Government Operations, *Special Inquiry on Invasion of Privacy,* 89th Cong., 1st Sess., p. 398 (1966). Hereinafter Gallagher Hearings. The power of higher civil servants, however, can also influence the adoption of negative discriminations such as political removal under "Schedule C." See Paul P. Van Riper, *History of the United States Civil Service* (Evanston: Row, Peterson and Co., 1958), pp. 445–46.

[13] U.S., *Statutes at Large,* XXXVII, 555 (August 24, 1912).

until recently opposition to them has often been extreme. For example, in 1943 New York's highest court argued that

to tolerate or to recognize any combination of civil service employees of the Government as a labor organization or Union is not only incompatible with the spirit of democracy, but inconsistent with every principle upon which our government is founded.[14]

In 1949, however, organized civil servants began a campaign, which culminated in a reversal of this opposition, to secure more formalized legal recognition and a greater role in determining working conditions in the federal bureaucracy.[15] By 1956 they had succeeded in obtaining the Democratic party's commitment to the "recognition by law of the right of employee organizations to represent their members and participate in the formulation and improvement of personnel policies and practices." [16]

During the presidential election campaign of 1960, Democratic nominee John F. Kennedy reaffirmed his party's earlier position,[17] and after his election he appointed the "President's Task Force on Employee-Management Relations in the Federal Service." [18] The task force was directed to study

[14] *Railway Mail Association* v. *Murphy,* 44 N.Y. 2d 601, 607 (1943).

[15] See Vosloo, *Collective Bargaining,* pp. 45–59, for a detailed account of this effort.

[16] *Ibid.,* p. 58. The statement was in the party's platform.

[17] *Ibid.*

[18] The task force was appointed on June 21, 1961. It consisted of Secretary of Labor Arthur Goldberg, Chairman; CSC Chairman John Macy, Jr., Vice Chairman; Director of the Bureau of the Budget David E. Bell; Postmaster General J. Edward Day; Secretary of Defense Robert McNamara; and Special Counsel Theodore Sorensen. See U.S., President's Task Force on Employee-Management Relations in the Federal Service, *A Policy for Employee-Management Cooperation in the Federal Service* (Washington: U.S. Government Printing Office, 1962).

the broad range of issues relating to federal employee-management relations, including but not limited to definition of appropriate employee organizations, standards for recognition of such organizations, matters upon which employee organizations may be appropriately consulted, and the participation of employees and employee representatives in grievances and appeals.[19]

The task force reported on November 30, 1961. It concluded that "the benefits to be obtained for employees by employee organizations, while real and substantial are limited," because "many of the most important matters affecting Federal employees are determined by Congress, and are not subject to unfettered negotiation by officials of the Executive Branch." [20] The task force also indicated that the creation of a uniform policy with respect to civil service unions was desirable because "lacking guidance, the various agencies of the Government have proceeded on widely varying courses. Some have established extensive relations with employee organizations; most have done little; a number have done nothing." [21]

Most of the task force's suggestions were incorporated into Executive Orders 10987 and 10988 [22] which were issued by Kennedy on January 17, 1962. The former, which was intended to establish "agency systems for appeals from adverse actions," was based formally on the assumptions that

the public interest requires the maintenance of high standards of employee performance and integrity in the public service, prompt administrative action where such standards are not met, and safeguards to protect employees against arbitrary or unjust adverse actions,

and that

[19] *Ibid.,* p. ix.   [20] *Ibid.,* p. 8.   [21] *Ibid.,* p. iii.
[22] U.S., *Federal Register,* XXVII, Part 1, 550, 551.

the prompt reconsideration of protested administrative actions against employees will promote the efficiency of the service, assist in maintaining a high level of employee morale, further the objective of improving employee-management relations, and insure timely correction of improper adverse actions.

The order required that "the head of each department or agency shall establish . . . a system for the reconsideration of administrative decisions to take adverse action against employees." It further provided that the CSC should issue regulations to put the order into effect and that grievance systems should be simple, orderly, timely, include one level of appeal and at least one hearing whenever practicable, that appeals should be in writing, and that employees should have the right to be represented by counsel.[23]

Executive Order 10988 was of greater importance. It was intended to promote "employee-management cooperation in the Federal service," and was premised on the beliefs that "participation of employees in the formulation and implementation of personnel policies affecting them contributes to the effective conduct of the public business," that "the effective administration of the Government and the well-being of employees require that orderly and constructive relationships be maintained between employee organizations and management officials," that "subject to law and the paramount requirements of the public service, employee-management relations within the Federal service should be improved by providing employees an opportunity for greater participation in the formulation and implementation of policies and procedures affecting the conditions of their employment," and that "effec-

[23] The order was to be effective on July 1, 1962. It excluded the Central Intelligence Agency, National Security Agency, Federal Bureau of Investigation, Atomic Energy Commission, and the Tennessee Valley Authority from its provisions.

tive employee-management cooperation in the public service requires a clear statement of the respective rights and obligations of employee organizations and agency management." The order provided that civil servants "shall have, and shall be protected in the exercise of, the right freely and without fear of penalty or reprisals to form, join and assist any employee organization or to refrain from such activity." [24]

Executive Order 10988 provided for three forms of recognition which might be accorded to employee organizations which were not "subject to corrupt influences or influences opposed to basic democratic principles," depending primarily upon the size of their membership within units and the proportion of employees in a unit designating an organization to represent that unit.[25] Informal recognition extended the right of employees to be heard, but it did not require management to solicit their views. Formal recognition required the agency to consult the organization "from time to time in the formulation and implementation of personnel policies and practices, and matters affecting working conditions that are of concern to its members." Exclusive recognition afforded an organization a more important role:

When an employee organization has been recognized as the exclusive representative of employees of an appropriate unit, it shall be entitled to act for and to negotiate agreements covering

[24] The term "employee organization" did not include organizations asserting the right, or imposing a duty, to strike against the government, advocating the overthrow of the government, or treating persons unequally on the basis of race, color, creed, or national origin. The order also specified that an employee could not be a representative of an organization if it constituted a conflict of interest or was incompatible with the law or the employee's duties.

[25] A unit was to be established on a craft, functional, installation, plant, or other basis which would "ensure a clear and identifiable community of interest among the employees concerned." No unit was to be established solely on the basis of organizational membership.

all employees in the unit and shall be responsible for representing the interests of all such employees without discrimination and without regard to employee organization membership. Such employee organization shall be given the opportunity to be represented at discussions between management and employees or employee representatives concerning grievances, personnel policies and practices, or other matters affecting general working conditions. . . . The agency and such employee organization . . . shall meet at reasonable times and confer with respect to personnel policy and practices.

In the absence of special circumstances, no unit could be established for exclusive recognition which included managerial executives, employees engaged in personnel work other than purely clerical, supervisors who officially evaluated the performance of employees and the persons they supervised, or professional and nonprofessional employees unless the majority of the former voted for inclusion in the unit.[26]

The order limited the scope of employee-management bargaining by specifying that the agency's mission, budget, organization, and technology were not subjects for negotiation. It also excepted the FBI and the CIA and provided that similar agencies could be excluded if it was determined that their inclusion would be detrimental to the national security. Section 14 of the order extended to all civil servants in the competitive service the rights afforded to veterans under section 14 of the 1944 Veteran Preference Act [27] to appeal demotions, dismissals, and suspensions for more than thirty days to the CSC.[28]

[26] By October 1967, eighteen employee organizations had exclusive recognition rights representing over a million federal employees. See Posey, *Public Administration Review*, XXVIII, 112.

[27] See chap. 5, *supra*.

[28] It should be noted that beginning with *Gadsden* v. *U.S.*, 78 F. Supp. 126 (1948), and especially since *Knotts* v. *U.S.*, 121 F. Supp.

The recent executive orders concerning federal labor relations have been clearly based on the belief that labor relations in the public service should, as far as possible under the circumstances, roughly parallel those in the private sphere, and they have afforded civil servants and their organizations an important means of challenging minor negative discriminations of the public employment relationship such as invasions of privacy and coercion to buy savings bonds or contribute to charities.[29] Moreover, they have increased the already important political power of employee organizations which may enable them to assume a greater role in the policy-making process, both in Congress and the executive branch, concerning the adoption or revocation of discriminations in the

---

630 (1954), provisions such as this one and other limitations on removal power have been of greater importance because the courts have been more willing to broaden "the scope of review to include a judicial determination as to whether the administrative findings were capricious, arbitrary or unreasonable, or whether such findings were supported by the record." *West* v. *Macy*, 284 F. Supp. 105 (1968). On the other hand, the courts have held that the provisions of Executive Order 10988 providing for union recognition are not appropriate for judicial vindication. See *Manhattan-Bronx Postal Union* v. *Gronouski*, 350 F. 2d 451 (1965) and *National Association of Internal Revenue Employees* v. *Dillon*, 356 F. 2d 811 (1968). Executive Order 10988 has been superceded by Executive Order 11491, U.S., *Code of Federal Regulations*, III, 191 (October 29, 1969). The new order, which is not to be fully implemented before January 1971, maintains the current trend toward granting greater labor rights to civil servants and their organizations. The order substantially continues many of the practices which developed under Executive Order 10988. Perhaps the most significant change is the establishment of a Federal Labor Relations Council to oversee and coordinate federal labor relations an to modify them on a continuing basis. Formal and informal recognition were also to be phased out and a new form of recognition—national consultation rights—was to be established. It is still too early to assess the impact of the new order.

[29] See discussion *infra*.

future. One public employee union leader, for example, has said that "collective bargaining is concerned not only with the economic status of the employee but also with the protection and extension of his rights and freedom." [30] Furthermore, the practices they developed encourage federal civil service strikes or other "job actions," despite their continued illegality.

Although some believe that "the outright prohibition of the right to strike by public employees is a denial of a fundamental and inherent right," [31] the right to strike is not one of unambiguous constitutional stature. However, the right or its absence is of obvious importance to the public employment relationship because it involves the ability of civil servants to determine the terms and conditions of their employment, including discriminations of the relationship. Executive Order 10988 was explicit in indicating the unacceptability of civil service strikes and a Presidential Memorandum of May 21, 1963, prohibited employee organizations from "calling or engaging in any strike, work stoppage, slowdown, or related picketing engaged in as a substitute for any such strike." [32] The outlawing of strikes, however, has not always prevented them, and civil service union leaders have suggested that the limited role which has been afforded to employee organizations encourages them to assert the right to strike or engage in strikes and other job actions in order to protect and expand their influence. For example, in 1962, Vaux Owen, President of the National Federation of Federal Employees which op-

[30] Arnold S. Zander, American Federation of State, County and Municipal Employees, AFL-CIO, "A Union View of Collective Bargaining in the Public Service," *Public Administration Review,* XXII (Winter 1962), 6.

[31] *Ibid.,* p. 8.

[32] U.S., *Federal Register,* XXVIII, Part 5, 5127, 5130 (May 21, 1963). Section 19 of Executive Order 11491 contains a similar provision.

posed Executive Order 10988 because it divided civil servants into management and employee groups, predicted that "collective bargaining will lead to the assertion of the right to strike and political pressure to repeal the law against strikes." [33] The same year, E. C. Hallbeck, President of the United Federation of Postal Clerks, AFL-CIO, stated that

the principal area of uncertainty now lies in the fact that federal employees both by law and their own sworn forbearance lack the muscle to reinforce their minimum positions with any effective economic weapon, such as the right to strike. It would seem to us, therefore, that the government managerial circles have an even greater obligation than private industry to be scrupulously fair. If they cling to some of the arbitrary attitudes that have long characterized federal bureaucracy, it is not impossible that we would consider new techniques which have been proved effective in the government service of other countries.[34]

Since that time, of course, federal employees have adopted new tactics, including picketing, "sick-outs," walkouts, and strikes; and the possibility of future federal civil service strikes has also been enhanced by an increasing reliance of state and municipal employees on them and an increasing awareness that sanctions against such strikes are often largely irrelevant.[35]

[33] Statement in Kenneth O. Warner, *Management Relations with Organized Public Employees* (Chicago: Public Personnel Association, 1963), p. 233. Most employee organizations were somewhat dissatisfied with the order because they had hoped for a law which would compel, in practice, all employees, except those of extraordinary independence, to join unions. See Vosloo, *Collective Bargaining,* pp. 75–76.

[34] Statement in K. O. Warner, *Management Relations,* p. 229.

[35] The most spectacular job actions were the professional air traffic controllers' "sick-out" and the postal strike of 1970. There was also a strike against the TVA in August 1962, there have been important instances of picketing, and there was at least one significant walkout.

III

A second important realm in which the perceived incompatibility between the roles of citizen and civil servant has recently declined and an area in which negative discriminations of the public employment relationship have been abandoned is that of the civil servant's privacy and freedom from coercion and big-brotherism. Interferences with the civil servant's constitutional right to privacy [36] through the use of polygraphs, personality tests, and various questionnaires have been common in recent years. In 1964 a House subcommittee investigating the use of polygraphs by the government found that eight agencies used them for investigating employee misconduct, three bureaus used them for medical purposes, and the CIA and NSA used them "as a routine part of preem-

---

See U.S., CSC, *Annual Report*, LXXXV (1968), 35; and Posey, *Public Administration Review*, XXVIII, 113. The ineffectual character of anti-strike legislation has been recognized by many. For example, Philadelphia Mayor James H. J. Tate stated that "antistrike legislation will not bring peace to the public sector of the economy. . . . Injunctions cannot halt rape in the alleys, collect refuse, teach children or disperse sewage." "Public Employees' Right to Strike," *Pennsylvania Bar Association Quarterly*, XXXIX (June 1968), 529. Similarly, during a New York City subway workers' strike, antistrike legislation was ignored because it would "never have got the subways running." "Labor Problems in Public Employment," *Northwestern University Law Review*, LXI (March–April 1967), 119. In 1966 there were about 150 public employee strikes, and the number for 1967 has been estimated at over 250. Recent public employee strikes have included subway workers, welfare workers, policemen, teachers, firemen, and public hospital workers. See Tate, *Pennsylvania Bar Association Quarterly*, XXXIX, 528; Gordon Nesvig, "The New Dimensions of the Strike Question," *Public Administration Review*, XXVIII (March–April 1968), 126, 128; Posey, *ibid.*, p. 113.

[36] In *Griswold* v. *Connecticut*, 381 U.S. 479 (1965), the Supreme Court found privacy protected by the First, Third, Fourth, Fifth, and Ninth Amendments.

ployment personnel screening." [37] The subcommittee found that although the tests were theoretically voluntary, in the latter two agencies they were practically mandatory. In summarizing the nature of much of the questioning, Congressman Gallagher stated, "I regret to say that the thread of outright voyeurism runs throughout too many of the cases that have come to my attention regarding the use of the lie detector." [38] For example, the following questions are said to be routine in the NSA:

When was the first time you had sexual relations with a woman? How many times have you had sexual intercourse? Have you ever engaged in homosexual activities? . . . in sexual activities with an animal? When was the first time you had intercourse with your wife? Did you have intercourse with her before you were married? How many times? [39]

During the 1960's several federal agencies began using personality tests and privacy-invading questionnaires. [40] The most common personality test used has been the Minnesota Multiple Personality Inventory which includes such true-false questions as "My sex life is satisfactory," "I believe in a life hereafter," "Christ performed miracles," and "There is

[37] U.S., Congress, House, Committee on Government Operations, Foreign Operations and Government Information Subcommittee, *Hearings, Use of Polygraphs by the Federal Government,* 88th Cong., 2d Sess., pp. 5–6 (1964). It has been estimated that over 20,000 lie detector tests have been administered per year. See William A. Creech, "The Privacy of Government Employees," *Law and Contemporary Problems,* XXXI (Spring 1966), 418.

[38] Quoted in Alan F. Westin, *Privacy and Freedom* (New York: Atheneum, 1967), p. 153.

[39] *Ervin Report,* pp. 21–22.

[40] Personality tests were used primarily in the Departments of State and Defense and the Bonneville Power Administration on a limited basis, and in the Peace Corps on a mass basis. See Westin, *Privacy,* p. 256, and Gallagher Hearings, pp. 176, 222.

little love and companionship in my family as compared to other homes." [41] Gallagher concluded that the information obtained through such tests could be misused because "confidentiality of government files is a myth. Such files float from agency to agency. Federal investigators in some instances are given access to information far removed from the subject of their inquiry." [42] A similar issue was raised when Form 89, a questionnaire originally designed for use by patients in government hospitals, was required on a mass basis for employees in the Department of Housing and Urban Development, NSA, Library of Congress, and Small Business Administration.[43] Among the form's questions were: "Have you ever had or have you now: Frequent or terrifying nightmares? Bed wetting? Nervous trouble of any source?" [44]

There have been other invasions of privacy. Beginning in 1965 some civil servants have been required to list

all assets, or everything you and your immediate family own, including date acquired and cost or fair market value at acquisition. (Cash in banks, cash anywhere else, due from others—loans, etc., automobiles, securities, real estate, cash surrender of life insurance; personal effects and household furnishings and other assets.) [45]

[41] See Westin, *Privacy,* pp. 260–68, for this and other tests.

[42] Gallagher Hearings, p. 398.

[43] *Washington Daily News,* November 11, 1966; quoted in U.S., *Congressional Record,* 90th Cong., 1st Sess., CXIII, No. 159 (October 5, 1967).

[44] *Ibid.* There was also a special section for women, asking, "Have you ever been pregnant?" and seven questions about the individual's menstrual cycle.

[45] *Ervin Report,* p. 26. This requirement began with the issuance of Executive Order 11222, U.S. *Federal Register,* XXX, Part 6, 6469 (May 8, 1965), which was initially intended to apply only to about 2,000 political appointees. However, it was allegedly extended to hundreds of thousands of others, many of whom were in the lower

During 1966, civil servants were also asked to state whether they were American Indian, Oriental, Negro, Spanish American, or none of these under regulations overtly intended to promote equal employment opportunity.[46] Other privacy-invading practices have included the use of "spy holes" in the men's rest rooms at the Pentagon,[47] phone tapping in the Internal Revenue Service,[48] closed circuit television surveillance in military installations, [49] two-way mirrors and other surveillance techniques in post offices,[50] and interviews which "could only have been the product of inordinately salacious minds." [51]

Coercion of employees and big-brotherism has also been widespread. In a Defense Department installation,

the office chief called meetings of different groups of employees throughout the day. . . A recording was played while the employees listened about 30 minutes. It was supposedly a speech made at a university which went deeply into the importance of integration of the races. . . . There was discussion of the United Nations—what a great thing it was—and how there could never be another world war.[52]

In other instances civil servants were urged to attend a lecture by a sociologist on the importance of integration, and a record

grades and non-policy-making positions. U.S., *Congressional Record,* 89th Cong., 2d Sess., CXII, No. 130 (August 9, 1966); *Washington Evening Star,* June 9, 1967; quoted in *Congressional Record,* CXIII, Part 19, 25433 (September 13, 1967).

[46] *Ervin Report,* p. 12.

[47] Robert G. Sherrill, "U.S. Civil Service: Washington's Bland Bondage," *The Nation,* February 20, 1967; quoted in *Congressional Record,* CXIII, No. 126 (February 21, 1967).

[48] *Ibid.*

[49] *Washington Daily News,* January 30, 1967; quoted in U.S., *Congressional Record,* 90th Cong., 2d Sess., CXIV, No. 103 (June 17, 1967).

[50] Creech, *Law and Contemporary Problems,* XXXI, 417.

[51] *Ervin Report,* p. 20.   [52] *Ibid.,* p. 15.

was kept of those attending;[53] employees were required "to attend film lectures on issues of the Cold War";[54] a record was kept of civil servants "who are participating in any activities including such things as: PTA in integrated schools, sports activities which are inter-social, and such things as Great Books discussion groups which have integrated memberships";[55] employees have also been requested "to participate in community activities to improve the employability of minority groups";[56] "to lobby in local city councils for fair housing ordinances, to go out and make speeches on any number of subjects, to supply flower and grass seed for beautification projects and to paint other people's houses";[57] and they have been required to participate in such groups as the Urban League and the National Association for the Advancement of Colored People.[58] The financial disclosure requirements led to "the establishment of counseling systems in the departments so that employees may go to their advisors before they or members of their families engage in outside activities, buy property, or seek credit."[59] Similarly, a Defense Department directive informed civil servants that "it is advisable to study and seek wise and mature counsel prior to the association with persons or organizations of any political or civil nature."[60] There has also been "outright coercion and intimidation of employees to buy everything from savings bonds to electric light bulbs for playgrounds,"[61] and in at least one

---

[53] *Ibid.*, p. 16.   [54] *Ibid.*   [55] *Ibid.*, p. 18.

[56] *Ibid.* Requests such as this one have often been enforced by the threat that "failure to participate would indicate an uncooperative attitude and would be reflected in . . . efficiency records" (*ibid.*, p. 9).

[57] *Ibid.*, p. 9.   [58] *Ibid.*, p. 17.

[59] *Congressional Record*, CXII, No. 114 (July 18, 1966).

[60] *Ibid.*, CXIII, No. 63 (April 25, 1967).

[61] *Ibid.*, CXII, No. 130 (August 9, 1966).

agency civil servants have been threatened with "possible reprisals and effects in their standing in the agency if they wrote to their Congressmen or exercised rights under the agency procedures to file a grievance complaint." [62]

Under pressure from congressional subcommittees headed by Gallagher, Congressman John E. Moss of California, Senator Ervin of North Carolina, and Senator Edward Long of Missouri [63] many of the foregoing practices have been restricted or abandoned entirely. The use of lookouts by the Post Office in men's rest rooms was discontinued in December 1964.[64] The Defense Department directive concerning organizational and personal associations has been canceled.[65] The CSC has prohibited denials of the right to file grievances and appeals or reprisals for exercising the right.[66] The use of financial questionnaires has been limited "to those positions in which the possibility of conflict of interest involvement is clear." [67] In May 1965 the CSC restated its policy concerning the use of personality tests:

The Commission does not itself use and prohibits agencies from using personality tests . . . in any personnel action affecting employees or positions in the competitive service. This does not, of

[62] U.S., Congress, Senate, Committee on the Judiciary, *Monthly Staff Report to the Subcommittee on Constitutional Rights,* February 1, 1967, p. 1.

[63] Long was chairman of the Subcommittee on Administrative Practice and Procedure of the Senate Committee on the Judiciary during *Hearings on Invasions of Privacy* held during the 89th Congress. Moss headed the subcommittee of the House Committee on Government Operations cited *supra.*

[64] Creech, *Law and Contemporary Problems,* XXXI, 417.

[65] *Washington Daily News,* June 1, 1967; quoted in *Congressional Record,* CXIII, Part 19, 25430 (September 13, 1967).

[66] *Ibid.*

[67] *Washington Evening Star,* June 9, 1967; quoted in *Congressional Record,* CXIII, Part 19, 25433.

course, relate to the proper use of such tests by a qualified psychiatrist or psychologist when, in his professional judgment, they would assist in his total study of an individual in connection with medical determinations for employment or fitness for duty.[68]

The Peace Corps, which is not under CSC regulations, eliminated 185 true-false questions from its test, which for technical reasons had not been scored previously anyway. These included "I feel sure that there is only one true religion," "I think Lincoln was greater than Washington," "There is something wrong with my sex organs," and "I deserve severe punishment for my sins." [69] Finally, in 1964 the armed forces and the NSA limited the conditions under which polygraphs could be used, and in 1965 the Defense Department limited their use to matters involving crime and national security and prohibited investigation into attitudes on political, religious, and social matters.[70]

Despite these changes, Senator Ervin has led an attempt, which may prove successful, to prohibit many of the remaining privacy-invading, coercive, and big-brother-type practices. His major arguments have been that these practices "will result in an intimidated, lack-luster, unimaginative and fearful civil service." [71] and that the racial questionnaires would result in a quota system for federal employment; [72] that "practices which [adversely] affect ten million citizens and their families can [adversely] affect an entire society"; [73] and that these practices are unconstitutional because "just because he

---

[68] Gallagher Hearings, p. 38. In other words they were limited to a few positions.

[69] *Ibid.*, pp. 242–45.   [70] Westin, *Privacy*, p. 234.

[71] *Congressional Record*, CXII, No. 114 (July 18, 1966).

[72] *Ibid.*

[73] U.S., Congress, Senate, Committee on the Judiciary, *Monthly Staff Report to the Subcommittee on Constitutional Rights*, May 5, 1967, p. 2.

goes to work for government, an employee does not surrender the basic liberties guaranteed every citizen under
our form of government." [74] Ervin, supported by all the major
employee organizations and such groups as the American
Civil Liberties Union, has introduced legislation "intended to
be a bill of rights for government employees." [75] The most
successful of these bills was S. 1035,[76] which would

prohibit indiscriminate requirements that employees and applicants
for Government employment disclose their race, religion or national origin; attend Government-sponsored meetings and lectures
or participate in outside activities unrelated to their employment;
report on their outside activities or undertakings unrelated to
their work; submit to questioning about their religion, personal
relationships or sexual attitudes through interviews, psychological
tests, or polygraphs; support political candidates or attend political
meetings. It would make it illegal to coerce an employee to buy
bonds or make charitable contributions; or to require him to
disclose his own personal assets, liabilities, or expenditures, or
those of any member of his family unless, in the case of certain
specified employees, such items would tend to show a conflict of interest. It would provide a right to have counsel or other person
present, if the employee wishes, at an interview which may lead to
disciplinary proceedings. It would accord the right to a civil action
in a Federal Court for violation or threatened violation of the act,
and it would establish a Board on Employees' Rights to receive and
conduct hearings on complaints of violation of the act, and to
determine and administer remedies and penalties.[77]

The Senate passed the bill on September 13, 1967, by a vote
of 79 to 4, but it was never reported out of committee in the
House.[78]

[74] *Ibid.*
[75] U.S., *Congressional Record,* 89th Cong., 2d Sess., CXII, No.
130 (August 9, 1966).
[76] Ninetieth Cong., 1st Sess.   [77] Ervin Report, p. 3.
[78] *Congressional Record,* CXIII, Part 19, 25457. Eleven of the sev-

IV

In recent years there have also been important demands for a revision of regulations concerning political neutrality, some actual revision, and significant state court decisions which have indicated that the degree of perceived incompatibility between the roles of citizen and civil servant and support for negative discriminations of the public employment relationship have been declining. In 1966, a bipartisan Commission on Political Activity of Government Personnel to study the existing provisions for political neutrality and make suggestions for their improvement was created by Public Law 89–617.[79] The commission, which reported toward the end of 1967, concluded that

---

enteen senators not voting would have voted for it if present. Senators Eastland, Hollings, Russell, and Stennis voted against it. The CIA, NSA, and the FBI were exempt from some provisions. Ervin reintroduced the same bill as S. 782 in the 91st Congress on January 31, 1969. The bill has been sponsored by 28 Democrats and 26 Republicans representing 38 states. The platforms of both major parties acknowledged the issue in the 1968 campaign. The Republicans, for example, stated "the increasing government intrusion into the privacy of its employees and of citizens in general is intolerable." See *ibid.,* 91st Cong., 1st Sess., CXV, No. 21 (January 31, 1969). Major opposition to the bill has come from the CSC. Chairman Macy, for instance, opposes "the current exclusive emphasis placed on the protection of individual rights with no concurrent recognition that individuals also have obligations." CSC, *Annual Report,* LXXXV, 38. He also believes that "it is important that legislation which deals with a significant aspect of personnel management be administered by an established central agency currently charged with the enforcement of other personnel legislation" (*ibid.,* p. 40). Ervin, on the other hand, believes that no basic changes concerning the problems involved will be forthcoming unless "the basic legal and administrative structures which can produce the injustices" are altered. See U.S., Congress, Senate, Committee on the Judiciary, *Monthly Staff Report to the Subcommittee on Constitutional Rights,* January–February 1969, p. 2.

[79] See U.S., Commission on Political Activity of Government Personnel, *Report* (Washington: U.S. Government Printing Office, 1968).

since 1939, when the Hatch Act was enacted, the American political system has changed dramatically. The growth of Federal responsibilities, the parallel growth of technology in Government, and the need for skilled personnel are eroding away traditional patronage schemes.[80]

It argued that

the best protection that the government can provide for its personnel is to prohibit those activities that tend to corrode a career system based on merit. This requires strong sanctions against coercion. It also requires some limits on the role of the government employee in politics.[81]

The Commission proposed, however, legislation which would expand, "within limits, the area of political activity permitted for Federal employees" [82] and which placed a greater emphasis on abolishing coercion. With respect to the latter, it suggested the establishment of an Office of Employee Counsel within the CSC to which civil servants could report instances of political coercion, intimidation, misuse of official authority, or other violations of the law.[83] The proposed legislation also provided for judicial review of adverse decisions.[84] Whether the Commission's bill, or any of its features, will be enacted into law remains to be seen. It is significant, however, that the CSC has also concluded that "1939 ground rules were not altogether suitable for the 1960's, [and] . . . recommended that permitted political activities be expanded, particularly at the local level; that protections afforded to public servants be strengthened; that the coverage of the law be clarified and

[80] *Ibid.,* I, 10.   [81] *Ibid.,* p. 3.   [82] *Ibid.*

[83] This suggestion was made despite the fact that the Commission found that political coercion was rather rare. See *ibid.,* p. 18. However, if some restrictions on political activity were abolished, coercion might increase.

[84] *Ibid.,* p. 51, sec. 1625 e.

modified; that deterrent and penalty provisions be made more equitable and effective; and, finally, that better means of administration and enforcement be provided." [85]

In *Wilson* v. *C.S.C.*[86] the scope of political activities for which a civil servant could be removed or suspended under the First Hatch Act was limited. An employee wrote a letter to a newspaper for publication which stated: "I respect Republicans as such. I respect Democrats as such. No one respects a renegade. Let's send Allan Shivers home." [87] The court reasoned that under the statute,

in each case . . . the critical distinction which must be drawn is whether an employee has expressed and communicated independent, personal opinions on political issues, or whether such employee with deliberation and as part of concerted political action, has sought the election or defeat of political candidates.[88]

The court concluded that the employee acted independently and held that in order to decrease the risk employees take by expressing political views the CSC should

resolve close questions—those in which genuine doubt exists as to the act of expression, the substance of the expression, or both— by taking evidence to indicate whether the statement of opinion does in fact represent active participation in a political campaign, and was so intended. Isolated or inferred contribution is not enough.[89]

In *Fort* v. *C.S.C.*[90] and *Kinnear* v. *San Francisco*[91] the California Supreme Court, and in *Minielly* v. *Oregon*[92] the Oregon Supreme Court, found provisions for political neu-

---

[85] CSC, *Annual Report,* LXXXV, 41.

[86] 136 F. Supp. 104 (1955).

[87] *Ibid.,* p. 104. Shivers was a candidate for nomination for governor by the Democratic party of Texas.

[88] *Ibid.,* p. 106.   [89] *Ibid.,* p. 107.   [90] 61 Cal. 2d 331 (1964).

[91] 61 Cal. 2d 341 (1964).   [92] 242 Ore. 490 (1966).

trality to be unconstitutional due to overbreadth. In *Bagley* v. *Hospital District,* the California court reached the same conclusion but implicitly raised the issue of whether the *United Public Workers* v. *Mitchell* [93] decision was still valid under the principles of the doctrine of substantial interest. The Court declared the doctrine of privilege to have been "utterly discredited" despite its antiquity, [94] and argued that the standards to be met in such cases were

(1) that the political restraints rationally relate to the enhancement of the public service, (2) that the benefits which the public gains by the restraints outweigh the resulting impairment of constitutional rights, and (3) that no alternatives less subversive of constitutional rights are available.[95]

Moreover, the Court appeared to invoke a form of the clear and present danger test rejected by *United Public Workers:* "The sweeping prohibitions of the statute and the directive are not necessary to the successful functioning of the civil service system." [96]

V

In recent years the Supreme Court has increased the constitutional rights of some civil servants by creating a positive discrimination of the public employment relationship with regard to the law of libel, and subsequently established a negative discrimination to more or less balance it. In 1896, the Supreme Court established the constitutional principle that

in exercising the functions of his office the head of an Executive Department, keeping within the limits of his authority, should not be under an apprehension that the motives that control his official

[93] 330 U.S. 75 (1947). See chap. 4, *supra.*
[94] 421 P. 2d 409, 412–13.   [95] *Ibid.,* p. 411.
[96] *Ibid.,* p. 416.

conduct may, at any time, become the subject of inquiry in a civil suit for damages. It would seriously cripple the proper and effective administration of public affairs as entrusted to the executive branch of the government, if he were subject to any such restraint.[97]

In *Barr* v. *Matteo* [98] the Court was presented with the issue of whether this principle applied to lower ranking civil servants as well. Barr, the acting director of the Office of Rent Stabilization, had issued a press release in which he announced his intention to suspend two employees because of their part in a plan for utilizing agency funds which had been severely criticized in Congress. The Court's judgment was in favor of Barr, but there was no majority opinion. Justice Harlan was joined by Justices Frankfurter, Clark, and Whittaker in an opinion in which he argued:

It has been thought important that officials of the government should be free to exercise their duties unembarrassed by the fear of damage suits in respect of acts done in the course of those duties—suits which would consume time and energies which would otherwise be devoted to governmental service and the threat of which might appreciably inhibit the . . . administration of polices of government.

. . . . .

To be sure, the occasions upon which the acts of the head of a department will be protected by the privilege are doubtless far broader than in the case of an officer with less sweeping functions. But it is because the higher the post, the broader the range of responsibilities and duties, and the wider the scope of discretion it entails. It is not the title of his office but the duties with which the particular officer sought to be made to respond in damages is entrusted—the relation of the act complained of to "matters com-

---

[97] *Spalding* v. *Vilas,* 161 U.S. 483, 498.
[98] 360 U.S. 564 (1959).

mitted by law to his control or supervision" . . . which must
provide the guide in delineating the scope of the rule which
clothes the official acts of the executive officer with immunity
from civil defamation suits.[99]

Harlan concluded that the speech involved was within the
line of duty and entitled to "absolute privilege." [100] Justice
Black concurred in the Court's judgment on the basis that

if federal employees are to be subjected to such restraints in re-
porting their views about how to run the government better, the
restraints will have to be imposed expressly by Congress and not
by the general libel laws of the states or the District of Columbia.[101]

Chief Justice Warren dissented in an opinion joined by
Justice Douglas. He argued against positive discrimination in
this area because it might lead to the destruction of "the
opportunity to criticize the administration of our Government
and the action of its officials without being subjected to unfair—and absolutely privileged—retorts." [102]

The positive discrimination established in *Barr* was neu-
tralized in *New York Times* v. *Sullivan*.[103] The issue was
whether a public official could recover libel damages for false
statements made by citizens with reference to issues of public

---

[99] *Ibid.*, pp. 571, 573–74.   [100] *Ibid.*, pp. 574, 576.

[101] *Ibid.*, p. 577. Black continued: "How far the Congress . . .
could go in barring federal officials and employees from discussing
public matters consistently with the First Amendment is a question we
need not reach in this case," but if he still adhered to his opinion in
United Public Workers it would appear that the realm in which such
speech could be prohibited was rather circumscribed.

[102] *Ibid.*, p. 584. Justice Brennan dissented on the ground that only
a qualified privilege was necessary. Justice Stewart also dissented.
He agreed with Harlan's reasoning but did not believe that the action involved had been taken in the line of duty. See also *Howard* v.
Lyons, 360 U.S. 593 (1959).

[103] 376 U.S. 254 (1964).

interest. The Court, per Justice Brennan, held that the public official could only recover if "he proves that the statement was made with 'actual malice'—that is, with knowledge that it was false or with reckless disregard of whether it was false or not." [104] Brennan's attempt to balance the *Barr* principle was overt: "It would give public servants an unjustified preference over the public they serve, if critics of official conduct did not have a fair equivalent of the immunity granted to the officials themselves." [105] The Court did not determine how far "into the lower ranks of government employees the 'public official' designation would extend," [106] but in *Rosenblatt* v. *Baer* [107] it held that the ruling "applies at the very least to those among the hierarchy of government employees who have, or appear to the public to have, substantial responsibility for or control over the conduct of governmental affairs." [108] Therefore, at the present time it appears that the domain of discrimination of the two kinds of libel action is approximately the same.

VI

In recent years there has been widespread dissatisfaction with negative discriminations of the public employment relationship and significant attempts have been made to reconcile the roles of citizen and civil servant. The most important expressions of this dissatisfaction and/or efforts at reconciliation

---

[104] *Ibid.*, pp. 279–80. [105] *Ibid.*, pp. 282–83.

[106] *Ibid.*, p. 283n. [107] 383 U.S. 75 (1966).

[108] *Ibid.*, p. 85. See also *Garrison* v. *Louisiana,* 379 U.S. 64 (1964). Justice Black, joined by Justice Douglas, concurred in *New York Times* on the basis that the First and Fourteenth Amendments prohibited states from awarding damages to public officials against critics of their official conduct. Justice Goldberg, also joined by Douglas, concurred, but argued that the validity of criticism of public officials should not depend on the motivations involved.

have been the executive orders concerning labor relations, the considerably successful attempts to prohibit invasions of privacy, coercion, and big-brotherism in the civil service and the extensive Senatorial support for the Ervin bill, the limitations imposed on the application of the First Hatch Act by the *Wilson* case, the suggestions of the CSC and the Commission on Political Activity of Government Personnel, the *Bagley* decision, and the *Barr* and *New York Times* cases. The present emphasis on equality of access to civil service positions, the partial decrease in the range of discrimination involved in regulations for loyalty-security since the latter half of the 1950's, and, of course, the emergence of the doctrine of substantial interest are also representative of current attitudes and practices concerning the public employment relationship. Furthermore, the Kennedy orders, the Ervin bill, and the Political Activity Commission's suggestions are indicative of a current emphasis on protecting civil servants from arbitrary actions and informal or illegal negative discriminations.

It is probable, although far from certain, that the present emphasis on reconciling the roles of citizen and civil servant and decreasing the importance of negative discrimination will continue if the size of public employment and the political power of civil service unions continue to grow, and if the perceived inability of the civil service to attract personnel of the desired quality continues and remains partially blamed on infringements upon civil servants' constitutional rights. It is also possible, but even less certain, that if the prestige, power, and perhaps social status of higher ranking civil servants and/or the civil service remains approximately at the present level or increases, the current emphasis will continue or conceivably tend toward positive discrimination as was the case prior to the development of the spoils system. In any event, it appears that the public employment relationship has entered, or is on the threshold of, a new phase in which the rights of civil servants will be greater and afforded more protection than in the recent and much of the distant past.

Conclusion

The relationship between the citizen and the state in public employment in America has been an important feature of United States political development from the founding period to the present time. The relationship has consistently been discriminatory and negative in direction, although there have been positive discriminations at various times, and the range of discrimination has varied widely. The negatively discriminatory relationship in the United States has been the immediate result of an apparent and perceived incompatibility between the role of citizen and that of civil servant, and of general tension between bureaucracy and democracy. The fundamental importance of the relationship has been twofold. It has been related to attempts to control the gross characteristics of bureaucracy by regulating the selection and behavior of civil servants. It has also been a partial determinative of the constitutional rights of the large and increasing number of citizens who are public employees as well. In recent years, as at various times in the past, the nature of the relationship has been widely debated in the courts, Congress, and executive branch of the government. The development of the public employment relationship in the United States cannot be correlated with one or two factors. Rather, it has been influenced by a wide variety of political, economic, and social forces. The evolution of the relationship can be summarized in the following manner.

Between 1776 and 1829 a negatively discriminatory relationship developed although there was an important tendency toward positive discrimination. Development during this period was largely influenced by legacies of colonial administration and the evolution of institutionalized political competition. During the founding period there was, as a result of the colonial experience, widespread suspicion of and hostility toward public officials. This attitude was influential in the establishment, by the Continental Congress, the Articles of Confederation, and the Constitution, of regulations for the behavior and selection of civil servants which abridged their ordinary citizenship rights. It was also at least partly responsible for the Constitution's basic caution toward appointed executive officials and for the outcome of the Decision of 1789, which, by allowing unrestrained removal of presidential officers, encouraged a negatively discriminatory public employment relationship. Although the selection of civil servants on the basis of their political opinions was present from the outset, the negative discrimination of political removal was added to the range of discrimination as partisan political competition became more important in the administrations of Presidents John Adams and Jefferson. In 1820, these discriminations were facilitated somewhat by the Tenure of Office Act. Throughout the period, however, civil service appointments tended to come from the upper social classes, kinship was important in recruitment, tenure was often *de facto* for life, and there was an important tendency to consider office to be a form of property. Consequently, office was sometimes informally inherited, removals for cause relating to character were usually accompanied by some kind of informal due process, and there was an important, although not dominant, tendency toward positive discrimination. During this period, many elements of the public employment relationship were present, including loyalty testing and political neutrality, which gained greater importance in later years. The degree and domain of various discriminations of the relationship during the period are difficult to estimate, but it appears that the range of discrimination was considerable.

The spoils system was introduced on the federal level in 1829 by President Jackson. It thoroughly altered the public employment relationship and created a highly politicized public personnel system and bureaucracy. Jackson found the principle of rotation in office useful for several reasons. It could destroy the concept of property in office and reduce the importance of the upper social classes in American politics. It could provide a rationalization for the civil service removals that he, as the first president since Jefferson to be elected in opposition to an incumbent administration, would find it politically desirable to make. It could also be of utility in solving the problems of superannuation and disability in the civil service which had resulted from previous reluctance to make removals. It was possible for the spoils principle to be applied in practice because there were no important legal restrictions on the executive removal power, despite some attempts to establish such limitations by the Whigs, and because, as the Supreme Court confirmed in *Ex parte Hennen* (1839), it was believed at the time that the Constitution did not limit the reasons for which a civil servant could be removed legitimately. It was also necessary for the nature of many civil service tasks to be relatively simple, and in agencies, such as the Patent Office and Life-Saving Service, which performed technical functions the spoils system was less important. The principle was continued in practice after the Jackson administration because there were strong political and economic pressures for one party to make political removals and appointments after the other had done so. Thus the Whigs accepted the principle after their electoral victory of 1840, and it was significant that the spoils system thrived during that period of United States history in which party control of the presidency changed most frequently.

Jackson's appointment ideology and the spoils system made the civil service more sociologically representative of the nation as a whole. The overall effect of the spoils system on the public employment relationship was, however, to extend the range of discrimination by increasing the importance of political appointment and removal, and by introducing coerced political activity and political assessment. The spoils era marked an important turning point in the evolution of the public employment relationship because it was the last time that partisan political activity on the part of civil servants would be encouraged and the last time that most of the more important negative discriminations would be determined and applied on an informal basis, rather than by law or formal regulation.

The civil service reform movement fundamentally reoriented the bureaucracy and had important consequences for the public employment relationship. The reformers, as a whole, were sociologically representative of a social group similar to that which had been politically important prior to the introduction of the spoils system. Their reforms, which were to be effected by law, were intended to relegate professional politicians, who thrived on spoils, to a minor place in the political system. They hoped to restore political leadership to men such as themselves, to raise the moral level of political life, and to make the civil service less corrupt and more efficient. Following Jackson, then, the reformers attempted to bring about fundamental political change by altering the character of the civil service. Their specific reforms were intended to apply almost entirely to that part of the civil service which they considered to be purely administrative or businesslike, and were meant to disassociate it from politics and politics from it. The primary success of the reform movement was immediately due to the assassination of President Garfield in 1881 and to the Republican party's defeat in the mid-term election of the following year. More fundamentally, the spoils system had created political and administrative effects which made it appear anachronistic as public policy began to become increasingly positive and as the nature of civil service tasks began to make more positions less suitable for unpracticed men.

The effects of reform on the public employment relationship were complex. With regard to equality of access to civil service positions, the reformers substituted merit and fitness of a practical nature for political selection in the classified service. They also sought to decrease the range of discrimination by eliminating coerced political activities and financial contributions. This attempt, however, was unsuccessful and the reformers' concept of an apolitical civil service encouraged the adoption of regulations prohibiting civil servants from taking active part in political campaigns and management. The result was to extend the range of discrimination considerably.

Toward the end of its importance as a political movement, reform encouraged the adoption of limitations on the executive power of removal which allowed civil servants to seek judicial redress for arbitrary removals and made informal negative discriminations somewhat more difficult to apply. Reform, like spoils, marked a turning point in the development of the public employment relationship and since its reorientation of the civil service the relationship has tended to center on specific issues, rather than on broad attempts to bring about fundamental political change.

Since the early 1900's, political neutrality has been an

important feature of the evolution of the public employment relationship and of the United States civil service. The basic rationale for the restriction of the political activities of civil servants has been to insure the overt impartiality of the bureaucracy and of individual civil servants, and to prevent civil servants, either under coercion or of their own volition, from using whatever political, economic, or social influence or authority accrues to them, by virtue of their official positions, in the partisan political arena. Although Jefferson formulated a concept of political neutrality and there were attempts to restrict the political activities of civil servants during the spoils period, the adoption of such restrictions was successful only after the reformers succeeded in establishing the desirability of nonpoliticized public personnel administration. After limited and/or ineffective executive orders by Presidents Grant, Hayes, and Cleveland, President Theodore Roosevelt, in 1907, promulgated a regulation prohibiting classified civil servants from taking active part in political management and campaigns. Roosevelt's order also prohibited these civil servants from expressing publicly their opinions on political subjects. The Civil Service Commission's interpretation of this regulation created a high degree of discrimination in the negative direction and made United States regulations concerning political neutrality among the most restrictive of any in democratic political systems.

In the 1930's, as the New Deal and the concept of the welfare state created important changes in the functions of the bureaucracy and its size, as the proportion of civil servants in the classified service declined, and as some newly established agencies were increasingly believed to be involved in state and local politics during President Franklin D. Roosevelt's purge, there were significant demands for extending the domain of discrimination concerning political neutrality to nonclassified

employees. These demands resulted in the enactment of the
First Hatch Act (1939), which basically extended the 1907
regulations to almost the entire civil service and in a rather
ambiguous fashion tended toward a decrease in the degree of
discrimination by not limiting civil servants' legitimate political expression to private statements. Political neutrality is
probably the most significant feature of the public employment relationship at the present time because it constitutes a
sizable part of the range of discrimination, and is of fundamental systemic importance.

The degree of citizen equality of access to civil service
positions has also been an important element of the public
employment relationship and one which is of overall significance to the political system as well. It is generally agreed that
the sociological representativeness of a bureaucracy affects its
integration with other features of a political system and its
performance, and that the inclusion or exclusion of groups
from the civil service affects their political influence and social
status. Historically, in the United States, there have been
important formal and informal abridgments of citizen equality
of access based upon social class status, kinship, race, religion,
sex, ethnicity, merit, fitness, veteran status, residence, and
political and other opinions. Many of these interferences with
citizen equality are clearly negative discriminations, but in
some instances this determination can be made only on an
ex post facto basis because the constitutional requirement of
equal protection is vague. Important developments in this area
have taken place since the late 1930's as President Roosevelt
and other officials attempted to unify the nation and increase
its productivity by prohibiting abridgments of equality based
upon race, color, religion, and ethnicity in the civil service
and in defense industries. These developments were also
furthered by the evolving civil rights movement. Since that

time racial, chromatic, religious, sexual, and ethnic equality of access have been guaranteed as a matter of policy. Moreover, it appears that at the present time negative discriminations based on any of these characteristics, except perhaps sex under certain circumstances, would be unconstitutional. In recent years, however, increased emphasis has been placed on formal negative discriminations involving the exclusion of individuals whose political and other opinions and behavior are thought to indicate that they are more likely than most citizens to use civil service positions to undermine the authority of the government or to engage in subversion.

Regulations intended to insure the loyalty of the bureaucracy and to prevent individual civil servants from using their special positions, authority, or influence for subversive purposes have had important effects upon the development of the public employment relationship. During much of the decade following World War II the nature of these regulations and the need for them was an extremely important political issue. Although there were regulations for loyalty-security during the Revolution, the Civil War, and World War I, it was not until the enactment of the First Hatch Act that loyalty-security became a lasting and fundamental feature of the civil service and of the public employment relationship. Modern provisions for loyalty-security were adopted largely as a result of World War II, the Cold War, the Communist victory in China, the widespread belief that the federal bureaucracy had been infiltrated by numerous subversives, the Korean War, and the McCarthy era generally. In practice these regulations led to a large domain and a high degree of discrimination in the negative direction by proscribing a wide range of unorthodox and unpopular opinions and behavior.

Constitutional issues presented by political neutrality, equality of access to civil service positions, and loyalty-security have also been important in the development of the judicial doctrines concerning the public employment relationship. The primary doctrines affecting the relationship have been those of privilege and substantial interest. Whereas the doctrine of privilege held that "the due process of law clause of the Fifth Amendment does not restrict the president's discretion or the prescriptive power of Congress in respect to excutive personnel," [1] the newer doctrine is based on the principles that "while there may be no constitutional right to public employment, there is a constitutional right to be free from unreasonably discriminatory practices with respect to such employment" [2] and "the government cannot condition admission to such employment . . . upon any terms that it may choose to impose." [3] The doctrine of substantial interest provides civil servants with greater substantive and procedural constitutional rights and has completely replaced the doctrine of privilege. Each doctrine has been composed of decisions on the issues involved in political neutrality, equality of access, and loyalty-security. It was, however, in the area of equal protection that the doctrine of privilege began to lose its influence, and in loyalty-security cases that it was rejected fully. Although the dominance of the doctrine of substantial interest is a very recent phenomenon, the principles upon which it is based were advocated by some members of Congress during debate on the Decision of 1789, and were the basis of such judicial opinions as Justice Bradley's dissent in *Ex parte Curtis* (1882) and the Virginia Court's decision in *Louthan* v. *Commonwealth* (1884).

In recent years there have been several other developments which have made, or attempted to make, the constitutional

[1] *Bailey* v. *Richardson*, 182 F. 2d 46, 58 (1950).
[2] *Whitner* v. *Davis*, 410 F. 2d 24, 30 (1969).
[3] *Bagley* v. *Hospital District*, 421 P. 2d 409, 412–13.

rights of civil servants more commensurate with those of other citizens. Civil servants have been afforded greater collective bargaining rights which, in the future, may enable them to play a greater role in the adoption or revocation of the more minor negative discriminations of the public employment relationship. They have also been granted the right to hearings on adverse personnel decisions and the right to present grievances. There have been significant demands for moderation of restrictions on the political activity of public employees, and some moderation has taken place as a result of *Wilson* v. *Civil Service Commission* (1955). The domain and degree of negative discrimination concerning loyalty-security have also been decreased in recent years, as have negative discriminations involving several areas of equality of access. The Supreme Court's decisions in *Barr* v. *Matteo* (1959) and *New York Times* v. *Sullivan* (1964) are reflective of the broad attempt to reconcile the roles and fundamental rights of citizens and civil servants which is presently taking place. It appears that barring a reversal of the current emphasis, civil servants will be afforded greater rights in the future than during most of United States political development since independence.

At this point, it is appropriate to note that within democratic political systems there are important alternatives to the discriminations of the public employment relationship adopted in the United States. The most significant differences, perhaps, can be found in the realm of political neutrality.[4] For example, in Sweden there are almost no restrictions on the political rights of civil servants. They may engage in political activity at all levels and can run for and be elected to any office while retaining their civil service employment. The only restriction

[4] See U.S., Commission on Political Activity of Government Personnel, *Report* (Washington: U.S. Government Printing Office, 1968), II, 168–71, Table 1.

on their political rights is that they cannot participate in the activities of political parties in their official capacity, but only as private citizens. In France, civil servants are allowed to express any political opinions except in a "rough and insulting" manner. They can participate in all political activity and management as citizens, but not in their official capacity. In most cases, they can also run for office at the local and national level. If they are elected to parliament they are placed in detached service and must be returned to active service if they so desire when they leave. They retain all pension and promotion rights while in parliament.[5] Japanese regulations concerning political neutrality, on the other hand, are closer to those of the United States, but somewhat more restrictive. Japanese civil servants, with some exceptions, cannot engage in political expression, in most political activity, or in political management. Violations are punishable by up to three years' imprisonment. Regulations and traditional restrictions in Australia, Great Britain, Western Germany, and Canada are more restrictive then those of Sweden and France, and more liberal than those of the United States and Japan.

There have been other variations as well. The degree of citizen equality of access to civil service positions and the characteristics upon which inequalities have been based have differed among democratic systems. For instance, it has been observed that "in Western European countries the main deviations from representative bureaucracy are in the distribution of employees by social class and, secondarily, though quite significantly, by religion."[6] Regulations and proceedings con-

[5] On the French civil service see Roger Grégoire, *The French Civil Service* (Brussels: International Institute of Administrative Sciences, n.d.). Grégoire concludes that "this extraordinary liberalism can only be explained by the country's political history" (pp. 360–61).

[6] Samuel Krislov, *The Negro in Federal Employment* (Minneapolis: University of Minnesota Press, 1967), p. 59. See also Brian Chapman,

cerning loyalty-security have been more circumscribed in Great Britain and France and considerably less politicized than in the United States. For example, in France, under a ruling of the *Conseil d'Etat,* applicants cannot be excluded on the basis of ideological beliefs or opinions, and dismissals for disloyalty are only sustained if the *fonctionnaire* has committed overt misconduct such as participation in spying or in antinational organizations.[7] Concerning labor relations with public employees, a difference in attitudes was evident in 1947 when civil services strikes were outlawed in the United States while French *fonctionnaires* were afforded the same labor rights as other citizens.[8] Finally, in practice, the range of causes for which civil servants could be removed legitimately has varied according to the procedural job security they have been afforded in different political systems. For instance,

in all Scandinavian countries except Finland the civil servant's right to his post is almost a vested right. In Sweden the Constitution not only guarantees the official against removal except after trial, but also protects him from any transfer except with his own consent. The Norwegian Constitution follows this very closely.

The Profession of Government (London: George Allen and Unwin, 1959), pp. 151, 284–85, 315–16; and V. Subramaniam, "Representative Bureaucracy: A Reassessment," *American Political Science Review,* LXI (December 1967), 1010–19. Although there has been little comparative analysis of the development of public employment relationships, Chapman's study provides some useful comparisons with regard to Western Europe.

[7] See Mark R. Joleson, "Legal Problems in the Dismissal of Civil Servants in the United States, Britain and France," *American Journal of Comparative Law,* XII (Spring 1963), 168.

[8] See Leonard D. White, "Strikes in the Public Service," *Public Personnel Review,* X (January 1949), 3; and Paul P. Van Riper, *History of the United States Civil Service* (Evanston: Row, Peterson and Co., 1958), p. 352.

. . . The Danish civil service law also protects officials from arbitrary dismissal or transfer.[9]

In France, protection against arbitrary removal has also been considerable. It has been observed that

the result of the French conception of public employment is that the civil servant has a full set of rights given him by statute and regulation. And, if these are violated, he may resort to the administrative courts just like any ordinary citizen whose personal or property rights have been infringed by the administration.[10]

Elsewhere, as in Great Britain, civil servants have been provided less legal protection than in the United States.

It is still too early to assess fully the political and administrative importance of the doctrine of substantial interest and related efforts to afford civil servants greater citizenship rights. However, at the broadest and most fundamental level recent changes in the public employment relationship will probably decrease the ability of political officials to control the selection and behavior of civil servants and therefore the gross characteristics of the federal bureaucracy. At the same time the change will probably encourage an increase in the role that civil servants will play in the political arena. Some years ago, President Harding's Secretary of Labor, James J. Davis, complained, "The simple fact is that I am am powerless to enforce changes which I desire because I am powerless to put in charge of these places individuals in sympathy with such changed policies." [11] Today, under *Pickering* v. *Board of Education* (1968) and other cases it is questionable in some instances whether officials can even remove civil servants who are openly opposed to government policy simply for

[9] Chapman, *Profession of Government*, p. 145.
[10] Joleson, *American Journal of Comparative Law*, XII, 158–59.
[11] Quoted in Van Riper, *History*, p. 287.

that reason. The possibility of civil servants engaging in public forms of opposition is far from hypothetical. For example, in March 1968 about 1,400 civil servants in the Washington, D.C., area signed the following open petition to the President:

From our position we have seen how the purpose and energy of government are drained by preoccupation with the making of war. We have seen how progress in foreign policy has been obstructed. We have seen how massive national resources are absorbed by a disastrous war while critical domestic needs are inadequately met. And seeing this we fear the political and moral consequences for the future of our country.

All this, together with the tragic and unnecessary suffering of the Vietnamese people, has troubled our conscience and now compels us to speak out to our colleagues and fellow citizens.

We call then for the war's end.[12]

If, in the future, civil servants increasingly exercise their newly guaranteed rights, it is reasonable to assume that their behavior will also effect the role of the bureaucracy in the political system. To a large extent, recent changes in the public employment relationship represent a rejection of the point of view that

the seat of reason and conscience resides in the legislature, whatever grudging concession may be made to the claims of the political executive, and a major, if not the major, task of constitutionalism is the maintenance of the supremacy of the legislature over the bureaucracy. The latter's sole constitutional role is one of neutral docility to the wishes of the day's legislative majority.[13]

[12] See David Sanford, "Our Uncivil Servants," *The New Republic,* CLVIII (April 6, 1968), 8–9. Some of the employees were in the Department of Defense, but none were in the State Department.

[13] Norton E. Long, "Bureaucracy and Constitutionalism," *American Political Science Review,* XLVI (September 1952), 808. Long opposes

These changes are clearly more compatible with the belief that "the theory of our Constitution needs to recognize and understand the working and potential of our great fourth branch of government, taking a rightful place beside President, Congress, and Courts." [14]

Although the trend toward affording civil servants greater rights appears likely to influence the role civil servants play in the political arena and the role of the bureaucracy, the actual changes which have recently taken place in the public employment relationship have been based primarily upon a conception of citizenship rights rather than upon a political theory concerning the bureaucracy vis-à-vis other elements of the political system. In this respect current developments differ greatly from the previous evolution of many of the most important features of the relationship. Pre-spoils practices, the spoils system, reform, political neutrality, and loyalty-security were all based, to a greater or lesser extent, upon a theoretical conception of what the role of the bureaucracy should or should not be. Regulations and practices effecting equality of access to civil service positions have often been founded upon similar conceptions, and even when they have been largely pragmatic in origin the normative aspects of the theory of representative bureaucracy have generally been only slightly below the surface. It appears therefore, that although major changes in the public employment relationship are not

---

this line of reasoning which underlies Charles Hyneman, *Bureaucracy in a Democracy* (New York: Harper and Bros., 1950). Hyneman believes that "to make our federal bureaucracy function as the faithful servant of the American people" (p. 5), as a rule it is necessary, among other things, "that Congress . . . specify in the statute every guide, every condition, every statement of principle that it knows in advance it wants to have applied in the situations that are expected to arise" (p. 81).

[14] Long, *American Political Science Review*, XLVI, 818.

necessarily dependent upon an explicit theoretical conception of the systemic role of the bureaucracy, any such change is likely to be of importance to that role. This interrelationship raises the issue of systematic integration of the bureaucracy once again, although in a new fashion. It also makes it reasonable to assume that, despite its historical susceptibility to unforeseen political, economic, and social forces, the development of the public employment relationship in the immediate future and the long-term viability and content of the doctrine of substantial interest will depend largely upon the effects of the recent increases in the constitutional rights of public employees, of the corresponding decrease in the ability of political officials to regulate the selection and behavior of civil servants, and of related influences upon the role of the bureaucracy in the political system.

Sources Cited

ARTICLES

Creech, William A. "The Privacy of Government Employees," *Law and Contemporary Problems,* XXXI (Spring 1966), 413–35.

Curtis, George William. "Irresponsible Executive Power," *Harper's Weekly,* XII (May 19, 1868), 306.

———. "Should the Black-Mail Be Paid?" *Harper's Weekly,* XXVIII (September 20, 1884), 612.

Cushman, Robert E. "The Purge of Federal Employees Accused of Disloyalty," *Public Administration Review,* III (Autumn 1943), 297–316.

Davis, John A. "Non-Discrimination in the Federal Services," *The Annals of the American Academy of Political and Social Science,* CCXXIV (March 1946), 65–74.

Dotson, Arch. "The Emerging Doctrine of Privilege in Public Employment," *Public Administration Review,* XV (Spring 1955), 77–78.

———. "A General Theory of Public Employment," *Public Administration Review,* XVI (Summer 1956), 197–211.

Emerson, Thomas I. and Helfeld, David M. "Loyalty among Government Employees," *Yale Law Journal,* LVIII (December 1948), 1–143.

Epstein, Leon D. "Political Sterilization of Civil Servants: The United States and Great Britain," *Public Administration Review,* X (Autumn 1950), 281–90.

Eriksson, Erik M. "The Federal Civil Service under President

Jackson," *Mississippi Valley Historical Review,* XIII (March 1927), 517–40.

Fellman, David. "The Loyalty Defendants," *Wisconsin Law Review,* CMLVII (January 1957), 4–39.

Fish, Carl R. "The Crime of Crawford," *American Historical Review,* XXI (April 1916), 545–46.

———. "Removal of Officials by the Presidents of the United States," *American Historical Association Annual Report,* I (1899), 67–86.

Friedman, Joseph M., and Tobias Klinger. "The Hatch Act: Regulation by Administrative Action of the Political Activities of Government Employees: I," *Federal Bar Journal,* VII (October 1945), 5–22.

Jahoda, Marie. "Morale in the Federal Civil Service," *The Annals of the American Academy of Political and Social Science,* CCC (July 1955), 110–13.

Jahoda, Marie, and Stuart Cook. "Security Measures and Freedom of Thought," *Yale Law Journal,* LXI (March 1952), 295–333.

Janowitz, Morris, and Diel Wright. "The Prestige of Public Employment: 1929 and 1954," *Public Administration Review,* XVI (Winter 1956), 15–21.

Joleson, Mark R. "Legal Problems in the Dismissal of Civil Servants in the United States, Britain, and France," *American Journal of Comparative Law,* XII (Spring 1963), 149–71.

Kaplan, H. Eliot. "Political Neutrality of the Civil Service," *Public Personnel Review,* I (April 1940), 10–23.

"Labor Problems in Public Employment," *Northwestern University Law Review,* LXI (March–April 1967), 105–34.

Long, Norton E. "Bureaucracy and Constitutionalism," *American Political Science Review,* XLVI (September 1952), 808–18.

Moberly, Robert B. "The Strike and Its Alternatives in Public Employment," *University of Wisconsin Law Review,* CMLXVI (Spring 1966), 549–82.

Murphy, Lionel. "The First Civil Service Commission," *Public Personnel Review,* III (January and July 1942), 29–39, 218–31.

Nesvig, Gordon T. "The New Dimensions of the Strike Question," *Public Administration Review,* XXVIII (March–April 1968), 126–32.

The New York Times, 1947, 1952, 1968, 1969, 1970.

Nikoloric, L. A. "The Government Loyalty Program," *American Scholar,* XIX (Autumn 1950), 285–98.

Posey, Rollin B. "The New Militancy of Public Employees," *Public Administration Review,* XXVIII (March–April 1968), 111–17.

Richardson, Seth. "The Federal Employee Loyalty Program," *Columbia Law Review,* LI (May 1951), 546–63.

Rose, Henry. "A Critical Look at the Hatch Act," *Harvard Law Review,* LXX (January 1962), 510–16.

Sanford, David. "Our Uncivil Servants," *The New Republic,* CLVIII (April 6, 1968), 8–9.

Schuman, Frederick L. "Bill of Attainder in the Seventy-Eighth Congress," *American Political Science Review,* XXXVII (October 1943), 819–29.

Schurz, Carl. "What is Reform?" *Harper's Weekly,* XXXVII (July 1, 1893), 614.

Subramaniam, V. "Representative Bureaucracy: A Reassessment," *American Political Science Review,* LXI (December 1967), 1010–19.

Tate, James H. J. "Public Employees' Right to Strike," *Pennsylvania Bar Association Quarterly,* XXXIX (June 1968), 527–32.

White, Leonard D. "Strikes in the Public Service," *Public Personnel Review,* X (January 1949), 3–10.

Wolgemuth, Kathleen L. "Woodrow Wilson's Appointment Policy and the Negro," *Journal of Southern History,* XXIV (November 1958), 457–71.

Zander, Arnold S. "A Union View of Collective Bargaining in the Public Service," *Public Administration Review,* XXII (Winter 1962), 5–13.

BOOKS AND PAMPHLETS

Adams, John. *The Works of John Adams.* Edited by Charles F. Adams. 10 vols. Boston: Little, Brown, and Co., 1850.

Andrews, Bert. *Washington Witch Hunt.* New York: Random House, 1948.

Aronson, Sidney. *Status and Kinship in the Higher Civil Service: Standards of Selection in the Administrations of John Adams, Thomas Jefferson, and Andrew Jackson.* Cambridge: Harvard University Press, 1964.

Barker, Charles A. *The Background of the Revolution in Maryland.* New Haven: Yale University Press, 1940.

Barth, Alan. *The Loyalty of Free Men.* New York: Viking Press, 1951.

Bell, Daniel (ed.). *The Radical Right.* Garden City: Doubleday and Co., 1964.

Bendix, Reinhard. *Higher Civil Servants in American Society.* Boulder: University of Colorado, 1949.

————. *Nation-Building and Citizenship.* New York: John Wiley and Sons, 1964.

Biddle, Francis. *The Fear of Freedom.* Garden City: Doubleday and Co., 1952.

Binkley, Wilfred. *President and Congress.* New York: Vintage Books, 1947.

Bonaparte, Charles J. *Civil Service Reform as a Moral Question.* New York: National Civil Service Reform League, 1889.

Bontecou, Eleanor. *The Federal Loyalty-Security Program.* Ithaca: Cornell University Press, 1953.

Brown, Ralph S., Jr. *Loyalty and Security.* New Haven: Yale University Press, 1958.

Chapman, Brian. *The Profession of Government.* London: George Allen and Unwin, 1959.

Civil Service Reform Association. *A Primer of Civil Service Reform.* No place: no publisher, no date.

Committee on Employee Relations in the Public Service. *Em-*

ployee Relations in the Public Service. Chicago: Civil Service Assembly, 1942.

Cunningham, Nobel E., Jr. *The Jeffersonian Republicans in Power.* Chapel Hill: University of North Carolina Press, 1963.

Curtis, George William. *Civil Service Reform Under the Present National Administration.* New York: National Civil Service Reform League, 1885.

————. *Orations and Addresses of George William Curtis.* Edited by Charles Eliot Norton. 3 vols. New York: Harper and Bros., 1894.

————. *Party and Patronage.* New York: National Civil Service Reform League, 1892.

————. *The Situation.* New York: National Civil Service Reform League, 1886.

————. *The Year's Work in Civil Service Reform.* New York: National Civil Service Reform League, 1884.

Deming, William C. *The Application of the Merit System in the United States Civil Service.* Washington: U.S. Government Printing Office, 1928.

DuBois, W. E. B. *Dusk of Dawn.* New York: Harcourt, Brace, and Co., 1940.

Eaton, Dorman B. *The Civil Service in Great Britain.* New York: Harper and Bros., 1880.

————. *The Spoils System and Civil Service Reform in the Custom-House and Post-Office at New York.* New York: G. P. Putnam's Sons, 1882.

————. *The Term and Tenure of Office.* New York: G. P. Putnam's Sons, 1882.

Farrand, Max (ed.). *Records of the Federal Convention.* 4 vols. New Haven: Yale University Press, 1911.

Fish, Carl R. *The Civil Service and the Patronage.* New York: Longmans, Green, and Co., 1905.

Foulke, William Dudley. *Fighting the Spoilsmen.* New York: G. P. Putnam's Sons, 1919.

————. *The Theory and the Practice of Civil Service Reform.*

Washington: National Civil Service Reform League, 1894.

Friedrich, Carl J., *et al. Problems of the American Public Service.* New York: McGraw-Hill, 1935.

Gellhorn, Walter. *Security, Loyalty, and Science.* Ithaca: Cornell University Press, 1950.

Godine, Morton. *The Labor Problem in the Public Service.* Cambridge: Harvard University Press, 1951.

Goldwin, Robert A. (ed.). *Political Parties U.S.A.* Chicago: Rand McNally and Co., 1964.

Graves, Edward O. *The Meaning of Civil Service Reform.* Geneva, New York: Geneva Civil Service Association, 1885.

Grégoire, Roger. *The French Civil Service.* Brussels: International Institute of Administrative Sciences, no date.

Halévy, Elie. *A History of the English People.* New York: Harcourt, Brace and Co., 1924.

Hamilton, Alexander, James Madison, and John Jay. *The Federalist Papers.* Edited by Clinton Rossiter. New York: New American Library, 1961.

Hofstadter, Richard. *Anti-Intellectualism in American Life.* New York: Vintage Books, 1963.

Hoogenboom, Ari. *Outlawing the Spoils.* Urbana: University of Illinois Press, 1961.

Hyman, Harold M. *Era of the Oath.* Philadelphia: University of Pennsylvania Press, 1954.

———. *To Try Men's Souls.* Berkeley: University of California Press, 1959.

Hyman, Sidney (ed.). *Beckoning Frontiers.* New York: Alfred A. Knopf, 1951.

Hyneman, Charles S. *Bureaucracy in a Democracy.* New York: Harper and Bros., 1950.

Irwin, James W. *Hatch Act Decisions.* Washington: U.S. Government Printing Office, 1949.

Jackson, Andrew. *The Correspondence of Andrew Jackson.* Edited by J. S. Bassett. 7 vols. Washington: Carnegie Institution, 1926.

Jameson, J. Franklin (ed.). *Essays in the Constitutional History of the United States in the Formative Period, 1775–1789.* Boston: Houghton, Mifflin and Co., 1889.

Jefferson, Thomas. *The Works of Thomas Jefferson.* Edited by P. L. Ford. 12 vols. New York: G. P. Putnam's Sons, 1904.

Kammerer, Gladys M. *Impact of War on Federal Personnel Administration, 1939–1945.* Lexington: University of Kentucky Press, 1951.

Kilpatrick, Franklin P., Milton C. Cummings, Jr., and M. Kent Jennings, *The Image of the Federal Service.* Washington: Brookings Institution, 1964.

Kingsley, J. Donald. *Representative Bureaucracy.* Yellow Springs: Antioch Press, 1944.

Krislov, Samuel. *The Negro in Federal Employment.* Minneapolis: University of Minnesota Press, 1967.

Labaree, Leonard Woods. *Royal Government in America.* New Haven: Yale University Press, 1930.

La Palombara, Joseph (ed.). *Bureaucracy and Political Development.* Princeton: Princeton University Press, 1963.

Link, Arthur S. *Wilson: The New Freedom.* Princeton: Princeton University Press, 1956.

Litwack, Leon F. *North of Slavery.* Chicago: University of Chicago Press, 1961.

Lubell, Samuel. *The Future of American Politics.* Garden City: Doubleday and Co., 1955.

McBain, Howard Lee. *De Witt Clinton and the Origin of the Spoils System in New York.* New York: Columbia University Press, 1907.

McMillin, Lucille Foster. *Women in the Federal Service.* Washington: U.S. Government Printing Office, 1941.

McWilliams, Carey. *Witch Hunt.* Boston: Little, Brown, and Co., 1950.

Morstein Marx, Fritz. *The Administrative State.* Chicago: University of Chicago Press, 1957.

National Committee on Segregation in the Nation's Capital. *Segre-

gation in Washington. Chicago: National Committee on Segregation in the Nation's Capital, 1948.

Neustadt, Richard E. *Presidential Power: The Politics of Leadership*. New York: John Wiley and Sons, 1960.

Owings, Donnell M. *His Lordship's Patronage: Offices of Profit in Colonial Maryland*. Baltimore: Maryland Historical Society, 1953.

Parton, James. *The Life of Andrew Jackson*. 3 vols. Boston: Houghton, Mifflin and Co., 1887.

Polk, James K. *The Diary of James K. Polk During His Presidency, 1845–1849*. Edited by Milo Quaife. 4 vols. Chicago: A. C. McClurg and Co., 1910.

Pritchett, C. Herman. *The American Constitution*. New York: McGraw-Hill, 1959.

Rogin, Michael Paul. *The Intellectuals and McCarthy: The Radical Specter*. Cambridge: M.I.T. Press, 1967.

Rosenberg, Hans. *Bureaucracy, Aristocracy and Autocracy: The Prussian Experience, 1660–1815*. Boston: Beacon Press, 1966.

Rossiter, Clinton, *et al. Digest of the Public Record of Communism in the United States*. New York: Fund for the Republic, 1955.

Ruchames, Louis. *Race, Jobs and Politics: The Story of F.E.P.C.* New York: Columbia University Press, 1953.

Sageser, A. B. *The First Two Decades of the Pendleton Act*. Lincoln: University of Nebraska Press, 1935.

Sayre, Wallace S. (ed.). *The Federal Government Service*. Englewood Cliffs: Prentice-Hall, 1965.

Schlesinger, Arthur, Jr. *The Age of Jackson*. Boston: Little, Brown, and Co., 1945.

Schurz, Carl. *Civil Service Reform and Democracy*. Washington: Good Government, 1893.

———. *Congress and the Spoils System*. New York: George G. Peck, 1895.

———. *The Democracy of the Merit System*. No place: National Civil Service Reform League, 1897.

————. *The Necessity and Progress of Civil Service Reform.* Washington: Good Government, 1894.

————. *Renewed Struggles.* No place: National Civil Service Reform League, 1899.

————. *The Speeches, Correspondence, and Political Papers of Carl Schurz.* Edited by Frederick Bancroft. 6 vols. New York: G. P. Putnam's Sons, 1913.

Shannon, David A. *Twentieth Century America.* Chicago: Rand McNally and Co., 1963.

Shils, Edward A. *The Torment of Secrecy.* Glencoe: The Free Press, 1956.

Spero, Sterling D. *Government As Employer.* New York: Remsen Press, 1948.

Swart, K. W. *The Sale of Offices in the Seventeenth Century.* The Hague: Martinus Nijhoff, 1949.

Sydnor, Charles S. *Gentlemen Freeholders: Political Practices in Washington's Virginia.* Chapel Hill: University of North Carolina Press, 1952.

Van Riper, Paul P. *History of the United States Civil Service.* Evanston: Row, Peterson, and Co., 1958.

Vosloo, Willem B. *Collective Bargaining in the United States Federal Civil Service.* Chicago: Public Personnel Association, 1966.

Warner, Kenneth O. *Management Relations with Organized Public Employees.* Chicago: Public Personnel Association, 1963.

Warner, W. Lloyd, *et al. The American Federal Executive.* New Haven: Yale University Press, 1963.

Washington, George. *The Writings of George Washington.* Edited by John Fitzpatrick. 39 vols. Washington: U.S. Government Printing Office, 1931.

Weber, Max. *Essays in Sociology.* Translated and edited by H. H. Gerth and C. Wright Mills. New York: Oxford Press, 1958.

Westin, Alan F. *Privacy and Freedom.* New York: Atheneum, 1967.

Weyl, Nathaniel. *The Battle Against Disloyalty.* New York: Thomas Y. Crowell, 1953.

White, Leonard D. *The Federalists.* New York: The Free Press, 1965.

————. *Further Contributions to the Prestige Value of Public Employment.* Chicago: University of Chicago Press, 1932.

————. *The Jacksonians.* New York: The Free Press, 1965.

————. *The Jeffersonians.* New York: The Free Press, 1965.

————. *The Prestige Value of Public Employment in Chicago.* Chicago: University of Chicago Press, 1929.

————. *The Republican Era.* New York: The Free Press, 1965.

Yarmolinsky, Adam. *Case Studies in Personnel Security.* Washington: Bureau of National Affairs, 1955.

CASES

Adler v. *Board of Education,* 342 U.S. 485 (1952).

Alston v. *School Board,* 112 F. 2d 992 (1940).

Baggett v. *Bullitt,* 377 U.S. 360 (1964).

Bagley v. *Washington Township Hospital District,* 421 P. 2d 409 (1966).

Bailey v. *Richardson,* 182 F. 2d 46 (1950); 341 U.S. 918 (1951); Transcript of Record.

Barr v. *Matteo,* 360 U.S. 564 (1959).

Beilan v. *Board of Public Education,* 357 U.S. 399 (1958).

Birnbaum v. *Trussell,* 371 F. 2d 672 (1966).

Bolling v. *Sharpe,* 347 U.S. 497 (1954).

Brooks v. *School District,* 267 F. 2d 733 (1959).

Butler v. *Pennsylvania,* 51 U.S. 402 (1850).

Butler v. *White,* 83 F. 578 (1897).

Cafeteria Workers v. *McElroy,* 367 U.S. 886 (1961).

Camero v. *United States,* 375 F. 2d 777 (1967).

Cole v. *Young,* 351 U.S. 536 (1956).

Commonwealth ex. rel. Rotan v. *Hasskarl,* 21 Pa. Dist. R. 119 (1912).

Cramp v. *Board of Public Instruction,* 368 U.S. 278 (1961).

Deak v. *Pace*, 185 F. 2d 997 (1950).

Elfbrandt v. *Russell*, 384 U.S. 11 (1966).

Ex Parte Curtis, 106 U.S. 371 (1876).

Ex Parte Hennen, 13 Peters 230 (1839).

Flannagan v. *Young*, 288 F. 2d 466 (1955).

Fort v. *Civil Service Commission*, 61 Cal. 2d 331 (1964).

Friedman v. *Swellenbach*, 159 F. 2d 22 (1946).

Frost Trucking v. *Railroad Commission*, 271 U.S. 583 (1925).

Fursman v. *Chicago*, 278 Ill. 318 (1917).

Gadsden v. *United States*, 111 Ct. Cl. 487 (1948).

Gardner v. *Broderick*, 392 U.S. 273 (1968).

Garner v. *Board of Public Works*, 341 U.S. 716 (1951).

Garrison v. *Louisiana*, 379 U.S. 64 (1964).

Garrity v. *New Jersey*, 385 U.S. 493 (1967).

Gilmore v. *James*, 274 F. Supp. 75 (1967).

Graves v. *Walton County Board of Education*, 410 F. 2d 1153 (1969).

Greene v. *McElroy*, 360 U.S. 474 (1959).

Herak v. *Kelly*, 391 F. 2d 216 (1968).

Hoke v. *Henderson*, 15 N.C. 1 (1833).

Howard v. *Lyons*, 360 U.S. 593 (1959).

Humphrey's Executor v. *United States*, 295 U.S. 602 (1935).

Jason v. *Summerfield*, 214 F. 2d 273 (1954).

Joint Anti-Fascist Refugee Committee v. *McGrath*, 341 U.S. 123 (1951).

Kelly v. *Herak*, 252 F. Supp. 289 (1966).

Keyishian v. *Board of Regents*, 385 U.S. 589 (1967).

Knotts v. *United States*, 121 F. Supp. 630 (1954).

Kutcher v. *Gray*, 199 F. 2d 783 (1952).

Lerner v. *Casey*, 357 U.S. 468 (1958).

Louthan v. *Commonwealth*, 79 Va. Repts. 197 (1884).

Lucia v. *Duggan*, 303 F. Supp. 112 (1969).

Manhattan-Bronx Postal Union v. *Gronouski*, 350 F. 2d 451 (1965).

McAuliffe v. *New Bedford*, 155 Mass. 216 (1892).

McDaniel v. *Board of Public Instruction,* 39 F. Supp. 638 (1941).

McLaughlin v. *Tilendis,* 398 F. 2d 287 (1968).

Meehan v. *Macy,* 392 F. 2d 882 (1968).

Meyers v. *United States,* 272 U.S. 52 (1926).

Mial v. *Ellington,* 134 N.C. 131 (1903).

Mills v. *Board of Education,* 30 F. Supp. 245 (1939).

Mills v. *Lownes,* 26 F. Supp. 792 (1939).

Minielly v. *Oregon,* 242 Or. 490 (1966).

Money v. *Anderson,* 208 F. 2d 34 (1953).

National Association of Internal Revenue Employees v. *Dillon,* 356 F. 2d 811 (1966).

Nelson v. *Los Angeles,* 362 U.S. 1 (1960).

Neusse v. *Camp,* 385 F. 2d 694 (1967).

The New York Times v. *Sullivan,* 376 U.S. 254 (1964).

Norton v. *Blaylock,* 285 F. Supp. 659 (1968).

Olson v. *Regents,* 301 F. Supp. 1356 (1969).

Parker v. *Lester,* 227 F. 2d 708 (1955).

People v. *Murrary,* 307 Ill. 349 (1923).

Peters v. *Hobby,* 349 U.S. 331 (1955).

Pickering v. *Board of Education,* 391 U.S. 563 (1968).

Railway Mail Association v. *Murphy,* 44 N.Y. 2d 601 (1943).

Rosenblatt v. *Baer,* 383 U.S. 75 (1966).

Saylor v. *United States,* 374 F. 2d 894 (1967).

Schneider v. *Smith,* 19 L. Ed. 2d 799 (1968).

Scott v. *Macy,* 349 F. 2d 182 (1965).

Shelton v. *Tucker,* 364 U.S. 479 (1960).

Sherbert v. *Verner,* 374 U.S. 398 (1963).

Slochower v. *Board of Higher Education,* 350 U.S. 551 (1956).

Spalding v. *Vilas,* 161 U.S. 483 (1896).

Steck v. *Connaly,* 199 F. Supp. 105 (1961).

Swaaley v. *United States,* 376 F. 2d 857 (1967).

Taylor v. *Taft,* 24 App. D.C. 95 (1904).

Thomas v. *Hibbits,* 46 F. Supp. 368 (1942).

Torcaso v. *Watkins,* 367 U.S. 488 (1961).

Uniformed Sanitation Men's Association v. *Commissioner of Sanitation,* 392 U.S. 280 (1968).

United Public Workers v. *Mitchell,* 330 U.S. 75 (1947).
United States v. *Lovett,* 328 U.S. 303 (1946).
United States v. *Rasmussen,* 222 F. Supp. 430 (1963).
United States v. *Robel,* 389 U.S. 258 (1967).
United States v. *United Mine Workers,* 330 U.S. 258 (1947).
Weiman v. *Updegraff,* 344 U.S. 183 (1952).
Weiner v. *United States,* 357 U.S. 349 (1958).
West v. *Macy,* 248 F. Supp. 105 (1968).
Whitehill v. *Elkins,* 389 U.S. 54 (1967).
Williams v. *Zuckert,* 372 U.S. 765 (1963).
Wilson v. *Civil Service Commission,* 136 F. Supp. 104 (1955).

PUBLIC DOCUMENTS

State

Maryland. *Lower House Journal.* Vol. XL.
North Carolina. *Colonial Records of North Carolina.* Edited by
William L. Sanders. Raleigh: Josephus Daniels, 1890.
South Carolina. *Statutes at Large of South Carolina.* Vol. III.

United States

Annals of the Congress of the United States. Vol. I.
Articles of Confederation (1781).
Atomic Energy Commission. *In the Matter of J. Robert Oppen-
heimer.* Washington: U.S. Government Printing Office, 1954.
Civil Service Commission. *Annual Report.* Vols. III, XI, XVIII,
XX, XXIII, XIV, LIV, LVII, LX, LXIII, LXV, LXXI,
LXXIII, LXXIX, LXXX, LXXXI, LXXXII, LXXXIII,
LXXXIV, LXXXV.
———. *Civil Service Act and the Rules Promulgated by the
President.* Washington: U.S. Government Printing Office, 1899.
———. *Civil Service Act, Rules, Statutes, Executive Orders,
and Regulations.* Washington: U.S. Government Printing Of-
fice, 1941.
———. *History of the Federal Civil Service, 1789 to the Present.*
Washington: U.S. Government Printing Office, 1941.
———. *Political Activity and Political Assessment of Federal*

Officeholders and Employees. Form 1236. Washington: U.S. Government Printing Office, 1939.

―――. *Political Activity of Federal Officers and Employees.* Pamphlet 20. Washington: U.S. Government Printing Office, May, 1966.

―――. *Report to the President.* Washington: U.S. Government Printing Offce, 1874.

―――. *Study of Minority Group Employment in the Federal Government.* Washington: U.S. Government Printing Office, 1966.

―――. *Veteran Preference in Federal Employment.* Washington: U.S. Government Printing Office, 1957.

Code (1964 ed.), Title V.

Code of Federal Regulations (1968, 1969), Titles III, V.

Commission on Government Security. *Report.* Washington: U.S. Government Printing Office, 1957.

Commission on Political Activity of Government Personnel. *Report.* 3 vols. Washington: U.S. Government Printing Office, 1968.

Compilation of the Messages and Papers of the Presidents of the United States, 1789–1897. Edited by James D. Richardson. 10 vols. Washington: U.S. Government Printing Office, 1896–99.

Congressional Globe. 25th Cong., 3d Sess., Part 1; 40th Cong., 2d Sess., Part 1; 41st Cong. 3d Sess., Part 1.

Congressional Record. Vols. XIV, LXXXIII, LXXXIV, LXXXVI, LXXXIX, CXII, CXIII, CXIV, CXV.

Constitution (1789).

Federal Register. Vols. IV, VI, VII, X, XII, XVI, XVII, XVIII, XX, XXVI, XXVII, XXVIII, XXX, XXXII, XXXIV.

House of Representatives. Committee on Government Operations. *Special Inquiry on Invasion of Privacy.* 89th Cong., 1st Sess., 1965.

―――. Committee on Government Operations. *Use of Polygraphs by the Federal Government.* 88th Cong., 2d Sess., 1964.

―――. Committee on Un-American Activities. *Hearings Re-*

garding Communist Espionage in the United States Government. 80th Cong., 2d Sess., 1948.

————. Covode Investigation. Report 648. 36th Cong., 1st Sess., June 16, 1860.

————. Defalcations. Report 313. 25th Cong., 3d Sess., February 27, 1839.

————. Document 212. 27th Cong., 2d Sess., May 9, 1842.

————. Executive Document 97. 40th Cong., 2d Sess., January 7, 1868.

————. Executive Document 8. 45th Cong., 1st Sess., October 25, 1877.

————. Report 741. 27th Cong., 2d Sess., May 23, 1842.

Journals of the Continental Congress. Vols. VII, XV.

Opinions of the Attorneys General. Vols. XIII, XXVI.

President's Commission on the Status of Women. *Report.* Washington: U.S. Government Printing Office, 1963.

President's Committee on Equal Employment Opportunity. *Report.* Washington: U.S. Government Printing Office, 1963.

President's Task Force on Employee-Management Relations in the Federal Service. *A Policy for Employee Management Cooperation in the Federal Service.* Washington: U.S. Government Printing Office, 1962.

Register of Debates in Congress. Vol. XI.

Senate. Committee on Civil Service and Retrenchment. Report 576. 47th Cong., 1st Sess., March 18, 1882.

————. Committee on the Judiciary. *Protecting Privacy and the Rights of Federal Employees.* Report 519. 90th Cong., 1st Sess., August 21, 1967.

————. Committee on the Judiciary, Subcommittee on Constitutional Rights. Monthly Staff Report. 1967, 1968, 1969.

————. Document 73. 21st Cong., 2d Sess., March 3, 1831.

————. Document 41. 22d Cong., 1st Sess., January 26, 1832.

————. Document 155. 23d Cong., 1st Sess., March 7, 1834.

————. Document 108. 23d Cong., 2d Sess., February 9, 1835.

————. Document 26. 27th Cong., 1st Sess., March 20, 1841.

————. Document 399. 28th Cong., 1st Sess., June 15, 1844.

Statutes at Large. Vols I, II, III, IV, V, X, XII, XIV, XVI, XXI, XXXVII, XL, XLII, L, LIII, LIV, LVI, LVII, LVIII, LX, LXI, LXIII, LXIV, LXVI, LXIX, LXXVIII.

UNPUBLISHED SOURCE

Rosenbloom, David H. "Individual Liberty Versus National Security." Master's dissertation, Department of Political Science, University of Chicago, 1966.

Index

Federal Service and the Constitution

Composed by Vail-Ballou Press, Inc.,
in 11 pt. Times Roman, 3 points leaded,
with display lines in Times New Roman No. 327.
Printed letterpress from type by Vail-Ballou Press
on Warren's No. 66 text, 60 lb. basis,
with the Cornell University Press watermark.
Bound by Vail-Ballou Press
in Interlaken Pallium bookcloth
and stamped in All Purpose foil.

B6.